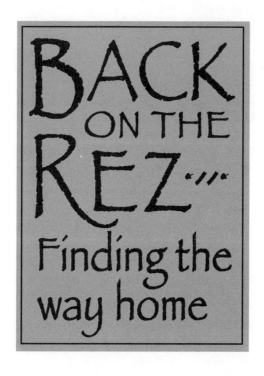

BACK ON THE REZ...

Finding the way home

BRIAN MARACLE

VIKING

VIKING
Published by the Penguin Group
Penguin Books Canada Ltd, 10 Alcorn Avenue, Toronto, Ontario, Canada
M4V 3B2
Penguin Books Ltd, 27 Wrights Lane, London W8 5TZ, England
Viking Penguin, a division of Penguin Books USA Inc., 375 Hudson Street,
New York, New York 10014, U.S.A.
Penguin Books Australia Ltd, Ringwood, Victoria, Australia
Penguin Books (NZ) Ltd, 182–190 Wairau Road, Auckland 10, New Zealand

Penguin Books Ltd, Registered Offices: Harmondsworth, Middlesex,
England

First published 1996
10 9 8 7 6 5 4 3 2 1

Printed and bound in Canada on acid free paper ∞

Canadian Cataloguing in Publication Data

Maracle, Brian, 1947-
    Back on the rez: finding the way home

ISBN 0-670-85915-X

1. Maracle, Brian, 1947-   . 2. Six Nations Indian Reserve (Ont.) - Social
conditions. 3. Six Nations Indian Reserve (Ont.) - History. 4. Iroquois
Indians - Ontario - Social conditions. 5. Indians of North America -
Ontario - Social conditions. 6. Indian reservations - Ontario. 7. Iroquois
Indians - Ontario - History. 8. Indians of North America - Ontario -
History. I. Title.

E99.I7M37 1996   971.3'47004975   C95-932051-2

Kenh iken khehyatonhse nène Ake'nihstenha
nok ne Rake'niha

«//«

For my mother and father

Acknowledgments

I am indebted to many people who helped me in the course of writing this book. First among them is Jackie Kaiser of Penguin Books, for her vision, belief and guidance in helping me shape and refine this book. Together with copy editor Catherine Marjoribanks, she helped me tell my story much more concisely and elegantly than I could ever have done on my own and for that, I am extremely grateful.

I also wish to acknowledge the special help I received from three exceptional librarians: Wendy Ancell of the union of B.C. Indian Chiefs in Vancouver, B.C.; Julia Finn of the Department of Indian Affairs in Hull, Quebec; and Winnie Jacobs of the Woodland Cultural Centre in Brantford, Ontario.

Another book-lover who made a special effort to help me find the information I wanted was the late Carol McComber of the Mohawk Nation Bookstore in Kahnawake, Quebec. Carol was enthusiastically dedicated to educating the world about the Onkwehonwe. She will be missed.

I am particularly indebted to Tawit (David) Kanatawakhon-Maracle and Tehahenteh (Frank Miller) for so patiently helping me with the Kanyen'kehaka language. I hasten to add, however, that they are not responsible for any errors or misinterpretations that may have been created by the way I have used their information.

(All the native language words in this book, incidently, are in Kanyen'kehaka. These words, though, should not be considered as the best or the only way to express, write or spell them, since other Mohawk speakers and other Mohawk communities—not to mention the Cayugas, Onondagas, Oneidas and Senecas—often use other words, other spellings and other writing systems to express the same ideas, objects and actions.)

My deepest thanks go out to many relatives, friends and colleagues who provided me with information, advice and encouragement at various stages of this work. Among them: Sue Bailey, Paul Barnsley, Diane E. Benson, Audrey Bomberry, Gloria Bomberry, Lillian Bradley, Ken Deer, Darrell Doxtdator, Angela Files, Gawitrha, Arnie General, Richard Green, Marge Henry, Martha Hill, Tom Hill, Wayne Hunter, Robert W. (Bob) Jamieson, Mary Jamieson, Dave Johns, Larry Mackenzie, Allan MacNaughton, John Maracle, Kitty Maracle, Leonard Maracle, Marilyn Maracle, Richard Maracle, Stan Maracle, Morningstar Mercredi, John Mohawk, Dennise Powless, Lynda Powless, Audry Powless-Bomberry, Kyle Skinner, Shirley Smith, Jake Thomas, Robert Venables, Anne Westaway and Morgan Wood.

For all your help, *nyawen'kowa sewakwekon*.

Six Nations Grand River Territory

Tsi nahoten kenton ne kawennasonha

//

What the words mean

Confederacy is a term that usually refers to the traditional government of the Iroquois embodied by the clanmother-appointed chiefs sitting in council. The Confederacy, also known as the League of Peace, was founded by the Peacemaker.

Great Turtle Island is the term used to describe North America. It stems from the Iroquois creation story in which the earth rests on the back of a giant turtle.

Handsome Lake, the English name of the Seneca war chief and prophet Skanyatariyo, is pronounced "skan-yah-da-LEE-yo" and means "beautiful lake." He is known as the founder of the longhouse / Handsome Lake religion.

Kanyen'kehaka is pronounced "ga-nyoon-geh-HAH-ga" and is commonly translated as "Mohawk." It literally means "people of the flinty ground." The word "Mohawk" stems from an Algonquin word meaning "cannibal." At Six Nations it is used to describe the "Mohawk" people and language.

Karihwiyo is pronounced "ga-ree-WEE-yo." It literally means "the good business" and is popularly known as "the good word." It is also called the Code of Handsome Lake and refers to the message preached by the Seneca prophet of the same name, a message he is said to have received in a series of visions at the end of the 1700s.

Kayaneren'tsherakowa is pronounced "ga-yaw-ne-RUNT-ser-a-go-wa" and it literally means "the great law." The Great Law tells the history and spells out the Iroquois form of government. The Peacemaker gave the Great Law to the Onkwehonwe when He founded the Confederacy, sometime before 1492.

Onkwehonwe is pronounced "ohn-gway-HOHN-way" and its literal translation is "real/first/original people." It is used as the equivalent of "Indian" or "native/aboriginal person." It can refer to an individual or a group of native people.

Peacemaker is the English name given to the supernatural man-being who, acting on instructions from the Creator, ended the blood feuds among the Iroquois and founded the League of Peace. He then gave the Great Law to the Onkwehonwe.

Rotinonhsyonni literally means "they make the house" and is pronounced "ro-dee-no-SHOW-nee." It can refer to the political institution known as "the Confederacy" or to the people of the Confederacy, "the Iroquois."

Shonkwaya'tihson is pronounced "sohn-gwa-yah-DEE-sohn" and is commonly translated as "the Creator." It literally means "He has finished making our bodies." The term comes from the creation story when Shonkwaya'tihson, then known as the Right-Handed Twin, created the Onkwehonwe from a handful of clay. Shonkwaya'tihson is also referred to in English as the Master of Life.

Contents

Tsi tyotahsawe
At the beginning

Mention the term "Indian reserve" to most Canadians and their minds fill instantly with several common images.

Indian reserves are hopeless puddles of poverty. People there live in shacks surrounded by garbage and wrecked cars. Everyone's on welfare. The men drink and beat their wives. The women play bingo and neglect their kids. The boys sniff gasoline and the girls have babies.

Everyone has a frightening or disgusting sickness—scabies, venereal disease, tuberculosis. The band council is always broke—it can't balance its chequebook let alone run a government. All the kids are dirty and have runny noses; they can barely read, if they go to school at all.

Worst of all, they just sit and complain about how much the government owes them. They're forever whining about their "rights" and bitching about how the white man has oppressed them. They always have their hand out but they won't lift a finger to help themselves.

What's more, the people are just plain weird. They eat raw meat from wild animals. They perform superstitious rituals. They hang onto primitive customs and insist on living in their backward state. The best thing they could do to better themselves would be to leave those hellholes and join twentieth-century mainstream society, but they won't even do that.

Luckily, not all Canadians think that way. What's more, the fact is that the reality of life on an Indian reserve is neither all that grim nor all that gloomy. Even on the "worst" reserves, the picture is not nearly as one-sided as the news media suggest. People have jobs. They go to work. They have nice homes. They're sober. They don't drink. Their children graduate from school. Now, there may not be all that many people enjoying the brighter side of reserve life in some communities, but there are *some*. In spite of these few bright spots, though, the facts and figures show that Indian life lags far behind the Canadian average. Statistics show that Indians are far more likely than the rest of the population to be unemployed, ill-housed, ill-educated, diabetic, tuberculous, sexually abused, alcoholic, imprisoned and suicidal. The numbers are well known, but they tell only part of the story. I've been to two hundred reserves in the United States and Canada and I know that the good side of reserve life includes many things that never get measured by pollsters and statisticians.

To understand the good things about a reserve it is necessary to understand first how we feel about the land. The ties that bind any group of human beings to their homeland are extremely powerful. The love of land transcends rational thought and competes on the highest level of human emotions. A people's love of their homeland equals—and often surpasses—the love of family and the love of life itself.

As for us—the Onkwehonwe, the Indian people—our ties to the land are stronger than most because we know from our teachings that our Creator, Shonkwaya'tihson, created the Onkwehonwe, the first human beings, with a handful of the very soil on which we now walk. We know from our teachings that the lands and waters of Great Turtle Island were made specifically for us by Shonkwaya'tihson. We know that the Creator placed us here, on this corner of Great Turtle Island, and He gave our people the knowledge of how to survive on this land. We know that He also gave us instructions on how we should respect the land, the waters, the plants, the animals, the fish and the birds. Lastly, we know from our teachings how we are to use the fruits of the earth to give Him our thanks. Our very being here on Great Turtle Island, then, stems from this one inescapable reality: we were born of this earth and to this earth. We believe in the deepest part of our soul that Great Turtle Island—North America—was divinely and expressly made for us by the hand of God.

Many things have happened since the time of creation. The majestic sweep of our homeland was stolen or swindled from us. We were pushed away from the lush river bottoms, pushed away from the prime fishing stations, pushed away from the best hunting grounds. We were pushed into barren and inhospitable regions. We were confined to these spaces called reserves and reservations. If we want to harvest the fruits of the land and remain true to the instructions of creation—and if we want to avoid arrest, prosecution and imprisonment—we have to confine ourselves to these cramped spaces. It's no wonder, then, that our love for the land, concentrated as it is in the reserves, is so passionate and intense.

The reserves mean many things to the Onkwehonwe. On one level, these postage-stamp remnants of our original territories are nagging reminders of the echoing vastness of what we have lost. On another, they are the legacy and bastion of our being. They are a refuge, a prison, a haven, a madhouse, a fortress, a birthplace, a Mecca, a resting place, Home-Sweet-Home, Fatherland and Motherland rolled into one.

Because they are the home of our elders, reserves are also sanctuaries of sanity in an insane world. The circle of elders holds a treasure-house of traditional wisdom, culture and language. Within the circle lies an unlimited fortune that is free for the asking for anyone seeking enrichment of mind and spirit.

Because most of them are far from the city, reserves are free from urban grime and crime; free from chaos and congestion; free from oppressive anonymity and anonymous oppression. The natural environment is a normal and vital part of everyday existence. Life on a reserve means that plants, animals, fish and birds are close at hand. And it is from living surrounded by these blessings of creation that we derive the soothing satisfaction and invigorating energy that give us peace and strength.

Lastly, because they hold the bulk of our population and because they constitute the little land base we have left, the reserves are focal points for political action and energy.

When most Canadians look at the balance sheet of life on reserves, they assess the pluses, represented by a short list of blessings, intangible benefits and debatable virtues, and weigh them against the minuses of often horrifying socio-economic conditions. And they probably conclude from this accounting that an Indian reserve is the least coveted listing in the universe of desirable addresses.

So why have I and so many other Onkwehonwe come home? What it comes down to, I think, is that the reserves have an inescapable magnetic hold on us. No matter how long we've been gone or how far we've been away, we return to the reserves as dependably and unfailingly as the salmon return to the rivers in the fall and the songbirds return to the fields and woodlands in the spring.

This book is specifically about one reserve—what the federal government calls Six Nations Indian Reserve #40—a block of land eight miles wide and nine miles long that straddles the Grand River south of Brantford, Ontario.

Six Nations is "my" reserve. It's my "rez."

It's called Six Nations because it includes members of the six nations (Mohawk, Oneida, Onondaga, Cayuga, Seneca and Tuscarora) of the Rotinonhsyonni, the Iroquois Confederacy. The Six Nations of the Grand River band council has 18,000 people on its membership rolls, making it the biggest, by far, of the 608 Indian bands in Canada. It has all the good features of other reserves and it shares many of the same problems—unemployment, inadequate housing, social problems—although not to the same degree. The one feature that distinguishes Six Nations from other reserves is the community's crippling political conflict, between the supporters of the elected band council and the supporters of the Rotinonhsyonni, the traditional government of the Iroquois people.

Although both my parents are from this reserve, my family moved away from here when I was five years old. As a result, I grew up in a small town in southern Ontario and two cities in western New York and lived my entire adult life in Vancouver and Ottawa. During my life in mainstream society, I earned two college degrees and achieved minor success in native politics and journalism. In my personal life, I failed at two marriages but did manage to help raise one wonderful daughter. In October 1993, I left a career on the fringes of Parliament Hill to start a new life back home on the Six Nations reserve. After forty years away, I returned—alone—to live in a battered log house in a community where I had few relatives, fewer friends and no job.

This is the story of my first year back on the rez.

Tsi teyotenerahtatenyons

//

When the leaves are changing

I have *arrived in the waning days of Indian summer, that gloriously invigorating and brown-tinted interlude between first frost and first snow. At this time of year, the predominant colour of this little corner of Great Turtle Island is not just one run-of-the-mill shade of brown. No, the countryside is a riot of earth tones competing for the eye's attention—chocolate, fawn, cinnamon, walnut, tan, rust, sepia, ginger, ochre, mahogany. There are enough rustic shades in every corner of the landscape to warm a crayon-maker's heart—from the coffee-hued ribs of freshly plowed fields, to the khaki-coloured banks of dried weedbeds, to the brooding, olive-toned stands of bare-limbed hardwoods.*

The warm days in this, summer's last gasp, are punctuated by increasingly chilly nights. The grass, now more brown than green, has stopped growing and gone to sleep. The trees, their bony fingers stretching skyward, stand stoically, as though being robbed at

6

gunpoint by the frosty thief of autumn. Scurrying through the leaves is a gang of squirrels, intent on stashing away a small mountain of walnuts. Soon, the rains of November will turn the pale dry carpet of fallen leaves into a darkened soggy pulp. Overhead, great flocks of geese, in long fluttering "V" formations, flap and honk their way southward.

Unlike my feathered friends, however, I will not be going south for the winter. No. Now that I'm finally here, I don't intend to go anywhere else. Like my furry friends, I will use the rest of Indian summer to ready myself for the winter to come.

Coming home

Before returning to Six Nations, I lived in Ottawa with my wife, Dora Hopkins, a Heiltsuk woman from Waglisla, a remote fishing village on the west coast of British Columbia, and our daughter Zoe. Although there were a lot of Indians and a friendship centre in Ottawa, it wasn't the same as living on a reserve. Not by a long shot. We didn't have any relatives in Ottawa. There were no Heiltsuk or Mohawk doings—no ceremonies, no potlatches, no socials. And even though we lived in Ottawa for thirteen years, we never considered it home; it was only the place we lived.

The longer we stayed there the more restless we became, especially Dora. Because her reserve was a lot further away than mine, she became increasingly homesick and her visits home grew progressively longer. As the years wore on, we both spent more and more time visiting our reserves, thinking about moving home. An obvious solution to our malaise, we knew, would be to move to either Waglisla or Six Nations. There were just three problems: 1) we didn't want to tear Zoe away from her friends; 2) picking either reserve would still leave one of us homesick; and 3) we couldn't get a house or "legally" live on either reserve because neither one of us was a member of our respective band.

By 1993, though, most of the barriers to moving back to the reserve had fallen. By then Dora, Zoe and I were "status Indians" under the terms of Bill C-31, the legislation that tried to correct the effects of sex discrimination in the Indian Act. Dora and Zoe were registered as members of the Heiltsuk Tribal Council and I was registered at Six Nations.

Also by that time, Zoe was in her last year of high school, headed to Toronto to attend university. With our daughter leaving home to make her own way in the world, Dora and I knew there was no more reason for us to stay in Ottawa, and it was then that Dora decided to return to Waglisla and I decided to come here.

Before we left Ottawa, Dora organized a traditional Heiltsuk potlatch. Before a hundred assembled guests, Dora gave me, as a final gesture of her love and respect, an exquisite button blanket featuring the Hopkins' eagle crest. She then formally and warmly welcomed me into her family. I was humbled and deeply touched by her kindness and generosity. In an odd but fitting way, her gesture cemented our care for one another into an unending relationship, and it made our inevitable leave-taking a little easier to bear.

The main purpose of the potlatch was devoted to Zoe's belated coming-of-age ceremony. Zoe emerged from ritual seclusion dressed in her potlatch regalia—a red-on-blue button blanket emblazoned with a huge eagle crest, and a woven cedar headdress trimmed with ermine and a dazzling abalone button. She then danced demurely and precisely to the steady rhythm of the Princess Dance, a symbolic example of young womanhood. After she was showered with gifts, Zoe announced to the crowd that she would sing a song she had written that day.

Standing straight, looking regal, poised and confident, she sang about our little family in a strong clear voice that never wavered. Her song, which still brings tears to my eyes, was the perfect healing touch that allowed us all to go our separate ways.

fly with the eagles
swim with the whales
see the mountains roll
feel the ocean in your soul
i know you cannot stay
so spread your wings and fly away
oh mother dear,
i know you hear
the land that calls your name

fly with the eagles
walk on the trails
write your words upon your scroll
speak the stories in your soul
i know you cannot stay
so spread your wings and fly away
oh father dear,
i know you hear
the land that calls your name

no longer your baby
i know now that maybe
it's time for me to grow
I'll walk away, but take it slow
enjoy each new day
my heart is with you all the way
may only good spirits guide you
to the homes that hold your names

Back on the rez

My new home is a steep-roofed, two-storey log house that is roughly one hundred and fifty years old. Despite efforts to modernize it, the house is clearly showing its age. The cement chinking is falling out, the window frames are crumbling and the roof shingles need to be replaced. The squared-off logs, although grey and deeply weathered, are in good shape—except for the bottom log on the west side, which has rotted out and given the house a pronounced tilt in that direction.

The house is in the northwest corner of the reserve, away from almost everything else. It sits on a large lawn, fifty yards back from a twisting gravel road that doesn't get much traffic. There are three houses immediately to the east of my home. To the north, just on the other side of the road, is the Grand River, murky and slow-moving. On the other side of the river are the fertile cornfields owned by non-Indian farmers. On the south side of my house there are hilly fields covered with weeds six feet high. To the west, there is a small creek and a hardwood bush. Given the populated and built-up nature of this corner of Great Turtle Island, I couldn't ask for a quieter, more peaceful place in which to live.

The house is much roomier than it looks from the outside, with nine hundred square feet of living space. There are windows all around, which admit plenty of light and provide panoramic views of the river and the surrounding greenery. Downstairs there is a spacious living room and a second large room I intend to use for an office. Up a narrow staircase there are two slope-ceilinged bedrooms, and tacked onto the back of the house is a shed-like addition that houses the kitchen and bathroom.

The house has electricity and running water. The stove, fridge, toilet and hot-water heater all work. There is even a television antenna on the roof. I have everything I need—except heat. (There are two rickety propane heaters downstairs but the propane tank is empty.)

Living in this house will be a constant test of my equilibrium. Because the floors slope so wildly, it requires a good sense of balance to walk through the house. There is such a slope in some places I'm almost tempted to put in a handrail. What's more, the walls and doors all lean at bizarre angles. One wall leans so much, in fact, I think I could hang a picture on it without using a nail—I'd just have to place it on the wall and it would stay there all by itself. Pretty soon I'll have to put blocks of wood under the downhill end of the couch, desk, table, beds, dressers and bookcases so that at least the furnishings in this house will be plumb and level.

The walls and the ceiling are panelled but the grooves on the panelling don't line up with anything else in the house. When I look at the floor, ceiling, walls, doors, windows, panelling and furniture, there are no parallel lines or right angles anywhere so I end up dizzy and cross-eyed. But what this place lacks in being plumb and level it more than makes up for in character and coziness. I know I'm going to like it here.

//

Three local guys helped me move in this afternoon, and my belongings are now stacked in boxes that are piled high in every corner of every room in the house. After unloading and returning the moving truck, I had just enough time to pick up some junk food, find the blankets, uncrate the television, plug it in and turn it on.

It so happens that my first day back on the rez, October 25, 1993, was the day of the federal election, so I promptly settled in to watch the returns. Although the house was *very* chilly, I swaddled myself in blankets and loved *every* frigid minute of my first night back home.

As the Liberal juggernaut rolled on and the final result became increasingly obvious, my mind drifted from federal politics to Indian politics. I didn't care whether the Liberals or the Conservatives won the election anyway because they both refuse to recognize the Iroquois Confederacy.

For that matter, my lack of concern about who forms the federal government extends to national Indian organizations like the Assembly of First Nations. Although I began working for native organizations in 1972, I don't care who leads those groups and I don't care what they say or do any more. That's because Indian organizations—and, for that matter, the federal treasury—won't solve the real problems of Indian communities. *We* are the only ones who can solve our problems. And the greatest problem we face is not legal, economic or social; it doesn't involve land claims, "self-government," health or education. No. Our greatest problem is spiritual, emotional and cultural.

Reflecting on this, I can now say that twenty-odd years after I started trying to solve Indian problems from Vancouver and Ottawa, I have finally done what I've always said other people should do: I have stopped trying to solve Indian problems from a distance. I have dropped out of the game of national Indian politics. I have left the city and come to live with my people on the land I have always considered my home.

Living away from the reserve for so long, cut off from the land, the people and the culture, left me with a nagging sense of loss. I did not feel spiritually or emotionally whole while I lived in the city. Now that I'm here, I'm still some distance from feeling whole, from feeling complete. But at least I know that I have moved within the circle. I am once again with my people in the physical, emotional, cultural and spiritual centre of our existence.

Over the years I have increasingly wanted to move back to the reserve, but the crazy thing is I don't really know this place. After all, I wasn't born here. I never went to school here. I never worked here. In spite of my many, many visits, I don't know the reserve very well and I don't know who's who or what's what. Although I have a slew of relatives here, the only member of my immediate family who lives on the reserve is my sister Dennise. My parents, two sisters and one brother live in Vancouver. Another sister lives in Pittsburgh and another brother lives in Rochester, New York. I also have aunts, uncles, cousins, nephews and nieces living hundreds and thousands of miles away, from Tennessee to Sault Ste. Marie. All the people in my extended family have strong emotional ties to the reserve, but the fact is that most of them have made their home in the outside world and will never live here again.

In spite of my lack of connections, I don't feel like a stranger—I feel I belong here—and I don't think I'm trying to create a home I never had, because I have always considered this my home. Before, when someone would ask me where I was from, I would be very specific and say I *lived* in Ottawa, Vancouver or wherever but I was *from* Six Nations. Now that I'm here, though, I know I'll have to make this—my spiritual and emotional home—a real home. I'll have to make friends. I'll have to make a living. I'll have to adjust to a totally new environment. It was only when a few of my Ottawa friends asked me if I was worried about fitting in that I realized I had given no thought to the matter. I know I'll have the odd problem now and then but I am not worried in the least. I'm lucky, I know, because many Indian communities do not welcome people like me who have been away so long. Fortunately, Six Nations is different. I think it's because so many of our people have had to move away to make a living that there is a sense of loss throughout the community and a genuine desire to have all of our people come home.

After the election coverage finally ended, I turned off the television and sat quietly in the darkness, wrapped in thought. The silence at the end of this long and unforgettable day was intensified by the fact that I was alone in the house. Zoe was in Toronto, Dora in Waglisla. Earlier in the evening, I called and told them that I had just moved in. They were both just as happy for me as I am for them. Although we are all where we want to be, we still miss each other very much.

As my eyes adjusted to the darkness I gradually began to recognize my radically new surroundings. I looked around this crazy old house—at the crooked doors, the leaning walls, the sloping floors. I looked at boxes and furniture piled every which way. I looked out the window and saw the river flowing blackly in front of the house. I saw the treetops waving in the wind. I saw the fields resting in the moonlight.

The river, the boxes, the fields, the floors, the trees—everything is all so unbelievably new. It's truly a new beginning for me and I am tremendously excited. I'm back on the rez. I'm home at last. And I can't wait for tomorrow.

Settling in

Moving into any new home brings with it the inevitable bother of unpacking, figuring out what goes where and trying to find a good place to buy groceries. But moving from the city to the outer fringes of a reserve, I have discovered, brings its own set of problems.

Although I knew it before, I fully realize now, after having lived in the city my entire adult life, that I have come to take many things for granted. If I wanted a drink of water, for example, I just turned on the tap. If the house was too cold, I turned up the thermostat. If I wanted my mail, I just opened the front door and there it was. When I wanted to get rid of my garbage, I put it out the front door and it disappeared. If I wanted to read a daily newspaper, I could subscribe to five different newspapers that would be delivered right to my door. If I wanted to watch television, I just picked up the remote control and flipped through two dozen cable television channels. Just about everything I wanted or needed was available at the tip of my finger.

My new life will not be nearly so simple or easy. For starters, one-half of this old house isn't heated and I have to do something about it before winter sets in, especially since my writing room is in the cold half. The tank for the propane heater that heats the other half of the house is empty and the thermometer shows that it is now eleven chilly degrees inside. At this point it looks as though I have three choices—to install another propane heater, to use electric space-heaters or to put in a wood-burning stove.

If I want mail delivered to the house, I'll have to walk the fifty yards down to the end of the lane every day. I won't mind that a bit because it will give me a chance to watch the hawks circling over the fields, see the ducks feeding in the river, listen to the guinea hens next door, smell the fresh air, be warmed by the sun and braced by the wind. There's no mailbox there now so it will mean digging a deep hole, getting a post and a regulation-size mailbox and putting it up, with the guaranteed certainty that it will be knocked over in a week or so by local teenagers with their version of Welcome Wagon.

When it comes to getting rid of my garbage, I have a choice. I can either pay twenty-five dollars every three months to have it picked up once a week or I can take it to the dump myself.

There doesn't seem to be much choice, however, when it comes to getting a daily newspaper delivered. It's either *The Brantford Expositor* or nothing. *The Expositor* is a pitifully thin link in the Southam chain and it is dreadfully shy of what I want in a daily newspaper. (And to think I used to complain about *The Ottawa Citizen*. Compared with *The Expositor*, *The Citizen* looks like *The New York Times*.) I don't know. I just can't see myself paying good money to walk down to the end of the lane every night to pick a tiny portion of yesterday's news out of the ditch. If I want any other paper, I'll have to get in my car and drive—either three miles into Ohsweken for *The Hamilton Spectator* or seven miles into Brantford to get *The Toronto Star* or *The Globe and Mail*.

As for water at the turn of a tap, I have all I want—for

the time being. There is a well next to the house and a pump brings it into the kitchen and bathroom. The problem is that the woman who tried to stay in this house last winter was forced out in January when the pipes froze, so before too long I'll have to investigate just what the problem is and figure out how to prevent it.

I don't know what I'm going to do about the television. There is an antenna on the house but all I get is two-and-a-half channels—Global, a local independent station and a fuzzy CTV. I won't miss all the stuff on cable TV I was able to see in Ottawa—the American channels, the music video channel, the sports channel and definitely not the home shopping channel, the weather channel or the real estate listings. What I do miss is CBC. It's not that I'm a CBC "fan"—it's more like I'm addicted. I'm a news junkie and I have to get my fix from CBC. In spite of its shortcomings, especially with regard to native issues, CBC News is the best of the bunch—by far. I just hope I can find a cheap way to get resupplied with a regular dose of the good stuff.

Home on the
political range

I am, at the very core of my existence, a political animal. I am fascinated by the political manoeuvres that bring people together and the political machinations that tear them apart. If anyone deserves credit for this aspect of my character, it's my mother, because she fuelled my interest in Indian people and Indian politics right from the start. I can still remember all of the circumstances of the night when I was a small boy and my mother first told me the wondrous story of how the earth and the first human beings were created. It was magic. As I grew up, she was always talking about Indian *this* and Indian *that*. It was her talking, I'm sure, that aroused my interest in Indian politics and instilled in me the urge to do something about the wrongs that were being perpetrated against the Onkwehonwe.

Most of the people here, in fact, have a heightened sense of political awareness by virtue of having grown up in an environment that forced them to defend their rights continually in their dealings with the government and with the white people surrounding them. For Onkwehonwe everywhere, that's normal. What makes the people at Six Nations hyper-political, more so than almost any other reserve in the country, is the paralyzing conflict between the Iroquois Confederacy and the elected band council.

To say that this community is split or divided would be incorrect, since it implies that at one time it was united. It never was. To understand the conflict here, it's necessary to understand the history.

When the American Revolutionary War started, most of the Mohawk, Onondaga, Cayuga and Seneca warriors fought alongside the British, while the Oneidas and the Tuscaroras sided with the Americans. The war devastated the Iroquois, no matter which side they fought on. In addition to their battlefield losses, most of the Iroquois villages were abandoned or burned to the ground by the Americans' scorched-earth campaign.

At the end of the war, the British compensated the Iroquois with land in Ontario for the lands they lost in New York. The governor of Quebec bought a huge tract of land from the Mississauga Nation. He set aside a strip of land six miles wide, on both sides of the Grand River, from its mouth on Lake Erie to its source south of Georgian Bay. In the deed that bears his name, Governor Haldimand gave it to "the said Mohawk Nation, and such others of the Six Nations Indians as wish to settle in that quarter... which them and their posterity are to enjoy for ever."

Led by Thayendanegea (Mohawk war leader Joseph Brant), nearly two thousand people from all six Iroquois nations left their camps in western New York and moved to the Grand River in 1784. But the people did not settle in one place. Instead, the various nations set up their own villages at different sites up and down the river. The present city of Brantford is located on the site of the largest Mohawk village. Once the people were settled here, the Iroquois Confederacy was re-established on the Grand River Territory and was the undisputed governing body here for 140 years.

In 1793, the deed to the lands along the Grand River that

the Mohawks and other Indians were "to enjoy for ever" was renounced by the lieutenant-governor of Upper Canada, who slashed the size of the territory by a third, saying Governor Haldimand hadn't meant to give the Six Nations that much land.

By the 1840s, most of the remaining Grand River Territory was sold off in a series of bitterly contested land deals. The scattered villages were then forced to relocate to the patch of land that became the present-day reserve, a plot measuring eight miles by nine miles downstream from Brantford.

(The history of how the original one-million-acre Grand River Territory was whittled down to its present 45,000 acres reminds me of the famous remark made by William Tecumseh Sherman, a nineteenth century American Army General who defined a reservation as "a parcel of land inhabited by Indians and surrounded by thieves.")

When they were dividing the territory into lots and assigning them to individual families, the chiefs purposely created tribal neighbourhoods. The Mohawks, Oneidas and Tuscaroras ended up settling in the centre and western half of the territory, an area known as the "upper end." The Cayugas, Senecas and Onondagas settled on the eastern or down-river end of the territory, an area known as "down below." As a result, the people who live in these areas are still known as "upper-enders" or "down-belowers."

Because many of the Mohawks, Oneidas and Tuscaroras adopted Christianity, while the Onondagas, Senecas and Cayugas retained their traditional religion, the terms "upper-ender" and "down-belower"—when delivered with an arrogant sneer—have evolved into nasty little put-downs. To some people, therefore, "down-belowers" are dumb, backward pagans while "upper-enders" are white Christian snobs. The name-calling isn't new—the two sides were calling each other "heathens" and "traitors" more than eighty years ago.

At the centre of the territory is the village of Ohsweken. It was originally called New Oswego, and was probably named after a Mohawk village (now the city of Oswego) at the eastern end of Lake Ontario. At the centre of Ohsweken is the old council house, a one-storey yellow-brick building the Confederacy chiefs built as their seat of government in 1863, four years before Canadian Confederation.

The Confederacy operates by the rules and procedures of the *Kayaneren'tsherakowa*, the Great Law, which relates the history and prescribes the government and religion of the Iroquois. Under the Great Law, each clan is represented by a chief who is appointed by the head woman, the clanmother. By the turn of the century, though, some of the people here were complaining about the lack of elections to the government of Canada, which was itself increasingly annoyed by the Confederacy's continued insistence that it was the legitimate government of sovereign, independent people. On October 7, 1924, the government's Indian Agent, backed by a force of twenty mounted RCMP officers, interrupted a meeting of the Confederacy chiefs and decreed that the people of the Grand River would, from that day on, be governed by Canada's Indian Act. They then confiscated the Confederacy's books, documents and wampum belts—the symbols of the oldest government on Great Turtle Island. Two weeks later, an election was held for chief and council, as provided for under the Indian Act. Just fifty-two people voted. Since then, the Government of Canada has turned a deaf ear to the Confederacy and has backed the elected band council with government money and the RCMP.

The supporters of the Confederacy refused to vote in the 1924 election and they have refused to do so since. Because it was created by the Indian Act, they see the elected band council as simply an arm of the federal government, while they regard the Confederacy as the only legitimate government of the Iroquois people. Confederacy supporters seethed with resentment for thirty-five years until their anger boiled over in March, 1959. More than a thousand Iroquois descended on the council house and occupied the building. From the steps of the council house, the Confederacy chiefs reasserted the independence of the Iroquois as a sovereign people. The uprising was eight days old when the Diefenbaker government sent in the RCMP riot squad to crush the resistance and hand the building back to the elected band council. And that's where things stand right now—the Confederacy still has the hearts and minds of most of the Iroquois people while the band council still has the council house, backed by the government's money, police and courts.

Today, 209 years after the Great Relocation, there are three distinct political factions in this community: 1) the Mohawk nationalists, who say that the reserve and the Grand River lands are Mohawk territory; 2) the Confederacy, which says that the land belongs to all six Iroquois nations; and 3) the elected band council, which says the land belongs to the eighteen thousand status Indians who are members of the Six Nations Indian Band.

The Supreme Court of Canada has ruled that the elected band council is the legal government here because, it said, Canada had the legal authority to impose the Indian Act elective system on the people of the Grand River Territory in 1924. In other words, might makes right. What Canada did here in 1924 and 1959 is exactly what Nazi Germany did in France in 1940, what China did in Tibet in 1950 and what the United States and the Soviet Union did in half a dozen countries each—it invaded a sovereign people's territory, abolished a popular government and installed a puppet parliament by force of arms.

The elected chief and council get annoyed when they are

called Canadian government puppets. They say that the band council is the legitimate government at Six Nations and they imply that most of the people here support the elective system. But since less than ten percent of the electorate voted in the 1993 band election, they don't come right out and say so.

I'm certain that most of the people at Grand River support the concept of traditional government and are fiercely opposed to the Indian Act and an elected band council. In an independent 1991 community survey, for example, 84 percent of the people here said they wanted the education system to be shaped by the Confederacy, not the band council.

For people who care about preserving and strengthening our culture, there is no choice. We are compelled to follow the instructions of the Peacemaker, the man who established the Iroquois Confederacy on the instructions of the Creator Himself.

We must lay grief aside

My family moved around a lot when I was growing up. It seemed as though I was always switching houses, schools, neighbourhoods and cities—even whole countries. One day, for instance, I would be singing "The Star-Spangled Banner" and the next day I would be singing "God Save the Queen." One day I would have to pronounce the last letter of the alphabet as *zed* and the next day it would be *zee*. One day the father of my country would be George Washington, the next day it would be Sir John A. Macdonald.

Our family, like hundreds of other Six Nations families, left the reserve in the 1950s in search of work. In those days my father—like his father and his brothers and all the other men in the Maracle family—was a carpenter. My father towed his growing family from reserve to city to town to city as he followed jobs in the construction trade.

Eventually he formed his own carpenter contracting business and put me to work when I was eight years old. My first job was stacking lumber, carrying water and cleaning up. When I was thirteen my father made me the "layout man." My job was to read the blueprints and mark out the location of every joist, stud, wall, window, door and rafter. At sixteen he added the job of foreman to my responsibilities. By the time I was eighteen I could build anything from a single-car garage to a thirty-six-unit apartment block. Not only that, I could build it fast and build it right. I learned to work hard and I learned to love hard work. For that I have to thank the boss, my father. He wasn't a tyrant and he rarely yelled or swore, at anyone, but he drove people with the force of his personality to work their hardest and do their best. In my case, he demanded more from my tender years and my skinny body than anyone else would reasonably have expected. It didn't matter that he was a giant of a man and I was a scrawny little kid; it didn't matter that he had years of experience and I had none. He expected me to live up to his standards—right then and there—and since I was so young and he *was* my father, I didn't know any better so I didn't question it. I didn't know that thirteen-year-old boys who weigh just 120 pounds shouldn't be expected to carry 75-pound bundles of roofing shingles up a two-storey ladder all day. After a half-dozen such trips I would be exhausted; my father and the other men would be teasing me and I would be crying from fatigue and frustration. But somehow, through my curses and tears, I found the strength to keep climbing that ladder.

I can still remember the stern commandments he delivered on the job:

"Never walk when you can run."

"Never carry two planks when you can carry four."

Over the years I absorbed and accepted all the uncompromising instructions he drilled into me, and now I am extremely grateful that I grew into manhood in my father's watchful shadow because his high expectations have become the standards I've set for myself.

One of the main reasons for my move back to Six Nations

was to be able to spend time with some very special people—the old-timers on this territory, who have many
things to teach me about the people, the culture and the
history of this place. People like Reg Henry. Well, I saw Reg
today, but it was for the last time. He died three days ago. I
went to his funeral this morning at the Seneca longhouse.
He was seventy years old.

I first met Reg and his wife Marge and their four daughters nearly thirty years ago when we lived down the street
from each other in Rochester, New York. At the time I was
in my last year of high school. I wanted to learn more
about my people but I was separated from the reserve by a
four-hour drive. I squeezed my parents for what they knew
and looked around for more. There was nothing. In those
days—the mid-1960s—there were no cultural programs or
activities for Indians in the cities. There was no such thing
as a native friendship centre. There were no native employment projects, no native student programs, no native
housing programs. In fact, there were no native organizations at all. Indians then were economic refugees from
reserve poverty, isolated bits of flotsam drifting in a white
urban sea. But then I found Reg Henry.

Reg was a member of the bear clan of the Onondaga
Nation. Not only did he seem to know everything about
what I wanted to learn, he was willing and caring and
patient enough to teach me. I remember the evenings he
spent trying to instruct me in the intricacies of the language, the drum, the rattle and the Rabbit Dance. It didn't
last long, though, because I soon went away to university,
while Reg and his family moved back to the reserve.

Reg then began to do the work that I'm sure the Creator
had in mind for him all along. He was a born teacher with
a gift for languages. His first language was Cayuga but he
also spoke Onondaga, Seneca and Mohawk. I knew him
best as the speaker of a by-golly, gee-whiz variety of

English that he delivered in a breathy nasal monotone.

Once he was back on the reserve, Reg began working to keep the Cayuga language alive. At the time Reg was, by his own count, one of just 200 people who still spoke the Cayuga tongue. (Twenty years later, the number of fluent Cayuga speakers is now just 137.) Reg taught the language in the elementary schools for six years. After that, and until he became unable to carry on, he worked at the local cultural centre developing Cayuga language and curriculum materials.

Reg became widely renowned for his language work and he was increasingly in demand to translate old documents. His work was so precise that the method he used to write the Cayuga language, with its distinctive spellings, accents and punctuation marks, was adopted by the local school system, universities, government and Cayuga speakers everywhere and is now known as the Henry orthography.

Because he was raised in its ways, Reg made the longhouse and its religion a central part of his life. The longhouse religion as practised at Six Nations is rooted in the traditional beliefs of the Iroquois that stretch back to the beginning of time. Today, there are four branches of the longhouse religion here. They are centred in the Seneca, Onondaga, Lower Cayuga and Sour Springs longhouses and are the focal points of traditional Iroquois culture. Since the traditional chiefs were ousted from the old council house in Ohsweken seventy years ago, the Onondaga longhouse also doubles as the meeting place of the Confederacy.

Despite its name, the Seneca longhouse has followers from almost all of the Six Nations, and one of the four head faithkeepers was Reg Henry. As such, Reg was responsible for ensuring that every word and every detail of every ceremony was faithfully and precisely conducted in accordance with longhouse tradition.

But the more he was called on, the less he was able to do. Reg was sick for several years with various ailments. The last time I saw him was in August, in between his numerous hospital stays. We sat together on his porch, shaded from a hot summer sun. He was upset at the time because he was unable to continue his work on the Cayuga language. "There is so much to be done," he said, with tears in his eyes.

Since I had always regarded Reg as the embodiment of human goodness, decency and virtue, I thought he was invincible. I was frightened, therefore, to see him so weak and troubled. I reached over, touched his arm and assured him that he would get better and soon be back to work. I told him that there was indeed a lot of work to be done and, I said, when I returned to the reserve I wanted him to teach me again. He smiled through his tears and agreed with me—more to humour me, I think now, than because he believed that he would ever be strong enough to work again. I never got to talk to him again.

Today the small Seneca longhouse was filled with more than a hundred of his family, friends and relatives. The men sat at one end of the longhouse, grouped in their clans; the women at the opposite end, grouped in their clans.

I stood outside the longhouse with almost two hundred others waiting to pay our respects. Half an hour after the service began we filed inside to say our final goodbyes, the men entering the men's door at the east end, the women entering the women's door at the opposite end.

As I stood before the open casket I took one long, last look at a man I had loved and respected for nearly thirty years. Reg was dressed in his best traditional clothes. He wore a fringed buckskin vest and a long blue ribbon shirt that had been sewn for his funeral two months earlier by his wife Marge and their daughters. His *kahstowa*, the one-feather Cayuga headdress, rested on his chest.

I was struck by a noticeable change in Reg's appearance. Gone were the signs of pain, trouble and stress that had marked his rugged features in recent years. In their place was a dignified and surprisingly vigorous expression. I knew then that Reg was ready to meet his maker with confidence and satisfaction, knowing he had done much of what he had set out to do so long ago.

I stood there thinking that I am one of the many people lucky enough to have known Reg Henry. He taught me many things about culture, language and history. He touched me with his dignity, humility, kindness and patience. As I stood there looking at my friend for the last time, my heart was heavy. The sorrow that was in my heart, and in the hearts of everyone gathered at the Seneca longhouse today, was meant to be lifted by the words of Skanyatariyo, the Seneca prophet known as Handsome Lake:

> When our friends depart we must lay grief aside.
> We must bury our grief in their grave. It is said
> moreover that you can journey with the dead
> only as far as the grave. When the body of the
> dead is buried we must become resigned to our
> loss. It can not be helped. Now let us journey to
> the grave with the body of the dead for it is as far
> as we can go...

With the service completed, the coffin was closed, carried outside and placed in an open grave in the plain cemetery next to the longhouse. Reg Henry, the gentle teacher, left this world in the way he would have wanted to—all the speeches were delivered in the Cayuga tongue and everything was done in accordance with longhouse tradition. I walked away from the cemetery knowing that in ten days' time, after the required death feast, Reg Henry will enter the Spirit World and be with the Creator in the land of everlasting happiness. I will miss him dearly then, just as I do now, but I shall grieve for him no more.

The Big Six

If you want to escape the noise, dirt, congestion and bustle of downtown Toronto all you have to do is drive ninety minutes southwest, to the spacious fields and peaceful woodlands of Six Nations.

This place, by the way, is also known by a number of nicknames. Most people living here call it "the reserve" or "the community." The term "rez" has been used only in recent years and seems to have been borrowed from Indians in the United States who live on *rez*-ervations. Some people here call this place "the Big Six" or "Grand River," and those who want to be politically assertive call it "the territory." (Depending on the occasion, I use all of the above.) Indians from other territories sometimes call it Brantford (wrong, since that's the city) or Ohsweken (not exactly, since that's the name of the small village in the middle of this big reserve).

People who are from here but who happen to be in town (off the reserve) often call it "the bush," and when they talk about returning to the reserve, they say they are going "donnabush" (down-the-bush). Many people still use the term even though much of the bush has been cut down and is now fields or farmland.

Although only about half of the 18,000 people on the Six Nations membership rolls actually live on the reserve, it still makes for a very large and very dispersed community. Only a thousand or so people live in the village of Ohsweken, most of them in a new subdivision behind the shopping plaza. The rest are scattered across the sprawling countryside. Their houses line the one hundred miles of roads on the reserve. Most people live in modern, well-kept bungalows, split-levels and ranch houses. But many live in battered trailers and crumbling farmhouses. A few live in basements while they wait, sometimes for years, to scrape together enough money to finish building the rest of their house.

The community can support many big-city services and businesses. For example, the reserve has a bank, supermarket, library, radio station, newspaper, arena, legion hall, driving range, doughnut shop, motel and funeral parlour. There are gas stations, jewellery stores, mini-malls, car washes, garages, video shops, clothing stores, flower shops, restaurants, craft shops, convenience stores, laundromats, lumberyards and limousine companies. If you live in Ohsweken, there are paved roads, a sewer system, natural gas, piped-in water, sidewalks, cable television and a stoplight.

But if you want to escape the hurly-burly of downtown Ohsweken, all you have to do is drive two minutes in any direction down the backroads that lead to homes, like mine, where the amenities are fewer and life is a little more basic.

//

With winter coming on, I still don't know how I'll heat the other half of my house but I do know that I don't like my options. Whatever I decide, I know that this winter the heat will gush from my drafty home like promises from a politician's lips.

I was abruptly reminded of this when I got my first propane delivery today. The bill was more than four hundred dollars. I can't imagine getting another propane heater to heat my writing room, not at those prices, and especially not when the propane man said he would be back every couple of weeks to fill the tank.

So, just as I have done a dozen times already this week, I asked my sister Dennise for advice. She has lived on the reserve for eighteen years and is a treasure-trove of local information. She knows a lot about the cost of home heating because she works for the natural gas company, and she heats her house with a combination of electricity and a wood-burning stove. She tells me if I think propane is expensive I should see what it costs to heat with electricity. *Hmm*.

Even if hydro weren't so expensive, I wouldn't select the electric heating option. The tiny electrical system in this house wouldn't be able to bear the extra load of space-heaters on top of all the appliances and computer equipment I use. Natural gas is not an option either because it will be years, if ever, before the gas company here extends its pipeline to this underpopulated corner of the territory.

So, if I want to write this winter without having to wear longjohns, sweaters, gloves and felt-lined boots, it looks as though I will have to put in a woodstove. Fortunately, I like the idea because it appeals to the rustic, back-to-nature side of me. I also like it because cutting, splitting, stacking and carrying all that wood will be good for my flabby figure. All I'll have to do is buy a stove, put up a chimney, get some wood and make a fire.

Yeah, right. As if that's *all* there is to it. Although I'm no stranger to heating a house the old-fashioned way, I've got a feeling there's a lot more to it than just throwing another log in the stove.

Aunt Ví and the travelling Mohawks

One of the things the Maracles can brag about is being a well-travelled family, but then, the Mohawks have always been great travellers. Long before the Europeans settled here, the Mohawks had journeyed to all parts of Great Turtle Island.

In the fifteenth century, the Mohawks reportedly travelled to Haiti. The museum in Port-au-Prince, a friend tells me, has a plaque that says Columbus brought a boatload of Mohawks with him on his second voyage there. The plaque does not explain where or how Columbus ever met the Mohawks, but it does say they escaped into the jungle and intermarried with the local Arawak people.

During the sixteenth and seventeenth centuries, the Mohawks routinely raided white settlements and Indian villages hundreds of miles away from their homeland in the Mohawk Valley, in what is now New York State. In the eighteenth century, Mohawk leaders were frequent visitors to the royal courts of London. All the Mohawk travelling in historic times, it should be noted, was done by the men and was done for either hunting, warfare or political reasons. By the nineteenth century, Mohawk men were still travelling—but only for employment. In 1884, for exam-

36

ple, a group of fifty Mohawks travelled to Africa and went up the Nile as part of the Wolseley Expedition to rescue General Gordon at Khartoum.

My family has done its part to continue the tribal tradition. During the 1880s, my great-grandfather, Peter June Maracle, toured the United States as a tomahawk-throwing performer in one of the Wild West medicine shows. His son, my Grampa Leonard, left the reserve and worked for several years in California during the 1920s. My parents began their far-flung travels while they were in the military during World War II. In recent years they have toured Peru and China and they're planning to visit Israel and Egypt next year.

As for me, I have been a tourist on the beaches of Hawaii, the boulevards of Paris, the canals of Bangkok and the markets of Tripoli. My work has taken me to out-of-the-way places in Canada (Canyon City, Nelson House, Moose Factory) and around the world—bush villages in Alaska, leper colonies in India and jungles in Papua New Guinea.

But all this Mohawk travelling—from birchbark canoes to jumbo jets—has come at a price. It is partly because of the ease with which we travelled, and it is partly because of our skills, confidence and adaptability, that the Mohawks today are a dispersed people and the Maracles are a far-flung family.

The first great dispersal came after the American Revolutionary War when the Mohawks left the valley in New York State that bears our name. Within a few decades Mohawks had settled in Quebec, Ontario, Ohio, Kansas, Oklahoma, Montana, Alberta, Washington and British Columbia. Within this century, the search for work has driven Mohawk individuals even further afield. (Many of the telephone books in major North American cities, for example, have at least one Maracle listed.)

My immediate family is scattered—split between British

Columbia, Pennsylvania, New York and Ontario. If I included my cousins, aunts and uncles, it would cover an even larger territory. The only time the Maracles get together these days is for a funeral, and we had one of those get-togethers for Aunt Vi today. She died peacefully last Saturday, less than a week after I moved back. She was eighty-three years old.

My parents flew in from Vancouver for the funeral. Other relatives drove in from Buffalo, Rochester, Hamilton, Fort Erie, Niagara Falls and I don't know where else.

Although I call her Aunt Vi, she was really my dad's aunt, my late Grampa Leonard's sister. She was born Violet Maracle and she married a Mohawk, Stewart Staats. Aunt Vi lived on the reserve almost all her life. She devoted herself to raising a family and was a lifelong member of the Seventh Day Adventist Church.

I didn't know Aunt Vi very well. Apart from one or two visits to her home, the only time I ever saw her was when I returned to the reserve for a funeral. But what I did know about her I liked a lot because she was always so bright, funny and cheerful.

The service for Aunt Vi was held at the funeral home in Ohsweken, led by a pastor from the Adventist church. It was identical to other family funerals I have attended over the years—an English sermon combined with Mohawk hymns sung by the Mohawk Singers, a group led by my uncle, John Maracle. The half-dozen singers, most of them grandmothers or grandfathers many times over, sat in the last two rows. There was no musical accompaniment, no sophisticated arrangement, no harmonizing—just a body of voices plodding together through the verses.

Most "Mohawk" hymns, incidentally, were translated from the English versions nearly three hundred years ago. When it is spoken, the Mohawk language has a rolling, almost singsong quality. Ordinarily, the words are hard to distinguish because of the breathy interjections that punctuate the predominantly nasal tone of the language. But when it is forced to conform to the rhythms of a hymn, the long, tongue-twisting words get stretched out and chopped into a chain of steady, bite-sized beats. Syllables that are usually almost silent get pronounced with the same stress and volume as those that are accented. The up-and-down rhythm of the spoken language gets flattened and the breathy punctuations evaporate, so that the musical quality of the spoken word is lost. It's much like what happens when the lyrics of a song are read aloud by a small child who has just learned to read—the music disappears in a chain of clearly enunciated and equally stressed syllables.

Nevertheless, there is another dimension to Mohawk hymns that makes them extraordinarily powerful. The nasal tone of the language becomes even more pronounced and, in an eerie but fitting way, the sustained nasal droning resembles the musical tones of a church organ and provides the singers with their own musical accompaniment.

Because Aunt Vi was elderly and had been in failing health, her death did not come as a great shock or surprise. The family members were as well prepared for her death and funeral as anyone can be, so everyone was quiet and composed during the service—until the singers began the first hymn. And then the crying started. The first few sniffles triggered some open sobs which led to even more weeping. By the time the first hymn was over, there were tears and red puffy eyes everywhere.

There is something about Mohawk hymns at a funeral that brings out the tears. It's not the lyrics, because the younger people didn't understand a word of them and they cried anyway. It's the *sound* of it all. For those of us who assemble from far-away places to bury one of our own, a Mohawk hymn is the sound that signals death, the sound that unlocks tears, the sound that triggers grief and sorrow.

//

At the top of a gentle rise overlooking a wide shallow valley, hemmed in by a ridge of trees and a green chain-link
fence, is a simple, well-kept cemetery not quite the size of
a football field, one of the two dozen graveyards on the
reserve. Squeezed between the fence and the tree line lie
the headstones, nearly one hundred and fifty of them.
Chiselled into a few of them are the clan symbol or the
Indian name of the deceased. Many of the headstones have
religious inscriptions. A few graves are adorned with withered floral tributes. Scattered among the gravestones are a
few cedar trees, a stand of spruce and some ornamental
shrubs. Everything is neat and orderly. The fence stands
straight and true. There is no litter. At the edge of the
cemetery next to the road is a hand-painted wooden sign
that says simply "Stump Hall Cemetery."

The name comes from the small white clapboard church
that used to stand by the road, a church known by everyone on the reserve as Stump Hall, though its proper name
was the Plymouth Brethren Church. It was founded by an
England-based sect that held communal meals and
believed every word in the Bible to be true. When the
brethren began their missionary work at Six Nations in the
mid-nineteenth century, they had no church and must
have used whatever was at hand because the Mohawks at
the time called the English preachers *rontsinowonrawaha*,
"those who speak standing on a stump." Even though the
white clapboard church was torn down twenty years ago,
the area is still known as Stump Hall.

This cemetery, now a community burial ground used by
just a few families, is Aunt Vi's final resting place. It also
holds the remains of my great-grandfathers Thomas and
Peter, my great-grandmothers Mary and Sarah, my
Grampa Leonard, my aunts Orma and Hilda, my uncle
Ronnie, and I don't know how many other aunts, uncles

and cousins. The tombstones here are granite pieces in a giant jigsaw puzzle. If I could ever figure out just how all these people are related, I could put the puzzle together and I would finally be able to visualize one-half of my family tree. Clearly, there is much for me to learn about the people buried here, much to understand about who they were and how they helped to make me who I am.

Because the cemetery is surrounded by open fields in all directions, the mood here is often lonesome, and today was no exception. The leaves have fallen from the trees overlooking the shallow valley, exposing skeleton branches that exaggerate the starkness of the scene. The weather was raw. A bitter wind that struck from grey, overcast skies made the chilly air seem that much colder.

On this harsh day, in this surreal setting, with her family surrounding the grave, Vi Staats was laid to rest. She was buried next to her husband under a headstone etched with both their names and the inscription "FOREVER WITH THE LORD." My father, an elder in the Adventist church, delivered the closing prayer. The graveside ceremony brought a solemn and dignified end to a funeral that added another Maracle to our common ground.

This funeral, like all the others, was a gathering of the Maracles, a summons to stand with the family. It was another death-triggered reunion that allowed the living to make an accounting of the number and health of those who remain. It was also a chance to take the measure of those who have joined the circle.

Before I moved back to the reserve, I often used to visit this graveyard. I didn't come here because I was sad or depressed. In fact, I did not come by conscious choice at all. Instead, I was pulled by a force I could not resist. I don't know what drew me here, but I didn't come to make a show of paying my respects because I always came alone. I was drawn to walk silently among the gravestones, to read the names of my people, to rekindle their memory, to walk on the soil that is mixed with their bones, to breathe the air that whispers their spirit. I always left that special place feeling stronger than when I came.

I have lived most of my life as a tumbleweed, pushed by the wind, pulled by gravity, drifting from one temporary landing to another. I have lived a restless and unsettled life—moving from one house, city and country to another, from one job to another, from one woman to another. Now that I am back on the rez, I don't have a job and I don't have a wife, my daughter has grown up and moved away, but at least I have the comfort and security of feeling I am home at last. This forty-six-year-old tumbleweed has finally stopped rolling. I am where I was meant to be.

Furthermore, I am comforted by the knowledge that this simple graveyard, this hallowed ground, is the final destination for me and all the wandering members of my tribal family. I have done more than my share of travelling and I know this simple graveyard will be the final destination in my life's journey. Stump Hall will be my last stop.

To the dump, to the dump, to the dump-dump-dump

It used to be that at the edge of many Indian reserves there was a sign saying, "NOTICE. THIS IS AN INDIAN RESERVE." Emblazoned with the Great Seal of Canada and signed by the Director of Indian Affairs, it went on to say that "Any person who trespasses on an Indian Reserve is guilty of an offence and is liable on summary conviction to a fine not exceeding fifty dollars or to imprisonment for a term not exceeding one month, or to both fine and imprisonment."

There is no such sign on the edge of this territory, at least not now. The only similarly official or ominous notice anywhere around here is the one posted at the entrance to the Six Nations landfill—the garbage dump. The dump, it says, is "FOR THE USE AND BENEFIT OF THE SIX NATIONS PEOPLE...TRESPASSERS WILL BE PROSECUTED." Another sign says, "PLEASE BE PRE-PARED TO STOP AND PRESENT IDENTIFICATION."

At the entrance to the dump is a small cement-block guard house. When I pulled up there this morning, the woman in the guard house looked me over and asked what I had in the back of my car. "Five bags of garbage," I told her. She took another look at me and my garbage-filled car and waved me through.

It used to be a lot easier to get into the dump a few years ago, I'm told. There was no guard at all then so anyone could drive right in. And that was the problem—just about anyone did. The private company that was supposed to be managing the dump was letting trucks from all over southern Ontario dump all kinds of stuff here. To make things worse, the company owner and another high-profile local businessman signed a deal with the band council to set up a recycling depot that would involve even more waste being delivered to the reserve. That news got everyone riled up, and at a community meeting attended by nearly three hundred people, a local environmentalist dropped a bombshell. She released a copy of an agreement between then-band chief Bill Montour and the Mayor of North York to develop a joint plan to dump Metropolitan Toronto's garbage on Six Nations. The crowd, by all accounts, went wild. No one, it seems, wanted anything to do with the two hundred and fifty promised jobs. A week later, the Confederacy banned outside garbage from being dumped on the territory. Two weeks later a group of environmental activists called SNAP (Six Nations Against Pollution) padlocked the entrance to the dump and granted access to reserve residents only.

I went to the dump today because I have decided to dispose of my garbage myself. I could pay a business here about two dollars a week to pick it up and dump it for me, but taking my own garbage to the dump just seems like the right thing to do. After all, one of the reasons I want to live in the country is to get "close to nature." The downside is that going to the dump will bring me close to a part of nature—rats, maggots and crows—that I really don't want to have much to do with.

The garbage controversy has left everyone in the community much more conscious of issues involving the environment. The band council eventually regained control of the dump and posted the guard to ensure that only band members use it. The problem is that while the band keeps a vigilant lookout for off-reserve garbage, nothing seems to be done about improving the way we deal with the garbage we create ourselves. There is no blue box recycling program, for example. That's understandable, in part, because outside municipalities lose a lot of money collecting and sorting the contents of all those blue boxes. But surely, it would pay to have giant blue boxes placed at the dump. People who use the dump could then put their old newspapers, bottles and cans in the bins and that would eliminate the collection and sorting expense. The band would then only have to deliver the stuff to a recycling plant. If the band wanted to get serious about recycling, it could also place containers there for fine paper, plastic pop bottles, cardboard and other reusable things in our garbage. And if it wanted to get *really* serious about protecting the environment, the band would do something to dispose properly of the hazardous waste that gets plowed under at the dump—used motor oil, paint cans, car batteries and I shudder to think what else.

So for the time being I'll continue to take my garbage to the dump. Leaving it at the roadside for someone else to get rid of is part of the lackadaisical, out-of-sight-out-of-mind urban attitude that got this community into the garbage mess in the first place.

Out of touch and loving it

Over the past two weeks I have been so busy unpacking and trying to get settled that I have begun to lose touch with the outside world. Just today, for instance, I realized I have not read a newspaper since I moved here.

Two weeks without reading a paper! It doesn't seem possible. I have read a newspaper, often two, almost every day for the past thirty years. A small forest must have been cut down to provide the newsprint for all the papers I've read. And now that I've finally broken the daily newspaper habit, I realize I don't miss the petty sensationalism, the staged events, the obsession with celebrities and the filler copy that passes for news.

I haven't completely lost touch, though. I listen to CBC Radio so I know something about "the news." I talk long-distance with people from the outside who presumably still read newspapers every day, and if another World War started, I assume they'd tell me about it. In that way, I'm becoming a lot like the people around me. Most of my neighbours and relatives don't read the paper every day and they don't seem to be suffering. The people in the coffee shops here don't talk about Bosnia or the Bloc Québécois.

The broken newspaper habit, though, is just one measure of the way I have dropped out of one world and entered another. I realized today, for example, that I have not hooked my computer back up to the Internet. Before I moved I was plugged into all the computer newsgroups about my two passions in life—fishing and native affairs. But there was so much information on the system it took me forty-five minutes a day just to skim it. Most of the postings on this electronic bulletin board were, for me, useless and irrelevant. I'm not terribly interested, for example, in an ongoing argument over the derivation of some word in the Dakota language, and I don't care what trout flies are working right now on the upper stretch of some river in Idaho.

And that was just reading the stuff! Heaven forbid if I actually replied to a message and got locked into one of those discussions that go on forever. I fought the urge to reply to some of the more inane and provocative postings because I knew I would end up sparring with some argumentative know-it-all who just has to have the last word (in other words, someone just like me).

So, in spite of all the dire warnings about how people who are not "plugged in" will be left behind in the coming revolution, I will not plug myself back into the Internet. I will continue, instead, to use my computer as a glorified typewriter and I don't care if I ever get back onto the information highway.

And as for getting plugged back into the world of television, I have stopped fiddling with the television antenna and I have given up trying to get CBC-TV. I will content myself therefore with the two-and-a-half channels I do get—and I will plan on doing a lot more reading.

The only problem is that getting something good to read will not be easy around here. Decent newspapers are hard to come by, there is no bookstore on the reserve and the band library, to put it as charitably as I can, needs a lot of work. But at least the corner stores here sell magazines. Boy, do they ever. At the front of the rack you'll find their top-of-the-line reading material—*The National Enquirer*, *Tattoo World* and *True Confessions*. At the back of the rack you'll find *Penthouse*, *Swank* and *Hustler*. But you won't find *Maclean's*, *Chatelaine* or even *People* magazine. You have to drive seven miles into Brantford for those. And even in Brantford you won't find *Harper's*, *Saturday Night* or *The New Yorker*. For those you have to drive thirty miles into Hamilton. I can give up the newspaper, the Internet and CBC-TV, but I can't give up magazines, so it looks as though I will be visiting Hamilton a lot more often than I thought.

//

After being back on the reserve for two weeks, I have taken stock of my new situation. Yes, I have lost touch with the outside world in some ways, but there are many new things in my life that more than make up for the loss of the old.

I am more active, for one thing, because there's a lot of physical work involved in whipping this old house into shape. I don't mind getting sweaty and tired. I don't even mind getting stiff and sore, because I can feel the physical labour strengthening my body, invigorating my mind and soothing my soul.

And after forty years of living under streetlights, I am especially thrilled by the nighttime sky. Every night before I go to bed I stand in the darkness and stare in awestruck wonder at a universe of dazzling lights twinkling in the infinite blackness.

There are lots of other things I like about being back on the territory.

When I call an office in Ohsweken (even some places in Brantford) and they ask me my name, I like being able to say "Brian Maracle." Period. That's because until I moved back here, whenever someone asked me my name I would say, automatically, "Brian Maracle. That's spelled M-A-R-A-C-L-E." But I don't have to do that any more because the people here know the name and know how to spell it. And they don't say, "Gee, what a funny name." If they say anything about my name, it's usually to ask if I am related to someone.

Another thing I like about living here is going into a store and bumping into guys I worked with twenty years ago in the States. I like being able to renew old acquaintances with guys like me who have finally moved home. I like being introduced to people at a coffee shop and finding out we're related. I like being able to see my sister, grandmothers, aunts, uncles, cousins, nieces, nephews and in-laws anytime and all the time.

What it comes down to, I guess, is that I love the sense of belonging I finally have. I love the warmth and security that comes from the feeling of being wrapped in a sheltering cocoon of family and community.

So maybe I am losing touch with the outside world. But I don't miss it at all. Not one little bit.

Taxophobia

So there I was, half asleep at three o'clock this morning, when I suddenly woke up and realized why everyone here, including the longhouse people, remind me of Christian fundamentalists—specifically, the ones who are always preaching "THE END OF THE WORLD IS NEAR."

You don't have to be around here for very long, less than a month in my case, to realize that the Indians here have a similarly unshakeable fear and belief that many of them loudly proclaim at every opportunity—"TAXATION IS COMING! TAXATION IS COMING!"

The people here are obviously suffering from taxophobia, the fear of impending taxation. They are particularly afraid that the government, through the band councils or by itself, will tax reserve land. It's this fear, I think, that makes the people fight back by insisting on being exempted from paying sales tax when they shop in town. If they don't get the exemption, they will leave the goods on the counter, walk out and drive twenty miles to another store—even if it's just to save fifty cents' tax. It's not the money, they say, it's the principle. And they're right.

The fact is that we must insist that the people and governments of Canada recognize our rights, all of them, no matter how seemingly small an issue is involved. If we don't, we open the door for the government to renege on any or all of our rights. Seen in this light, insisting on a fifty-cent tax exemption is not about saving money or even about protecting our rights. What it's about—and I don't think I'm exaggerating or being overly dramatic when I say this—is fighting to preserve the little land we have left.

The people here are alarmed by the way the taxation noose has slipped ever tighter around the reserves— Indians are being forced to pay the GST, provincial sales tax and income tax in more and more situations. A lot of people have been running around like Chicken Little, issuing dire warnings about the coming of the Taxman. Their alarms are finding a receptive audience because the taxophobics here generally don't know what the federal government, the provincial government, the band council or the Confederacy is doing about anything.

The ironic thing about this situation is that the more government chisels back on our tax exemptions, the more some white people scream about the ones we have left. They're the ones who argue loudly, "We're all Canadians. The past is past. Everyone is equal. No one should be tax-exempt."

The reeve of a neighbouring township has been hollering lately about how the Six Nations band council has bought land, added it to the reserve and reduced the township's tax revenues. I can just imagine her wailing: *Those Indians have the nerve to buy back the land we stole from them and they're not going to pay taxes on it. It ain't fair!*

The twist in this little story is that this reeve, a white woman, is a status Indian. She married an Indian man back in the days when the government gave white brides a status card entitling them to all Indian rights and privileges, including tax exemptions. So this reeve, who complains about Indians gobbling up her township and not paying taxes, has been seen on the reserve using her status card to buy tax-free gasoline. (Presumably, she also uses it in town to save money on sales tax.) What drives people around here crazy is that her public complaints are widely and frequently reported but her private hypocrisy is not.

Some of the complaints against Indian tax exemptions are rooted in the racism that has been passed down in this area from father to son and mother to daughter for over two hundred years. The people who complain these days are probably descendants of the men who used clubs and pitch-forks in the 1840s to drive the Iroquois off the land on the north side of the Grand River while the authorities stood by and did nothing. They may also be related to the town fathers of Brantford who petitioned the federal government in 1914 to have the Indians from Six Nations packed up and moved to Manitoulin Island like so many cattle because, they said, we stood in the way of development.

These people should be aware of certain realities. The Iroquois have always maintained that we are citizens of sovereign Indian nations and, as such, are immune from Canadian taxation. The opponents of Indian tax exemption might ignore our pleadings, but aboriginal and treaty rights *were* recognized and entrenched in Canada's constitution in 1982, and these treaties guaranteed immunity from Canadian taxation.

One of the earliest treaties is known as the Two-Row Wampum. The "Two-Row" is made from wampum—purple and white beads made from clam shells that are strung together in a wide belt. Two parallel lines of purple beads run the length of the white belt. One line represents the Iroquois, the other, the Europeans. The belt signifies that our two peoples will travel the river of life separately, the Iroquois in their canoes, the Europeans in their boats. The agreement provides that both peoples will stay in their own vessels and neither side shall interfere with the course or progress of the other. Contained within this treaty of friendship and mutual non-interference is the recognition, among other things, of Indian immunity from European taxation.

Although most treaties are silent on the issue of taxation, it is clear from the oral record that past Indian leaders clearly intended to retain our traditional immunity from alien taxation. (The Supreme Court of Canada, incidentally, has ordered the government to interpret the treaties in the way they would have been understood by the Indians who signed them. The court also says that a treaty right for one Indian nation is a treaty right for all.) Treaty 8, signed in 1899, leaves no doubt about the matter. In their report to Ottawa, the federal treaty commissioners said, "We assured them that the treaty would not lead to any forced interference with their mode of life, that it did not open the way to the imposition of any tax."

And because of all this, the federal and provincial governments have long recognized that Indian people are legally entitled to specific tax exemptions. The Indian Act, for example, exempts the property and income of Indians on reserves from taxation. Some provincial governments, like Ontario's, have exempted Indians from provincial sales tax—an exemption that recognizes that Indians here, like tourists from other provinces, are not Ontario citizens.

Before I tried to go back to sleep this morning I made a point of turning on the light and writing down my little observation about the connection between Christian fundamentalists and Indian taxophobics. I also couldn't help thinking at the time that while I understand the need to be vigilant and ever-ready to defend our rights against all comers, I don't think the threat to tax reserve lands is worth worrying about—yet.

But, I thought, there are plenty of things we should be

worrying about, things that few other people seem to be paying any attention to, things that have moved way past the threat stage and are doing serious damage right now to our personal and collective well-being—things like television, bingo, junk food, alcohol, golf, Nintendo and a thousand other Euro-Canadian elements that are overwhelming our culture.

And just when I started to think that maybe I should start warning people, doomsday-like, about all these dangers that are already here to stay, I realized that I'm probably suffering from a phobia of my own, a fear of foreign cultural elements. I think I have Europhobia.

One pail of water

In the old days, people around here used to get their water by going outside, throwing a pail down a well and hauling the water up, hand over hand, pail after pail, day after day. That's just how my sister Dennise (or, more accurately, that's how her husband Gary) had to get water until just a couple of years ago. It never occurred to me, at least not until Stan Maracle told me, that getting water could be even harder than that.

Stan (I call him Uncle Stan but he's really my dad's uncle) is seventy-nine years old. Although old age has withered him a bit, he is still nearly six feet tall, weighs nearly two hundred pounds and is stronger and more active than many men just half his age. He has a fringe of salt-and-pepper hair on the sides and back of his otherwise bald head. Seen face-on, he has the square-jawed, bullet-headed look of a grandfatherly Mr. Clean, minus the earring.

On first introduction, Stan is quiet, modest and extremely polite. Beneath his well-mannered demeanour, though, is a tough and unyielding core that is all business. For people who know him, he can be, with a little prodding, an earthy and entertaining storyteller with a hearty laugh and a gap-toothed smile.

Stan grew up on the reserve and worked with his hands all his life, first as a farmhand, then as a logger, later as a hard-rock driller. But for the past fifty-two years he, like all the other men in the Maracle family, has been a carpenter. During that time he has built or remodelled thousands of apartments, homes, garages and offices. In fact, he's still at it. He just finished building a level floor in my writing room so that my computer won't slide off my desk any more. And right now, he's doing the trim carpentry on a cousin's new house. The only concession he makes to his age these days is that he doesn't do any heavy lifting and he goes home in the early afternoon to take a nap. Once he finishes his current job he'll be looking for another one, not so much because he needs the money (he does) but because he genuinely likes to work and he would be bored to tears sitting in his seniors' apartment with nothing to do.

Over the past several years I have spent a lot of time with Stan. I like to practise my Mohawk on him and ask him questions about himself, our family and the reserve. Because his memory is so sharp and extensive, his answers are chock-full of asides and colourful details. In our discussions of current events, he has a keen and penetrating mind that searches out inconsistencies, and he delights in puncturing half-baked arguments with a sharply pointed question.

Stan frequently sprinkles his conversation with elements of his moral code. He is quick to glorify hard work. He believes in giving and getting a day's work for a day's pay. He places great stock in being "a man of your word" and "doing unto others as you would have them do unto you." And he celebrates fairness, honesty and thrift in a personality marked with hard-headed, no-nonsense practicality.

Because he is so confident of his abilities and untroubled by his limitations, Stan is very secure in his self-image and he flat-out doesn't care what anyone else thinks of him. The other day I went to pick him up at his apartment so we could go to a restaurant. He had just finished getting dressed when I arrived; he was wearing a wash-and-wear sport shirt and permanent-press pants. Casting a critical eye on the crease in his pants he said, "I guess they look all right."

I told him I wasn't in any rush and that if he wanted to iron them, he could.

"Ha!" he said. "I don't even own an iron. I just take my clothes out of the dryer and put them on a hanger. If people don't like the wrinkles in my pants," he harrumphed, "they can look the other way."

Stan is a plain man with simple tastes and he makes no apologies for it. He's a meat-and-potatoes guy and he rarely eats anything else. It's risky to try to get him to eat even the simplest Chinese or Mexican dishes—a *fajita*, say, or almond *guy ding*. More exotic fare or the latest food fad is simply out of the question. "I don't eat that shit," he'll sniff.

When he was thirteen years old, his father (my great-grandfather, Peter June Maracle) took him out of the eighth grade and put him to work full time on the family farm. Stan is not an educated man as a result and he doesn't read very much, but I am still amazed at how much he knows about the most obscure bits of ancient history, far-flung religions and Old World geography.

What I like best about being with Stan is listening to his stories of life on the reserve in the old days. Because he comes from a time when the Indian way of life was radically different, his stories are couched in a distinctly old-fashioned vocabulary. He might say, for instance, "We took a cutter to Jack's shivaree."

Cutter? Shivaree?

Or when he describes a piece of land, he'll often say something like: "You go past the swale on the old Jake Fish farm and it's ten chains east of the hedgerow."

Swale? Chains? Hedgerow?

And as for "Old Jake Fish," *Jake* was probably an old man when Stan was a boy, and yet Stan talks about him as if I might know who he is. If I look the slightest bit quizzical, though, Stan will give me a complete rundown on Jake Fish's family tree, showing how we might be related to him, as well as an accounting of how the Fish property came to be owned by whoever has it now.

Sometimes when I tell Stan that I don't know who or what he's talking about, he will tease me by snorting with disgust, "And I thought you were an educated man. You went to college and you still don't know nothin'."

Mostly, though, Stan loves to explain what life was like in days gone by. The other day, for example, we were in my garage and I held up a rusty old tool and asked him what it was. "It's a hayknife," he said. When I gave him a blank look, he said with a grin, "I'll bet you don't even know what a hayknife is." I gave him another blank look. "Well," he said, "when you're building a haystack..." But he stopped, thought about that for a second, looked straight at me and asked, "I'll bet you don't know how to build a haystack, do you?" Before I could give him yet another blank stare, he proceeded to show me with a few hand gestures how to use a pitchfork to build a haystack. "You have to place and handle the hay just so. It's like any material, you have to learn how to work it. You just don't pile it up."

Stan ended the lesson of the hayknife by explaining that it was used in the winter to cut blocks of hay out of the haystack to feed to the cows. There were other rusty old tools in the garage, but I decided to save my questions about them for another day.

Because "the old days" are frequently at the front of his mind, Stan often doesn't recognize the significance of some of the things he says. Recently, for example, he was telling me about the various places he had lived on the reserve. He said that in 1933, the year he dug the well, he was living on the family farm on Sour Springs Road. He was about to go on but I stopped him.

"Wait a minute. What do you mean, you dug a well?"

"I dug a well."

"By hand?" I asked incredulously. Being familiar only with the present-day practice of digging wells—you call up a professional well-drilling company that sends out a truck-mounted mechanized drilling rig, a work crew, steel pipe and concrete well casings—it never occurred to me that there might still be people alive today who had done such a thing by hand.

"Yes," was all he said, as though digging a well was such an everyday occurrence that it was not worth talking about. He was about to go on and tell me where he lived in 1934 when I stopped him and dragged the whole well-digging story out of him, question by question, detail by detail.

"Had you ever dug a well before?"

"No."

"How did you know what to do?"

"My father told me what to do and I just did it."

"How did he know what to do?"

"I don't know. That's just one of the things you learned how to do in those days."

I learned that Stan began digging the well on the family farm when he was eighteen. Before that he had hauled water from a creek a couple of hundred yards away. Using only a pick and shovel he dug the well six feet in diameter without using cribbing or braces. Stan says the well was straight and true because he used a wooden gauge his father made to keep the well plumb. That winter he and his father took a team of horses and a sled into the bush behind the farm. They cleared the snow cover off the ground, removed a couple of feet of topsoil and then, with a sledgehammer and cold chisel, quarried several tons of limestone which they hauled back to the well site. The next summer's digging took Stan to the forty-five-foot level and a thin layer of blue clay. When he broke through the clay, water started to seep in. That's when his father, who was seventy years old at the time, climbed down into the well. He used the stone they had quarried to line the well and keep it from collapsing.

With the last stone in place, Stan covered the well and waited—waited for the water to rise, for the sediment to settle and the water to clear. A week later he went to the well, uncovered it, dropped down a pail, filled it, lifted it out and took a drink.

At this point in the story Stan looked at me with twinkling eyes and a wide-open smile. Then, loudly emphasizing every word, he said, "Oh, that was good water. It really tasted nice."

He sat there for a minute, not saying anything, thinking back more than sixty years, remembering the taste of a drink of water he had drawn from the bowels of the earth with little more than his bare hands. He shook his head, made a tight-lipped smile, looked up and stared at the ceiling as the memories washed over him.

Then he turned to me. When he went back to the well the next day, he said, there was no water, only a jumbled pile of stone. The well lining had collapsed and the stones had fallen in on themselves. Stan said he was ready to go back down into the well, pull the stones out and try to re-line it but his father said it was too dangerous. There was nothing more to do, he said, but fill in the hole.

"Are you kidding?" I boomed. "You dug a hole six feet wide and forty-five feet deep. You quarried and hauled a couple tons of stone. You spent a year doing all that and all you got was *one* pail of water?"

"Yep."

And with a silly grin on his face he added, "But, oh, that was good water. It really tasted nice."

One of my fondest childhood memories involves well water.

When I was a boy, my family lived for a time with my great-grandmother, Sarah Thomas, in a simple frame house my parents built on the upper end of the reserve near Thomas's Corner. Gramma Thomas, who was sixty-nine years old when I was born, was the matriarch of a huge branch of the Maracle family tree.

I loved her place, for many reasons: partly because the house was built by my parents; partly because it was surrounded by fields and woodlands and was the best playground a kid could ever have; but mostly because it was Gramma's place and she lived there.

After my family moved to the States we returned several times a year to visit and stay with her, and I continued these visits long after I was on my own. Twenty years ago, I spent an entire winter living in that house with her. I cut wood, kept the fire going and hauled water from the well. Gramma lived in that house almost until the day she died in 1978, at the age of one hundred.

One of the things I will always remember about being in that house was the pail of well water that stood on the counter inside the back door. Hanging next to the pail was a ladle—a cheap aluminum saucepan with a long thin handle. I loved to take the ladle and dip it into the pail, hold it to my lips and drink slowly and deeply from what I still think was the best-tasting water in the world. It didn't have any chlorine, iron or sulphur in it so it smelled, looked and tasted better than city water. A lot better. City water, to me, tasted like the discharge from a chemical factory, while the water from Gramma's well had the cool, sweet and refreshing taste of a tumbling mountain stream.

The well water in this house of mine is also delicious but it just doesn't seem to taste quite as good as the water at Gramma Thomas's. The only way I think I could recapture that taste would be to uncap my well, throw down a pail, drag the water up hand over hand and drink it from a saucepan.

I appreciate good water, especially now that everybody in the village of Ohsweken is plagued by bad water. They get their water from the community's water plant on the Grand River, and for the past couple of years it has been contaminated with small amounts of cancer-causing NDMA (Nitrosodomethylamine). While the band tries to find the source of the pollution and solve the problem, there is a ban on drinking tap water in the village. People and businesses, therefore, have to drive to the fire hall and fill their own containers with drinking water from a tanker truck.

Ohsweken's problem, and Stan's story of a year's work for a pail of water, is a reminder to me that I shouldn't take my own water for granted. So is the fact that the woman who tried to live in this house last winter had to move out because the pipes froze. So, having every intention of staying in this house all winter, I set out three days ago to keep my water supply from freezing up.

The house has a water pump in the utility closet that feeds water from the well into the kitchen and bathroom. The first thing I did was scout out the problem. There are two plastic pipes connected to the water pump that disappear down a hole in the floor of the utility closet and lead to the well. The house doesn't have a basement, so I went outside and squirmed my way underneath the back of the house. The two plastic pipes, I discovered, were exposed to the air for about three feet, from the floor to the ground. If

I wanted to have running water in the house all winter, I knew I would have to protect those pipes from freezing.

My plan was to wrap them in electrical heating cable and insulate the heck out of them. Because I didn't know anything about heating cable, plastic pipe or insulation, I spent a day buying materials and talking with a stationary engineer, a plumber and several hardware salesclerks. That was Monday.

On Tuesday, I put on my work clothes and gathered all my tools and materials. Before I wriggled underneath the house and started wrapping the pipes, though, I had to drill a hole through the floor of the utility closet so I could plug the heating cable into a wall outlet. I decided not to drill it next to the wall because I didn't want to hit the electrical wire that powers the outlet. No sir, no sense doing something dumb like that.

I decided instead to drill it next to the water pump—that way the heating cable could be wrapped around the pipes and emerge through the floor right next to the pump and be plugged into the wall. What's more, the drill bit would be kept away from all those electrical wires.

So I started drilling. And drilling. And drilling. *Boy, these old houses have thick floorboards*. The drill bit kept sinking and sinking and the wood shavings kept foaming out of the hole but still the drill bit didn't burst through the floor into the crawl space below. *What's the problem? I'm nowhere near the floor joist.* I pulled the drill out a couple of times to check on its progress and nothing seemed to be wrong. So I pushed the drill even harder.

Suddenly I was hit full in the face by a cold wet blast. I pulled out the drill and a geyser exploded from the hole in the floor. The water was blasting out of the floor, hitting the ceiling and raining back down. It was hitting the walls and soaking everything in-between, me included. I was standing in the middle of a gushing fountain and I couldn't see a thing. I had to keep my hands in front of my face because it was like getting blasted with a fire hose. A split second after the geyser erupted the water pump kicked in to keep up the pressure. Only then did I realize what I had done. I had missed the electrical wires—oh yeah, by at least three feet—but I had drilled right through one of the plastic water pipes.

This wasn't the first time I'd made a boneheaded blunder while trying to make a home improvement. I've made so many of them, in fact, that some years ago I developed a set routine to cope with whatever disaster I unleashed. The key to my routine is staying calm and rational. I sit for a minute and quietly contemplate the situation while silently cursing my tools, my materials, my helpers or myself. (Okay, so sometimes the cursing isn't silent.) I shake my head, again and again, and try to estimate how much it will cost to fix my mistake and how long it will take to do it right.

This time, though, I took one quick water-logged look around and decided that this was no time for quiet contemplation. Water was gushing everywhere. It was soaking the tools, the kitchen supplies, the ironing board and the vacuum cleaner. There was so much water on the floor it was flowing out of the closet and into the kitchen. Through the drips on my glasses I could see the dustpan floating away. More ominously, though, was the fact that the water was splashing all over the hot-water heater, the water pump, the lamp and my drill—all of which were still plugged in. As I stared at the menacing merger of water and electricity I looked down and saw that I was standing in a rapidly widening pool of water.

Holy lightning juice! What the hell do I do now? Dry off my glasses so I can see? Contain the flood? Take all the stuff out of the closet? Get out of the water? Put on rubber boots? Unplug all the appliances? Plug the hole? Shut off the power in the house? Turn off the water pump?

Looking back, I realize that I should have shut off the power. I should have left the closet (and thereby kept myself from getting electrocuted), walked to the main electrical panel located in my writing room and thrown the switch that would have shut off the appliances and the water pump and stopped the geyser. Problem solved.

But no, that would have been too easy. I decided, for some reason, to try to shut off the water pump instead. The problem was that I didn't know how. Although I've lived in this house for a month, I've never had a reason to shut it off or even give it a close look. All I knew was that the pump was a chunky engine the size of a bulldog with a maze of pipes, hoses and spigots leading in all directions. It was jammed between the wall and the hot-water heater and normally I could see only one side of it. The trouble was I couldn't see anything because of all the water that was gushing out of the hole right next to the pump. And with the engine roaring and the pressurized water exploding, it was so noisy in that confined little space I couldn't think.

From the throbbing vibrations that came through the floor, I could feel the pump pounding away, straining to maintain the water pressure. There had to be an on–off switch somewhere, I knew. The problem was, where? I held my breath and leaned over the pump, into the full force of the geyser. I was determined to feel my way around in the hope of finding a switch to end the chaos. As I explored the engine with my tender, vulnerable and oh-so-valuable fingers, I tried not to think of all those metal parts throbbing, pounding and grinding away. I probed every inch of that pump. I pushed, flicked and manipulated everything that felt like a switch but the engine kept pumping and the water kept gushing. I was out of breath and nothing was working. It was almost panic time.

And then, as if by magic, the pump stopped. There was

no more roaring and shaking. The geyser was still exploding out of the hole in the floor but over the next sixty seconds it slowly subsided and finally stopped altogether. Except for the water dripping off the ceiling, there was silence. Trying to account for my good fortune, I looked around and saw an electrical switch on the wall just inches above the pump. The pump was connected to the switch by an electrical cable that was in plain sight. In my desperate thrashing and groping, I had apparently leaned against the switch and, unintentionally, turned off the pump. Soaked to the bone, I slumped in exhaustion and sighed with relief.

That was two days ago. Yesterday I faced up to the job of repairing the damaged water pipe. I dreaded the job because it had to be done in the cramped little crawl space under the house. I dreaded that crawl space, partly because of the dirt, the mud and the thick hanging cobwebs, but mostly because it was home to several species of insects, reptiles and rodents. Taking a deep breath, I wormed and twisted my way under the house and cut out the damaged section of pipe. I then spent most of the day shopping for a piece to replace it.

When I got home, I wriggled back into the crawl space with the pipe, the fittings, some clamps, a measuring tape, a torch, a lighter, a hacksaw, a wrench, a screwdriver and a flashlight. I couldn't sit up down there—there was barely enough room to lift my head—so I had to lie on my back in the dirt and the mud, hoping I wouldn't see a pair of little beady eyes staring back at me. After two hours of cutting, fitting, re-cutting, squeezing, heating, twisting, pushing, tightening and wrestling with the pipe, the clamps and the fittings—after two hours of grunting, sweating and cursing in that cold, dark and muddy coffin-like space—the water pipe was finally fixed.

I walked into the utility room and turned the water pump back on. The repair job wasn't pretty but the pump worked and there weren't any leaks. I was about to puff myself up with a sense of accomplishment when I realized that after two days of solid work, I was just back to my original starting point.

So today I set out to finish the job once and for all. I drilled another hole in the floor of the utility closet—away from the wires *and* from the pipes. Taking a deep breath and crawling under the house yet again, I managed to wrap the heating cable and insulation around the pipes without any problem. When I plugged the heating cable into the outlet—and nothing blew up—the job was finally finished.

So now, after all the work, expense and aggravation—after narrowly escaping electrocution, drowning and mutilation—I think I have finally managed to protect my water pipes from freezing this winter.

Looking back on the past three days, I've come to realize that this drawn-out comedy of errors hasn't been all bad. It's given me a better understanding of the workings of the water pump, for one thing. More important than that, though, is the fact that it has also driven home the full meaning of the old saying, "You never really appreciate something unless you work for it."

That thought was foremost in my mind as I stood, tired and thirsty, by the kitchen sink this afternoon, still wearing my muddy work clothes. As I opened the cupboard, got a glass and turned on the tap, the pump in the utility closet started chugging to keep up the pressure. As the water rippled down the side of the glass and wiggled its way to the top, I thought of the work that had gone into getting this one glass of water. I held that glass of water to the light of the window and looked at its shimmering clarity and tiny sparkling bubbles. I put that glass to my lips, tilted my head back and drank slowly and deeply from the most delicious water in the world.

As I savoured the taste, I couldn't help smiling and thinking of my Uncle Stan. And I couldn't help saying aloud, "Oh, that's good water. It really tastes nice."

By their architecture ye shall know them

Iroquois is the name that the French gave to our people 450 years ago. The word is Algonquin in origin and the experts can't agree on exactly what it means. But going by one scholarly explanation, what I think happened was this: the French asked the Algonquins who their southern neighbours were and the Algonquins said, "They are *Irinakhoiw*"—"real snakes."

Needless to say, we "Iroquois" don't quite see ourselves as a form of slithering lowlife; we like to think that we occupy a slightly higher, more noble and dignified plane of existence. (Other Indians who know us well—and who have collided with our abundant self-confidence—would probably say that we think we are the Creator's gift to Great Turtle Island.)

Naturally, we don't call ourselves "real snakes" in our own languages. Each of the Six Nations uses basically the same word to describe ourselves. In Mohawk, the name we use for the people of the Six Nations is not "Iroquois," it is Rotinonhsyonni. Loosely translated it means "people of the longhouse."

In the old days, a longhouse was built by driving long poles into the earth in two rows about twenty feet apart.

The tops of the poles were pulled over and lashed together to form a long, tunnel-like frame which was then covered with sheets of elm bark. In the middle of the longhouse were firepits about every twenty feet or so, and each fire was shared by two families. These days the Iroquois use a communal building as a centre for social gatherings, religious ceremonies and political meetings. This building, whether it is made of logs or two-by-fours and plywood, is still called a longhouse.

If other aboriginal peoples were also identified by their traditional housing, then the Navajo would be known as the people of the hogan, the Inuit would be called the people of the igloo and the Blackfoot would be called the people of the tipi. When I look around the Big Six these days, I think we should call ourselves RotiATCOyonni instead—the people of the Atco trailer. Those hideous tin bins are everywhere! But they don't house families, they house smoke huts. The Atco trailer is the standard building of the cigarette trade around here.

The cigarette trade is said to employ six hundred people on the territory today in various capacities. It is, by far, the largest local employer. (At least a half-dozen of my relatives are involved in the transportation, wholesaling and retailing ends of the business.)

The way the cigarette trade operates is this. Tobacco companies are obliged to collect federal and provincial sales tax—about $28 a carton—on all the cigarettes they sell in Canada. But since they do not collect tax on cigarettes exported to the United States, a few American companies buy millions of tax-free Canadian cigarettes and arrange to have them "smuggled" back over the border at Akwesasne. The cigarettes are then transported to Six Nations and sold in local smoke huts at a whopping discount, tax-free, thereby attracting thousands of bargain-hungry nicotine addicts from all over southern Ontario.

What makes all these Atco trailers a real eyesore, compared with the portable classrooms that have been on the reserve for years, are all the garish signs that are parked in front. You've seen them—those portable billboards with that ghastly yellow light, light so bright it can be seen on Mars. If you live near one of those signs (and I am *so* grateful I don't), you can forget about seeing Orion, the Great Bear, Cassiopeia or any of the other treasures of the night sky. All you'll see is that nuclear-yellow sign beaming its tawdry message: "CHEAP SMOKES—ALL BRANDS—FREE LIGHTER."

There are more smoke huts springing up all the time. According to the newspaper there are eighty here already, and from what I see, there are new ones going up every week. A year or so ago, when the cigarette trade really started to take off, there were relatively few retailers. They sold name-brand cigarettes for about $35 a carton—$10 less than the price in a store off the reserve. As more and more people got into the business, though, the law of supply and demand kicked in and a price war started. Now, name-brand cigarettes sell for as little as $20 a carton at a smoke hut in the middle of the territory, less than half the off-reserve price. On the edge of the territory prices are $6 to $8 higher per carton—apparently there are plenty of white buyers who would willingly pay a higher price to avoid entering the heart of the territory and being surrounded by all those *Indians*.

As prices fell, the profit margin shrank from as much as $14 to just $2 a carton for many retailers, but the lower prices have attracted even more customers. There are so many buyers, in fact, that I don't go anywhere near "cigarette alley" on Saturday or Sunday. Caravans from Brantford, Hamilton, St. Catharines, Kitchener, London, Toronto and as far away as Windsor stream onto the territory for tax-free cigarettes. The traffic jams around the smoke huts are so bad, the roads look like parking lots. And it's even worse on the first weekend of the month, after the government cheques come in.

With all that business, you'd think the retailers would be ecstatic. Wrong. They *used* to be happy because they were making a dumptruck full of money every day. (Some of the larger dealers, it is said, were making over $1 million profit a year.) But now, with all the increased competition, some of them are only making a *suitcase* full of money every day, a lot of them are barely scraping by, and they're all upset. So they held a meeting yesterday at which almost every retailer was present. By the end of the meeting, with the height of the Christmas shopping season just around the corner, they came up with a solution. They formed a cartel—just as the Arabs did with their oil in 1973—and everyone at the meeting agreed to sell at the same inflated price. Overnight the price went from $20 to $32 a carton.

Obviously, these merchants hope to maintain the same volume of business and increase their profits by something like 600 percent. But I wonder, do these guys ever ask themselves why we pay less for gasoline now than we did in 1973? Do they know why the Arab oil cartel fell apart? Don't they know that the Arabs were done in by old-fashioned greed?

From what I hear, there are a lot of greedy guys in the cigarette business at Six Nations. These guys will be under tremendous pressure to hold their cartel together, so things could get nasty. For example, one smoke hut was burned down recently, I'm told, because the owner dropped his prices. And four of the biggest retailers on the territory have refused to join the cartel and are refusing to raise their prices. Sounds like trouble.

Just as the retailers are split, so is the community. There are many people here who say retailers should sell tax-free cigarettes only to Indians because, they say, white people should not be allowed to benefit from Indian tax exemptions. And there are a couple of stores here, I'm told, that do refuse to sell cigarettes to white people, thereby forfeiting the chance to make *big* money. Although I applaud these retailers for making the financial sacrifice to practise what they preach, I have to question their logic. After all, while they refuse to sell tax-free cigarettes to white people, they presumably still sell them soda pop, potato chips and magazines—tax-free. This racially based policy, when carried to its illogical conclusion, would mean that if the day ever came when cigarettes (or anything else for that matter) were cheaper in town than on the reserve, the merchants of Brantford would be justified in turning the tables: "We don't sell cigarettes to Indians," they could say. "Go back to the reserve and pay higher prices there."

There was a "random poll" conducted this past summer by the *Tekawennake*, the weekly newspaper on the reserve, that said that 66 percent of the people questioned who had an opinion wanted the smoke huts to "disappear." The paper also claimed that most of those people wanted the police to do the job. But even the elected band chief—a vocal opponent of the smoke huts—questioned the validity of the poll.

It's my guess that half the people here support the tobacco trade. In addition to the employment it provides, it also indirectly benefits every local business. Among the most visible beneficiaries are the off-reserve car dealers. The roads here are filled, most conspicuously, with young men driving huge four-by-four pickups with tires the size of half-grown elephants. And an astonishing number of local limousine companies have sprung up in the past year. In fact, this reserve now has more limousines than taxicabs—no kidding!

Most of the criticism directed at the tobacco trade stems from the fact that the extra income it generates is not evenly distributed within the community. Leading the opposition are many of the Confederacy chiefs. They, and others, complain that the "cigarette people" are cashing in on our collective immunity from taxation for their private profit. I've run into a few of the complainers myself and our conversations usually go something like this:

"Are we Canadian citizens?" I'll ask.

"No," they'll say.

"Are we subject to Canadian tax laws?"

"No."

"As Onkwehonwe, are we citizens of an independent sovereign nation?"

"Yes."

"So should our people be in the business of collecting taxes for a foreign government?"

"No, but..." And that's when their anger and jealousy gets the better of them. "It's not right that just a few people are getting rich," they'll complain. "The whole community should benefit."

Great idea. The trouble is that, the way things are now, there is no possible way it will ever happen. The cigarette trade at Six Nations is a textbook illustration of what happens when recession-ravaged nicotine junkies stumble into Smokers' Heaven—a lawless, no-tax jungle ruled by the raw forces of King Capitalism. Neither the Confederacy nor the band council can control the cigarette trade. Trying to do so is like trying to shovel sand with a pitchfork.

But, according to a recent issue of the *Tekawennake*, band council chief Steve Williams—pitchfork in hand— says he'll give it a try. Williams, who was reelected last month, said at the time that his top priority would be controlling the sale of tax-free cigarettes and gasoline.

Hmmph. If Williams thinks he can tame the tobacco dragon and take the golden eggs it lays, he is hopelessly naive. Either that, or it's not sand he's slinging with that pitchfork.

The fix is in

Today, the first Sunday of December, would have been ideal for visiting friends and family—there was no snow and the ground was frozen rock-hard. With conditions like this, you don't have to worry about tracking slush or mud into people's houses.

Around here, I've discovered, visiting is quite a bit different than it was in Ottawa, where my (white) friends would visit only by appointment. I would bump into them on the street and they would say, "We should get together sometime."

And I would say, "Good idea. Why don't you come over to my place?"

"Okay," they would say. "When?"

"How about next week?"

"What day?"

"It doesn't matter. Any day."

"How about Thursday?"

"Sure."

"Oh, I forgot. I can't do it then. How about Wednesday?"

"Great."

"What time?"

"Anytime."

"How about seven?"

"That's fine."

"Wait a minute. I'll still be downtown. How about seven-fifteen?"

"Anytime. Really."

And then, two days before their scheduled visit, they would call and confirm it.

"Are we still on for Wednesday evening?"

"You bet."

"Is seven-fifteen still good?"

"Yeah. Seven, seven-fifteen. It doesn't matter. Anytime."

"My meeting might run late so I might not get there till seven-twenty-five."

"That's fine. Anytime. Really."

And, on the day in question, an hour before the scheduled-and-confirmed visit, they would call one last time.

"I'm just checking to see if we're still on for seven-twenty-five."

"Ready and waiting."

"Okay. I'll be leaving here in about ten minutes and I might get to your place a couple minutes early."

"Great. I'll see you when you get here."

Now, I know that my friends were just trying to be courteous and thoughtful while cramming the most into their hectic lifestyles. In addition, I know that such behaviour is more than just an extension of time-management business practices into the social arena; it is considered, in Ottawa circles anyway, as the mark of a cultured and well-mannered person.

Well, that's not the way people visit on the Big Six. *Uh-uh*. Around here no one calls ahead. *Ever.* Instead, people visit by just dropping in out of the blue. Their gregarious approach to visiting is somewhat akin to a contact sport. Sometimes I think the object of all the surprise visits is to score points by catching the visitees in their underwear, in the shower or, best of all, sitting down having something to eat.

After thirteen years of staid and proper Ottawa living, I became an enthusiastic devotee of full-contact visiting almost from the day I moved back here. Living alone as I do, I welcome the company and the chance to talk to someone besides my cat. I also like to get out of the house and make surprise visits of my own. Sunday is my favourite day for visiting. I like to get in my car and drive, with no set route or destination in mind. When I see a friend's or relative's car in their driveway, I pull in and stop for a visit. And so on, until the day is done.

But I didn't go visiting this past Sunday because I was half expecting someone to stop by. A notice published in the *Tekawennake* two weeks ago said a door-to-door survey would be conducted on the reserve over a ten-day period to gauge the feelings of local residents regarding the establishment here of "a legal gaming entertainment facility"—a casino. Sunday was the last day of the survey, and although I've been home most of the time, I haven't been contacted. I was hoping to get the chance to meet the survey-takers and ask some questions myself, so I decided to spend Sunday at home.

Casinos are really hot in Indian country right now. Every news report about the millions being made by some tribal casino somewhere seems to trigger another report that another band is building its own casino to cash in on all the easy money. For its part, though, Six Nations hasn't been seized by casino fever—yet. Although the band council muses every once in a while about setting one up, it hasn't amounted to anything but talk. But if their discussions ever get past the talking stage, I would expect a sizable protest campaign to spring up.

The curious thing about the lack of enthusiasm for a casino in this community is that the Iroquois have always been a gambling people. One of the four sacred rituals of the Mid-Winter Ceremony, for instance, is a gambling game. It dates back to the time of creation when the Right-Handed Twin, a good-minded being, and his mischievous brother, the Left-Handed Twin, were battling for control of the earth. To settle their feud, they played the peach pit game. The Right-Handed Twin won the game and the battle. He went on to create the first human beings, the Onkwehonwe, and is known by the Iroquois as Shonkwaya'tihson, our Creator. Today, the Onkwehonwe still play the peach pit game during the Mid-Winter Ceremony to honour and entertain Him.

The game is played using a large wooden bowl containing six peach pits that are blackened on one side. It's a team game; half the clans in the longhouse make up one team, the other clans make up the other team. One player from each team takes a turn shaking the bowl, slams it down and counts the way the peach pits land. If five of them, or all six, land with the black or white side up, the team wins a certain number of beans (or kernels of corn). When one side has amassed all the beans, it wins the game and all the bets that have been wagered.

Before the game, the people on both sides of the longhouse bet on their "team." But they don't bet money, they bet traditional objects—a rattle, a piece of beadwork, a ribbon shirt, a lacrosse stick. The items are matched up in pairs of roughly equal value—a rattle bet by one side is tied together with a rattle bet by someone from the other side. After the game, the paired items are then distributed among the winning side.

In colonial times, the Iroquois were known to gamble with reckless abandon. They would bet heavily on lacrosse games, with the stakes being held by the chiefs. The act of betting, it was said by a nineteenth-century observer, "was more important to Indian spectators than the monetary value of the items won, for it made them active partici-pants in the contest.... They would wager a new gun against an old gun [because] they would rather bet against something than not bet at all."

Another observer, writing at the same time, said that the Hurons (cousins of the Iroquois) often gambled and lost everything they owned—and more: "A man who lost all he owned bet his hair, which he also lost—the winner cut it off; another gambled his little finger and had it chopped off upon losing, without showing signs of pain."

Many other Indian nations played lacrosse and they all, apparently, gambled on the outcome. Among the Choctaw, it has been reported that players would sometimes go so far as to bet their wives and their children—the idea being, presumably, that the fear of losing their families would incite them to play like mad demons.

Lacrosse is still the number-one summer sport around here, but hardly anyone bets on it any more. Instead, they play bingo. They also buy raffle tickets, 50/50 tickets, scratch-and-win tickets and Nevada "pull-tab" tickets. And with computerized terminals in most of the corner stores here, they also buy a lot of provincial lottery tickets. I'd bet that the people on the reserve spend a *minimum* of a mil-lion dollars a year on various forms of gambling.

Despite the acceptance and popularity of gambling, though, I think the longhouse community will mount a campaign to oppose the establishment of a casino. The opposition will probably be based on one of the taboos issued by the founder of the longhouse religion, the Seneca chief and prophet Skanyatariyo (Handsome Lake). In one of the visions he had in 1799, Skanyatariyo was taken on a guided tour of a Hell-like realm ruled by a Devil-like being called the Punisher. The occupants of the Punisher's realm were Indians who had sinned on earth, and their fate was to suffer excruciatingly painful tortures

designed to fit their sins. Skanyatariyo warned his followers about the punishments they would face:

> The Punisher called out in a loud voice and
> commanded two persons to appear before him.
> Now when they stood before him he handed
> them what seemed a pack of red hot iron cards.
> Then he forced the two to sit down facing each
> other and compelled them to shuffle the cards
> and as they did flames spurted out from between
> them. So they cried out in great agony, sucked
> their fingers in their mouths, handled the cards
> again until their flesh was eaten away and the
> meat fell off.

Based on this vision, the longhouse religion clearly prohibits poker and blackjack. But I don't know if
Skanyatariyo's card-playing taboo was meant to cover all
forms of gambling, given the widespread nature of gambling in Iroquois country. In his landmark study of the
Iroquois, for example, Lewis Henry Morgan found that betting on games was totally accepted by the spiritual leaders
of the Iroquois. Writing in 1851—thirty-six years after
Skanyatariyo's death—Morgan said: "This practice was
never reprobated by their religious teachers, but, on the
contrary, rather encouraged, [and] it frequently led to the
most reckless indulgence."

Skanyatariyo's warning against card-playing could be
used to oppose a casino, I suppose, if it were interpreted as
a taboo against all forms of "white man's gambling"—
roulette wheels, crap tables, slot machines and the like.
The trouble with this argument, of course, is that the
white man also invented bingo, lotteries, Nevada tickets,
raffles and 50/50 draws. What's more, the longhouses
themselves sell raffle tickets and hold 50/50 draws, and I

have even seen one longhouse chief involved in selling Nevada tickets, with all their slot-machine imagery.

Given the tangled history of our people's attitude to gambling, I was very interested when I first read about the casino survey. Properly done, it would help the community decide what to do. The problem is that the "independent polling company" conducting the survey is affiliated with a pro-casino development group. *Hmm.* It also seems that in 1990 one of the companies in the development group conducted a similar poll which found, supposedly, that a whopping 72 percent of the people here support "gaming." *Hmm. Hmm.*

If there was ever any belief in the survey's impartiality, the company president destroyed it when he said in the *Tekawennake*, "It is hoped that the community as a whole supports the initiative and will realize the indirect and direct benefits that a gaming facility will provide." Profits from a casino, he added, could go towards recreation facilities, an ambulance service and programs for senior citizens.

Even though I waited all day Sunday for the survey-taker, nobody came. It's too bad because I was really looking forward to it—especially after a friend of mine told me about the encounter she'd had.

"Do you support a casino?" the survey-taker asked.

"No," she said.

And then, my friend reports, the verbal onslaught began. "What's the matter?" the survey-taker demanded. "Don't you want the kids on this reserve to have a swimming pool? Don't you think our kids deserve decent recreation facilities? Don't you realize a casino will bring hundreds of jobs here? Don't you want our people to be able to work on the reserve without having to go to town?" And so on.

Knowing what I know now about this "survey," I fearlessly predict it will show that an overwhelming majority of the people here are frothing at the mouth to get our own casino.

If I had been interviewed, I would have told the survey-taker that I don't think we should base our plans for prosperity on anything that preys on people who are overwhelmingly poor and ill-educated. We should be in the business of trying to make people stronger, not prey-ing on their weaknesses. But it doesn't really matter what I think, because the fix is in.

Playing it safe at the old folks' home

My Gramma Lillian lives in Iroquois Lodge, the old folks' home in Ohsweken. Gramma is eighty-nine and is a great-great-grandmother twelve times over. Despite her age, she is still alert and in full command of her wits. She is, however, clearly feeling the effects of old age. She can't walk more than a few steps so she spends most of her days in a wheelchair. She has had various problems with her ears for many years and is half deaf. Today was the second time I've taken her to the ear doctor in a month.

Finally, though, after months of testing, treatment with antibiotics, periodic cleanings, ointment and a new hearing aid, she can hear properly, and at long last, I can carry on a normal two-sided conversation with her. In the past, most of our conversations consisted of her saying something and me nodding my head. I had to shout so she could hear me. My shouting and her *"What did you say?"* replies were stressful for both of us so I tended to keep my end of the conversation to a minimum. Now, I'm looking forward to many long talks. I want her to tell me old-time stories about our family, the reserve and, especially, about herself—starting with how she lost the tip of the index finger on her left hand.

When I wheeled her back into her room at the Lodge today, she told me to shut the door. She didn't really have to tell me this because I knew she'd want her door kept closed at all times to keep drafts out of her room. She has poor circulation and is always complaining about the cold, so she keeps her room hot enough to melt butter. Even in July she bundles up in sweaters, sweat pants and thick socks.

Gramma has lived in the Lodge ever since my sister Dennise and I moved her there from an old folks' home in the States a year ago. Iroquois Lodge is a wonderful place in its own right, but especially so compared with the place she used to live in—a county nursing home that should have been called Death's Conveyor Belt because the staff there pumped the residents full of drugs to keep them quiet and easy to manage.

Although Iroquois Lodge is a new building, it lacks some of the modern amenities usually found in such a facility. I can't understand, for example, why it doesn't have one of those buttons that open the door for people in wheelchairs. It's such a hassle getting Gramma in and out of that building. I mean, if the bank on this reserve can have an automatic door, why can't the nursing home?

Well, anyway, Iroquois Lodge has something far more important. Since almost everyone on staff is an Indian from the reserve and is therefore related to one or more of the residents, the residents get the kind of loving care that family members provide, rather than the indifferent ministrations that come from strangers just doing a job. In fact, the first time I entered the Lodge I felt a rush of excitement at the sight of so many Indians living together as one big family.

I get a warm, homey feeling walking through the place, but I also get a funny twinge, because part of me knows, deep down, that I might be looking at my future home. That should be the last thing on my mind, I know, since I'm

in perfect health and the prospect of living in an old folks'
home is, I hope, some forty or fifty years in the future. But
every once in a while I find myself looking around and
imagining myself as one of the old men living here.

I'm not afraid of getting old. And while I don't look forward to the aches, pains and illnesses, I do look forward to
a sense of peace and contentment and the satisfaction of a
life well lived. I'm already looking forward to visits from
grandchildren I don't even have yet, young ones who will
help me revisit the joy, vigour and excitement of youth. I
can't wait to break into a full-faced smile of unrestrained
delight at the mere sight of my grandchildren coming to
visit me. Just like the smile my Gramma Lillian always
gives me when I step into her room.

People who meet Gramma for the first time probably
think she is quiet and shy, bashful almost. But she can be
cranky, especially when it comes to her meals and her
room temperature. Although she won't spare anyone's feelings if something displeases her, she tries to keep her
tongue in check because she doesn't want to be known as a
complainer. Gramma is definitely not a jokester, but she
can be devastatingly funny when she unleashes one of her
cutting observations.

Today she explained why she wanted me to shut the door.
It seems that someone has told her that one of the women
across the hall is a witch. "She even looks like a witch."
With her eyes narrowed and a nod of her head for empha-
sis, she said flatly, "She can turn you into a horse."

She looked to me for reaction but I didn't say anything.

"Do you believe in stuff like that?" she asked.

I answered her with a question of my own. "Do you
believe it, Gramma?"

And this woman, who claims to have forgotten most of
her Mohawk—who can't count higher than six in a language she knew intimately as a child—effortlessly spat out

a long, tongue-twisting Mohawk word I didn't understand. "She's a witch," she added in English.

Gramma knows about witches, she says, because her father was killed by a witch. It happened some sixty-odd years ago, just after she had given birth to her second son, my Uncle Tom, at the family homestead near Thomas's Corner. Her father was sick in bed at the time, she said, and when she carried her newborn son into her father's room, a woman was there who "did something" to his feet. Gramma says she didn't know who the woman was or what she did but a moment later her father was dead.

So now, Gramma says, part of her believes in witches and part of her doesn't. To protect herself, she intends to keep her door closed and to keep away from the woman across the hall—"Just to be safe."

I looked at my grandmother, this sweet old lady sitting there with a half-smile on an angelic face framed by a cap of fluffy white hair. I looked at the Bible on her dresser, at the verse of Scripture on the wall, at the cassette tape of hymns sitting on her nightstand. I thought back to the stories about how the Mohawks renounced their "pagan" ways and converted to Christianity two hundred years ago. I balanced that history with the stories I have been told of people in recent years who have been "witched" by bad medicine; by the stories of people who have witnessed fantastic things—flying heads, the little people, disembodied hands and corn-husk dolls coming to life. I thought of all this history and looked at my grandmother, who has been a churchgoing woman for just about her whole life, and knew that despite the supposed triumph of Christianity over "paganism," some of the old beliefs are still very much alive.

I don't know which of the dozen old women in the Lodge my grandmother is talking about. Some of them are confined to wheelchairs. Others wander the hallways endlessly.

Some of them don't seem to be aware of their surroundings while others are alert, friendly and talkative. I don't know which one of these women is the witch. But as I made my way out of the Lodge today, I made sure I had a kind word and a smile for all the old ladies.

Just to be safe.

Smoke didn't get
in my eyes

Finally, finally, finally: my woodstove is up and working. The job took me a week—about six days longer than planned. I learned a lot in the process, mostly by making mistakes. But at least these mistakes weren't nearly as dumb, dangerous or catastrophic as the one involving my water pump. (Well, maybe one of them was kinda dumb, but if I hang a large picture in the middle of the bedroom wall upstairs, no one will be able to see it.)

My big worry all week was installing everything properly so that the system would "draw" well: so that cold air would be drawn into the stove and all the smoke would get sucked out the chimney. Because of where I put the stove, the chimney ended up surrounded by the tall spruce trees that are right next to the house. I was worried that the air circulation around the trees might cause a downdraft and fill the house with smoke. If that happened, I would face two equally unpleasant choices (after I'd cleared the smoke out of the house): I would either have to cut the trees down (no way) or add another thirty feet to the chimney to make it taller than the trees (impossible). So today, once the chimney was secured to the house and the chimney cap was in place, I filled the stove with paper, kindling and firewood, lit a match, said a little prayer and held my breath as I set the paper afire.

In seconds the fire in the belly of the stove was blazing. Looking anxiously through the window in the stove door, I could see the smoke roiling furiously inside. I stood up and quickly examined the joints in the stovepipe leading through the ceiling to the second floor. There was no smoke in sight so I ran upstairs and looked at the joints in the stovepipe up there. No smoke there either. I then ran outside, stood under the trees and looked at the chimney top enveloped in spruce boughs. Black smoky curls were billowing out from under the rim of the shiny new chimney cap. They hung in the frosty air for an instant and then were whipped away by the wind. What a beautiful sight.

With more than a little bit of self-satisfaction I came back inside, threw some more wood in the stove and plopped down in front of the fire with a cup of coffee and a big smile on my face. It was getting cold outside, the ground was frozen, and a glance at the calendar showed that it was December 8. The longest night of the year was less than two weeks away. As I sat there looking at the flames, soaking up the warmth, I couldn't help thinking, *"Finally, I'm all set for winter."*

And then I remembered I was missing just one little thing—a small mountain of firewood. But, hey, after overcoming the problems I've had with the stove, the water pipes and the other hassles of moving in, how hard could it be to get a little wood?

Tsi kanye'onh

//

When the snow has fallen

Ordinarily, *when Mother Nature sprinkles a layer of snow across the landscape, her artistry is that of a painter. It's as if she is airbrushing the countryside, softening the contours of the terrain ever so delicately. Whether her snow-coating is dry, light and fluffy or thick, wet and heavy, the countryside still looks more or less the same. Even with a thick coating of the deepest snow, all the features of the landscape are still in proportion; everything just looks a little bloated and puffy.*

But there are a few days every winter when Mother Nature the genteel painter becomes Mother Nature the brawny sculptor. These are the days when she cracks a blizzard's whip across the face of the land, sending rivers of air whipping in every direction. When she has finished windblasting her snow-covered canvas, the air is brilliantly clear and bitterly cold. The sky is a dazzling shade of neon blue and everywhere, everywhere, there is the eyeball-searing whiteness.

In the blizzard's wake the once-familiar terrain is transformed into an alien landscape. The snowbanks are monumental, awesome and elegant. In some of them, the wind has gouged out great swooping hollows that hang suspended like ocean breakers. In open spaces, the storm has whipped and moulded feathery snowflakes into long willowy snowdunes, the ripples echoing across the fields, their course and contour shaped by the wind. Everywhere there are the snow-chiselled features of a miniature earthscape—snowy mountains and mesas, icy canyons and caverns.

But Mother Nature's artistry does not last because, just as quickly as it was created, the exquisitely sculpted snowscape begins to wear away. The sun and wind round off the ridges, fill in the hollows and blur the image of winter's beauty.

Trouble in the schoolyard

Trouble's coming. The first public sign of it is buried in a notice in the latest issue of the *Tekawennake*. The notice says that a local committee has been empowered to take over control of the school system in this territory from the Department of Indian Affairs. On the surface, this development—local control of education—looks like a good thing, a change that's long overdue. But there's trouble written all over it.

The problem is not so much *what's* being done as *who's* behind it—the Six Nations band council. Most of the people here have passionate feelings and deeply rooted beliefs about education, and since most of the people here generally distrust the band council, this new committee could be in for a very rough ride. Unlike the band's other program areas—economic development, for example—education is an issue the people here don't intend to leave to some committee of "experts."

Six Nations people feel strongly about education in part because they have been involved in "white man's schooling" since at least 1713, when the Mohawks, still living in the Mohawk Valley, built their own schoolhouse. Things didn't work out at that time, though, and the school closed four years later, perhaps because it was run by an Anglican minister whose mandate was to "convert the heathens." Now, almost three centuries later, many would say that little has changed—non-Indian people are still in charge of the schools and are still determined to mould our children in their image.

The Iroquois, it's safe to say, had definite ideas about what they wanted—and didn't want—in the way of education. In 1744, for example, chiefs from the Six Nations were engaged in treaty negotiations with the government of Virginia. After the main business was settled, the Virginians mentioned their college at Williamsburg and said that "If the chiefs of the Six-Nations would send down a half-dozen of their sons to that College, the Government would take care that they should be well provided for, and instructed in all the Learning of the white People." The next day one of the Iroquois chiefs thanked the Virginians for their generous and well-meaning offer. Then, he added:

> Several of our Young People were formerly
> brought up at the College of the Northern
> Provinces; they were instructed in all your
> Sciences; but when they came back to us, they
> were bad Runners, ignorant of every means
> of living in the Woods, unable to bear either
> Cold or Hunger, knew neither how to build a
> Cabin, take a Deer, or kill an Enemy, spoke our
> Language imperfectly; they were totally good for
> nothing. We are however not the less obliged
> by your kind Offer, tho' we decline accepting it;
> and to show our Grateful Sense of it, if the
> Gentlemen of Virginia will send us a dozen of
> their Sons, we will take great Care of their
> Education, instruct them in all we know, and
> make Men of them.

One of the first of our people to be educated in a "white man's school" was Thayendanegea (Joseph Brant). He studied English, math, Latin and Greek and completed his schooling in 1763. One of the first things he did after the relocation to Grand River in 1784 was establish a school in the Mohawk village. A century later, there were twelve small schools on Six Nations, nine controlled by the Anglicans, two by the Methodists and one by the Confederacy chiefs. Even in those days, 90 percent of the teachers were Indians from the reserve who had been educated at the Mohawk Institute, the local residential school.

In 1933, all the schools on Six Nations came under the control of the Department of Indian Affairs, where they have remained ever since. In 1973, though, the Trudeau government adopted the slogan "Indian Control of Indian Education" as government policy. Since then, most of the Indian bands in Canada have taken over the control and administration of the schools on their reserves. The most glaring exception is Six Nations. Despite the pride that even the band council takes in its "independence," the Department of Indian Affairs still decides who the teachers will be on this reserve and what they will teach.

It should be mentioned that even though the department controls them, most of the people who actually run the schools—the teachers, principals and administrators—are Indians from this reserve. In fact, for several years the department's superintendent of education here was one of the Cayuga Confederacy chiefs. (Many Confederacy supporters, however, openly questioned how anyone could give orders on behalf of the Department of Indian Affairs— of all government agencies—and still be a chief.)

Even though many local people are involved in running the schools, the government is still very much in charge. When a job competition was conducted for a principal's position earlier this year, the person who won was an

Indian woman who had grown up on the reserve, become a teacher, earned a Master's degree and her principal's papers. The ideal candidate, right? Not according to the Department of Indian Affairs, which awarded the job instead to a francophone white woman who had never been to Six Nations. The reason? She had just been laid off from a reserve school in northern Ontario and was on the government's priority hiring list. (She eventually decided not to accept the position after elected chief Steve Williams complained.)

For its part, the Department of Indian Affairs desperately wants to get out of the business of running the schools on this territory and it wants to give the job to someone else. So six years ago the department began funding a band committee to organize a local school board. As a result of that work, the Six Nations Education Board was established this fall. Although it claims to be a politically neutral body that represents everyone here, the education board is, in fact, little more than a self-appointed committee with no real community backing. Despite its lack of credibility, the band council gave the education board its blessing this month, and that's what all the fuss is going to be about. In a "memorandum of understanding," the band council empowered the board to be *the* education authority on Six Nations. The board will now try to negotiate a funding agreement with Indian Affairs so that it can begin running the schools next fall. In trying to do this, the board will have a gun at its head because the department has already said that if the Six Nations Education Board isn't ready to take over the schools by September 1, the department will give the job to a third party—the Brant County Board of Education, perhaps, or the New Credit First Nation or, improbably, the Catholic Church.

When the news about this band council–education board deal gets out, I predict that a lot of people are going to be very angry. That's because for months, if not years, the people here have been led to think that the schools might end up being controlled by the Confederacy, or at the very least, that the band council would cease to have anything to do with them. This latest turnaround, therefore, will probably come as a slap in the face to many people.

I wouldn't be surprised to see the people mount a school boycott, as they did five years ago. At that time all the one- and two-room schools on the territory were found to be chock-full of asbestos. The parents demanded that all the dilapidated ninety-year-old schools on the reserve be torn down and replaced by new ones. The department refused and insisted that the schools were safe. The parents and teachers—mostly women—fought back and organized a highly charged boycott that lasted for three months. Eventually the government was forced to admit that the schools were unsafe. In short order, the government then ordered emergency repairs, brought in portable class-rooms and okayed the construction of large modern replacement schools.

The school takeover deadline is now a little more than eight months away. And given all the players in this little drama—the band council, the Confederacy, the education board, the parents, the department—just about anything can happen in the meantime.

There's one born every minute

Wood buying, I have discovered, is a lot more complicated than I thought.

First of all, there's the matter of finding someone who has firewood and is willing to sell some. The big wood-sellers won't take on any new customers at this time of year, I've learned, because they're worried they will run out before the winter is over, leaving their long-time big-volume buyers without any wood.

Then there's the matter of price. A long time ago, wood was sold by the cord—a pile of wood four feet high, four feet wide and eight feet long. Nowadays wood is still sold by the cord, but the pile has shrunk to what is called a "face" cord—one-third the size of an old-time cord. Around here the going rate for a face cord these days, delivered, is between fifty and sixty dollars. Although I've heard plenty of stories of people delivering wood for forty dollars a cord, they're like Elvis sightings—numerous and hard to pin down.

The most difficult part of buying wood, though, is the knowledge factor. You have to know your wood. And you have to know the difference between good wood and bad.

That point was driven home in a story my Uncle Stan

first told me several years ago. It seems that in the early part of this century Indians from the reserve used to go to the public market in Brantford to sell vegetables, hand-made baskets and firewood to the townsfolk. As Stan tells it, one of the men he knew used to sell firewood at the market from a trailer on the back of his truck. The man was a sly character and he didn't stack the wood neatly in the truck so a buyer could judge how much there was; he just threw it into the trailer in a jumbled pile. The wood was usually poplar, pine or some other softwood that is easily cut but burns quickly and gives off little heat.

As the matrons of Brantford made their rounds of the market, they would come up to the man, look over the wood and ask the price.

"A dollar-fifty," the man said, "delivered."

In response the women would invariably ask, "Is that for a cord?"

And the man would say, "Oh, no, ma'am. This is much bigger than a cord." And then, sweeping his arm over the jumbled pile of wood that amounted to little more than half a cord, he would add, "It's a dollar-fifty a *load*."

A lot of women didn't know much about buying wood but they always knew enough to ask, "Is it hardwood?"

And the man would always answer the same way. He would pick a big stick of wood out of the pile and rap it soundly with his knuckles. "Oh, yes, ma'am," the man would say. *Knock, knock, knock*. "It's very hard wood. Just see for yourself."

The woman would then reach out with a dainty hand and rap the wood just as the man had done. Invariably she quickly pulled her hand back and massaged her knuckles to soothe the sting. She would then agree, "You're right. It *is* hard wood."

At this point in the story, Stan would explode in a fit of laughter at the memory from so long ago. He loves to tell the story and I love to hear it because it illustrates a favourite age-old stereotype—that of the poor country bumpkin pulling a fast one on a rich, ignorant city-slicker.

Bearing that story in mind, I was very careful when I began calling up the wood-sellers in the area. I would ask them, "What kind of wood is it?" (I wanted to hear that they were selling one of the hardwoods, preferably maple, birch, beech, cherry or oak.) "When was it cut?" (It should have been cut months ago for it to dry out or "cure" properly.) "Is it split?" (It had better be.) "How long are the sticks?" (No sense buying wood that is twenty-four inches long when it won't fit into my stove.)

Yesterday, after nearly two weeks of shopping around, I finally found what I was looking for—someone who sold only hardwood and had some for sale. I asked the seller what kind of wood he had, and he said, "Oh, some cherry and oak but it's mostly maple."

Thanks to Stan I know there's a difference between sugar (hard) maple and red (soft) maple—soft maple burns a little faster and gives off a little less heat than hard maple—so I asked him, "What kind of maple?"

When he said "hard maple," I went to look at it. It was split in quarters, it was just the right length and it was stacked in cords. Judging from the weathered face of the grain, it had been cut quite a while ago and was well-cured. The price was sixty dollars a cord, delivered—a bit steep, but at this time of year I wasn't going to quibble. So I ordered two cords and had them delivered today.

A fire was blazing in the stove when Stan came over for dinner tonight. As he sat in the rocking chair next to the stove, soaking in the warmth, rocking back and forth, back and forth, I went to the wood-rack and pulled out a stick of wood and handed it to him. I didn't say anything because I was fishing for a compliment. I wanted him to tell me what an expert wood-buyer I was. Stan, it should be understood, is a man who grew up with wood-burning stoves and worked as a logger and a carpenter. He knows his wood.

Stan hefted the stick in his hand and examined the grain. He gave it a quarter-turn, examined the bark and handed it back to me. He then uttered his two-word verdict. "Soft maple," was all he said.

I realized then that I had failed the wood-buying test. Someone had shown me a pile of wood, said it was hard maple and I'd bought it. I didn't say anything to Stan. I just turned away and put the stick back in the rack, doing my best to hide my embarrassment.

Oh, I know I could have done worse. Soft maple burns a lot better than softwood so my house will still be warm this winter. And at least I'll know what soft maple looks like when these two cords are gone and it's time to buy some more. But this whole episode made me realize one thing—although I like to think of myself as a son of the forest, when it comes to buying firewood I am no different than those ignorant city-slickers who were fooled in the Brantford marketplace seventy years ago.

The war is on

The closer winter comes the colder it gets—for most of us, anyway. The cigarette merchants, however, have been feeling the heat lately. Force-fed a diet of news stories about the "lucrative and illicit" tobacco trade, swapping gossip about the government's possible moves, defending themselves against complaints of their neighbours while warily eyeballing each other's prices, the cigarette people are clearly under a lot of pressure.

If there were no buyers, they are quick to point out, there would be no sellers, but still, they grumble, the heat of the news coverage is directed at them. They also complain that the tobacco trade is, in their eyes, perfectly legal and, given the cutthroat competition, not that lucrative. Despite their arguments, however, they are losing the battle of public relations—on all fronts.

They probably laughed off the government's threat to impose a quota on the delivery of "legal" cigarettes to the territory, given the fact that most of the cigarettes sold here are "smuggled" and therefore almost unstoppable. I wonder, though, if they're laughing quite as hard at today's newsflash from the RCMP—the cops are threatening to start confiscating the cars of people leaving the territory in

possession of as little as one package of "contraband" cigarettes. It used to be that the RCMP would confiscate a car
only if the driver had forty cartons or more. This drastically
lower level is clearly meant to clamp down on the tobacco
trade by frightening off the white middle-class buyers who
travel to the reserve to buy their smokes.

Judging by a drive through cigarette alley today, I'd say
that the greatest threat to the prosperity of the tobacco
trade is not external, it is right here on the reserve. If the
cigarette people didn't already have enough headaches, I
noticed that the price war has started again. Actually, it
was impossible not to notice. Every smoke hut is trimmed
with Christmas lights and has a roadside sign decorated
with pictures of Santa Claus, reindeer and candy canes,
screaming that their price is lower than next door's. The
prices have dropped back down to $22 and less.

It took three weeks but the joint effort at cigarette price-
fixing appears to have met its inevitable fate. The cartel is
broken. I didn't notice exactly when the price war started
but it's now just two days before Christmas. So much for
the season of "Peace on Earth, Good Will Toward Men." In
its place, the Christmas sentiment here is, "The war is on.
Every man for himself."

Noyah, Noyah

T hrough the window this morning I saw a van crunch to a stop in the gravel driveway. Four excited kids piled out, ran up to my house and pounded on the door, laughing and shouting at the top of their lungs, *"Noyah! Noyah!"* I threw open the door, welcomed them in and responded in kind, *"Noyah! Noyah!"*

Grinning and full of giggles, their eyes flashing, the four youngsters thrust their bulging plastic bags at me for the treats they have come to expect on New Year's Day. I held out my offering—a heaping plate of Indian Cookies—to a welcoming chorus: "Indian Cookies!" "Can I have two?" "Oh boy!" *"Nya'wen."*

The van driver was Audrey Powless-Bomberry, my sister's sister-in-law. With her was her brother Richard and, between them, their four kids. They were my first *Noyah* visitors.

Noyah (with the accent on *yah*) is a local New Year's tradition. In the morning, children are taken around to the homes of friends, neighbours and relatives for treats. In the afternoon, the grown-ups go visiting. The practice probably began in the seventeenth century when the Iroquois, living alongside Dutch settlers in the Mohawk

Valley, would have learned about the calendar and New Year's merrymaking. The expression *Noyah*, meaning "Happy New Year," probably comes from the Dutch term *Nieuw Jaar*.

Nowadays, when so many people on Six Nations are so fiercely committed to resisting white influences and upholding our own traditions, *Noyah*, despite its European origins, seems to have escaped the carping and criticism directed at almost every other institution on the reserve. I think it's because we have, over hundreds of years, made *Noyah* our own. In fact, Six Nations is the only community I know, Mohawk or otherwise, that still celebrates *Noyah*.

Because of *Noyah*, New Year's Day is my favourite day of the year. I like it because there is more visiting today than there is during the hit-and-run, gimme-gimme action of Hallowe'en. In fact, I think of *Noyah* as Indian Hallowe'en—treats and socializing without the costumes and the teenage vandalism. I also like *Noyah* because it involves the whole family and is popular with all segments of the community. The split in this community over religious, political and cultural matters is wide and deep, but *Noyah* bridges the differences and allows everyone to take part in a shared activity.

When the old-timers talk about going *Noyah*-ing back at the turn of the century, they are quick to point out that they walked miles to visit the widely scattered farmhouses. If they were lucky, they say, a team of horses and a bobsleigh might have taken them around. Nowadays, though, there are few horses, fewer bobsleighs, and sometimes there isn't any snow on New Year's Day. Throw in the fact that there are more people to visit and longer distances to travel and it's little wonder kids get driven around the reserve by their parents. "That's just more evidence," the old-timers good-naturedly grumble, "that kids have it easy these days."

One thing that hasn't changed over the years are the treats people hand out. Some people give out candy and fruit but the most highly prized handouts are still home-made doughnuts, cookies, tarts, pastries and other treats baked just for the occasion. People who buy them are teasingly said to be cheating.

Knowing that, I didn't intend to cheat on my first day hosting *Noyah* visitors. Although I could have made ordinary cookies and doughnuts from a cookbook, I wanted to try my hand at Indian Cookies because everyone here raves about them. I also wanted to make them because I don't think I've ever had one. Although my mother tells me I went *Noyah*-ing when I was a little kid, I don't remember any of it and I don't remember Indian Cookies.

So yesterday I borrowed a recipe from Audrey. I started making the cookies late last night and everything was going fine until I discovered that the recipe didn't say how much flour had to be added in the final mix. I didn't know if it was supposed to be two teaspoons or two cups so I kept adding flour until I ran out. That coincided, luckily, with my assessment that the dough was just the right texture. At least I hoped it was.

The Indian Cookie I ended up making was a light, spicy affair filled with raisins. It was the size of a hockey puck and it was more of a biscuit than a cookie. Since I didn't know what they were supposed to look like or taste like I was more than a little anxious when Audrey, Richard and their gang arrived. I was doubly anxious because Audrey, a lifelong resident of the reserve and a former home economics teacher as well, is someone who knows a lot about Indian Cookies.

Once seated at the kitchen table, the grown-ups sampled my cookies and immediately judged them "delicious." Second helpings quickly disappeared in another round of compliments. Such praise, coming as it did from such seasoned gourmets of *Noyah* fare, had me patting myself on the back—I was a successful *Noyah* host the first time out.

Later on more members of the Powless gang showed up—my sister Dennise, her husband Gary, their three kids and a niece. They too liked the cookies. My house was the last stop on their route so we settled down to play card games, board games and computer games with the kids. We played, laughed and ate our merry way through the rest of the afternoon.

At the end of the first day of the new year, this house of mine was filled with lingering echoes of joy. I could still see the indentations in the rug from the children and grown-ups who had lain on their tummies playing games. The walls were still coated with the tumbling laughter of little boys and little girls. The smell of fresh-baked cookies still hung in the air. I turned out the lights but I couldn't bring myself to close my eyes on this wonderful day so I walked to the window of this darkened house and looked out. I gazed at the star-speckled sky and the snow-covered fields glistening in the moonlight, and I was filled with a glow that hugged me, warmed me and comforted my body and soul. I stood there alone, in the dark and in the silence, with a smile on my face and tears of joy in my eyes.

It felt so good to have been part of a one-of-a-kind ritual that celebrates friendship, family, tradition and sharing. It felt so good to know that I have helped, in a small way, to keep this wonderful tradition alive. It felt so good to know that I have helped give my niece, my nephews and five of their cousins the kind of magic and memories that can make a grown man cry.

Oh, it's been a great day. A truly wonderful day. *Noyah. Noyah.*

Democracy in action

For the past seventy years—ever since it was imposed by armed force in 1924—the elected band council has been the target of unrelenting scorn by the vast majority of people in this community, who express opinions like these: *They're not the real government on this reserve. They're just out to help themselves and their families. They're puppets of the Department of Indian Affairs. They're ripping off the people. They just do what the white man tells them to do. They couldn't run a lemonade stand.*

From the little I know about the band council, the criticisms are a little exaggerated, but there is a nugget of truth in most of them.

Although the elected council operates a raft of government programs, it has no inherent authority because almost everything it does has to be approved by the Department of Indian Affairs—land transfers, additions to the band lists, settling a will and budget requests, especially budget requests. Even a by-law to prohibit littering can be vetoed by the Minister of Indian Affairs.

Oppressive bureaucracy is a fact of life for Indian bands everywhere, but Six Nations is one place where people have little sympathy for the headaches and frustrations the band council has to endure. In spite of the band council's claim that it is working in the best interests of the community, the fact that it is a creation of the Canadian government—which refuses to recognize the Confederacy—means that many people here regard the band council as little more than a gang of collaborators, sell-outs and traitors.

Band elections here are conducted under the terms of the Indian Act and are held every two years. The election plan for this reserve was laid down by the government's Indian Agent in 1924 and hasn't changed since. The reserve is divided into six districts and the residents in those districts elect two councillors each. The chief councillor, "the chief," is elected from across the reserve. In the election held last fall, only 770 of the 18,000 people on the Six Nations band list voted.

Because of the lack of interest in the band council system, councillors are often elected by acclamation. That's how six out of twelve councillors were elected this past October. In a similarly unconvincing manner, band chief Steve Williams was reelected. He received 305 votes in a three-way race—less than 40 percent of the turnout and less than 2 percent of the people on the band list. Nevertheless, Williams emerged smiling on election night to speak about his "mandate." Having beaten the second-place finisher by just 18 votes, Williams said he was "relieved people had confidence in me."

Williams and the twelve councillors are in charge of more than two hundred employees and a budget of nearly $40 million. Although most of the money gets spent properly, there are numerous horror stories of mismanagement. The irony is that the band likes to think of itself as educated, progressive, businesslike and, above all, professional. Supporters of the elective system see the Confederacy, on the other hand, as a bunch of uneducated doddering old chiefs who can never agree on anything. The fact is that the band is about a million dollars in debt and has bounced cheques all over the county. Last July, the newly hired band manager issued a scathing report on the way the band administers its whopping budget. Although the band has twenty bookkeepers, he said, no one had an overall picture of its finances. "Financial management is non-existent," he reported. And to this day, I'm told by someone who knows, when the band gets a bill from a supplier showing a credit on its account, the band routinely sends the company a cheque in that amount.

It's not just financial mismanagement that angers people. Last August, according to the *Tekawennake*, the council put a piece of prime riverfront land up for sale. It advertised for bids and said that only band members who did not already own land could enter the bidding. But it also said it would not necessarily accept the highest bid—that the names might be put in a hat and the new landowner would be determined by a lucky draw. Sure enough, the guy who met all the bidding qualifications and who apparently bid the most did not get the land. *So why bother to ask for bids if they're just going to pick names out of a hat?* As one sore loser told the *Tekawennake*, "I had no idea the band was so rich it could sell community assets and not get the highest price for them."

I've been victimized by the system myself. A year ago, after seeing the band advertise an acre of land for sale, I submitted a bid of $1,100. I was later informed by the band that the land was sold to a relative of a neighbouring landowner—for $300. Events like these are just some of the horror stories I know about—and I've been back on the reserve less than three months. It's no wonder I laugh when I hear the words "band council" and "businesslike" used in the same sentence.

While I "know" many other unflattering things about the

band council and its operations, most of it is based on hearsay and rumour. Although my general lack of first-hand information never stopped me from bad-mouthing the council in the past, I recently decided it was time I measured my opinions and "knowledge" of the band council against reality. So tonight, for the very first time, I went to a meeting of the Six Nations band council.

I didn't know what to expect but I was extremely curious. I wanted to see the people who supposedly represent the progressive, educated and professional faction—the best and the brightest—of this community. I wanted to see the entity that the Government of Canada recognizes as the law-making authority and the only legitimate voice of this community. I wanted to see the band council at work, to see the blessings of democracy in action. It was not a pretty sight.

Tonight was the first meeting of the "new" council that was elected last October. (Since ten of the twelve councillors and chief Steve Williams were reelected, the council is not really all that new.) The council meets in the band's headquarters, a squat brick-and-glass building on the main drag in Ohsweken. The band has its own high-ceilinged council chamber the size of a large classroom. At the front of the room is a row of six framed colour prints, each one labelled with the name of one of the six nations of the Iroquois, showing a man's head wearing the *kahstowa* (the traditional headdress) of that particular nation. In front of the prints is a raised dais where the chief, the band manager and the recording secretary sit. The twelve councillors sit in high-backed swivel chairs at a U-shaped desk facing the dais, and at the back of the room are thirty-two chairs for the press and the public. The walls are decorated with various pieces of native artwork having no particular relevance to Six Nations. There are two pictures of military warships on one wall. A picture of Mohawk poet Pauline

Johnson sits on the floor, propped against the wall.

After a Christian prayer from one of the reserve's white ministers, Steve Williams convened the meeting and launched into his inaugural address. He told the councillors that as chief he would maintain decorum during the meetings and would not tolerate profane language. He warned them not to use their positions on council for financial profit or to further their personal goals. And then he told them they must wear "proper business attire" to council meetings. Williams was well dressed himself. He wore a blue suit, white shirt and a yellow striped tie. (Although his pencil-thin moustache and slicked-down hair reminded me of the stereotypical used-car salesman, Williams is a siding contractor by trade.)

His "proper business attire" remark seemed to be aimed at Dave Johns, one of the two newly elected councillors, who just happens to be Williams's number-one political adversary. Johns is an outlandish character in his own right, particularly when measured against the middle-class values of the rest of the council. A twenty-nine-year-old owner of a combination gas bar/smoke hut, Johns is a short, chunky man with a moustache and goatee, and he's better known by his nickname—"Muskrat," or "Muskie" for short. At the meeting tonight Johns was wearing his usual outfit—high-top sneakers, sweat pants, sweat shirt and golf gloves. His hair was covered by a bandana and a baseball cap he never took off.

What really distinguishes Johns, though, is his politics. He is a renegade who detests the band council. He says, for example, that Steve Williams can do whatever he wants because the band council has lacked the courage to exercise its own leadership. Johns doesn't much care for the Confederacy either because his loyalties lie with the Mohawk Warrior Society. The only reason he ran, he says, was to find out what the council did in all its closed-door meetings, and to share that information with the rest of the community. He was elected by acclamation.

Williams concluded his opening remarks by outlining what he saw as the three major issues facing the community—cigarettes, gambling and membership—and he said that under his leadership, council would be doing something about all of them. He didn't say anything about the plans by the Six Nations Education Board to take over the schools this fall.

The meeting began, as scheduled, promptly at 7:30 p.m. Traditionally, it seems, the first item of business is to hear out any visitors or band members who want to appear before the council. The first such person tonight was a New Credit band member, a female law student at the University of British Columbia. She was speaking on behalf of a female Six Nations band member who was also a law student at UBC. The woman asked the council to give the two of them $1,200—not for law books, tutors, seminars or anything to do with the study of law. No. They wanted the money so they could fly from Vancouver to Toronto to play in a hockey tournament for law students.

The councillors asked the woman if she had approached the band's education office for money. "They don't have any for this purpose," she replied. They asked if the money was needed for equipment. "No, it's just for travel and accommodations." Finally, after ten minutes of questions and hemming and hawing and not wanting to say "no" to her face, the council voted to give the Six Nations woman $600 and send a letter to the New Credit band council encouraging it to give the other woman the other $600.

I was flabbergasted. I looked around to see if anyone else in the room shared my disbelief but there were only eight other people in the gallery—six Indians and the white reporters from *The Expositor* and the *Tekawennake*. No one seemed to be disturbed.

I didn't know what was worse: that the council—supposedly a law-making body—listened to a personal plea for hockey-and-travel cash; that the council gave them the money; or that the council made its decision without ever discussing the band's financial situation. This is a businesslike way to handle money? This is an efficient way to run a government? I don't think so. Compassionate, perhaps. Businesslike, efficient, professional—no.

The meeting then descended into farce when it came time for "chief and council reports." Williams gave a report of a trip that he and councillor Roger Jonathan had taken to England just before the Christmas holidays. They had gone there to rededicate a ship in the Royal Navy, but just what they had to do with "rededicating" a British warship was not explained. I suppose the ship might have been named the HMS *Ohsweken* or some such thing, but I doubt it.

Like a small child breathlessly recounting his first visit to Disneyland, Williams then eagerly blurted out the highlights of the trip. I scribbled furiously so I wouldn't miss a word:

> "We got to see the Crown jewels. Up close. We
> had special passes. We got to see them for an
> hour, we didn't get rushed through like the
> tourists do. One of the diamonds is 519 carats
> and it's not insured. We took a tour of the Tower
> of London, St. Paul's Cathedral and Westminster
> Abbey. We went to Plymouth for the rededica-
> tion ceremony and visited the ship and talked to
> the officers. They liked our gift, it was a soap-
> stone carving. We went to a pub for dinner and
> had a good time. We went to the ship's dance
> and a young lady won a car in a raffle. We met a
> countess and an earl. They live in a castle and

they're related to the Queen. They're really nice
people. He's the sixth-richest man in England. I
laid a business card on him and mentioned our
land claims and the $37 million we are owed in
our trust accounts, so I got a little business in."

According to Williams, the trip was a roaring success.
The only down-side, he declared, without realizing how it
would sound to thousands of struggling stay-at-home
Indians, was that it rained all the time and he and Roger
Jonathan couldn't play golf. *This is the guy who runs this
reserve? This is the guy who is negotiating with government on my behalf? This guy is supposed to be my chief?* I
didn't know whether to laugh or cry.

Although tonight was the first time I'd ever heard Steve
Williams speak or seen him in action, I had heard plenty
about him before I came to the meeting. People around
here bad-mouth him as though he alone is responsible for
all the reserve's problems. People say he doesn't listen to
anyone and does whatever he wants. I haven't heard *anyone*
say a good thing about him in the last two months. In fact,
the criticism is so vicious and one-sided that when I went in
there tonight I half expected to see Williams with cloven
hoofs, a barbed tail and horns sticking out of his head.

What I saw instead was a run-of-the-mill politician who
appeared desperately eager to please everyone in the room
by blunting any harsh words and downplaying any point of
contention. His favourite expressions seemed to be: "I can
understand that," "I agree with you" and "I know what
you're saying."

The councillors didn't raise any questions about the
British boondoggle. They didn't ask what the trip cost,
whether it was justified or what the two of them were
doing there. They didn't say anything at all, but I imagined
them all thinking, *"How come Roger got to go?"*

An even more disturbing revelation about the way the band operates came during an impromptu discussion on access to information. That's an important issue around here since half the reserve operates on gossip and hearsay and the other half doesn't know anything at all about what's going on. It is, in fact, all but impossible for even the most interested and determined community member to find out what the band is doing. The radio station does not cover the council meetings and the *Tekawennake* and *The Expositor* cover only a few highlights. Public attendance is low, probably because the meetings are so long. By 10:30 tonight, after meeting for three hours, the council had completed only half the points on the agenda. By then the only observers left in the gallery were the two reporters and me.

Dave Johns opened the can of worms by complaining that the band office had refused to give him the minutes of band council meetings for the previous two years—even though he was an elected band councillor. Johns then demanded to know the council's policy on this issue.

Williams, who campaigned on a platform of open government in 1991, then explained the facts of life to the new councillor. Anyone who wants information has to put their request, in writing, to the elected band council, stating what they want and why they want it. The council then decides whether or not to grant the request. Some people, Williams pointed out, have been turned down. If the request is granted, the band charges ten dollars an hour to conduct the document search, though the first two hours are free. It also charges ten dollars an hour (it calls this a "severance charge") to delete "non-pertinent information" from the documents. The photocopies themselves cost one dollar per page.

Whoa! No wonder no one knows what's going on around here.

Despite his pointed questions to Williams about the unfairness of the policy and how it was administered, Johns failed to rouse his fellow councillors. They sat on their hands and said nothing.

By the end of the meeting, nearly four hours after it started, the matter of cigarettes, a casino and band membership—issues that Steve Williams identified as major community concerns—had not been mentioned.

Chief stumbles over sewer

Two weeks ago, on the night of January 5, five men and one woman drove to the edge of a cornfield on the south bank of the Grand River two miles upstream from the centre of Brantford. They unloaded a few tarps, some clothing, food and water and began heading for their destination—an unoccupied island in the middle of the river the size of an extra-long football field. In the arctic blackness the six people inched their way over a treacherous ice bridge and scoured the unnamed island looking for driftwood. They built a fire, set up camp and settled in to wait through a long and frighteningly cold night.

They were there to stop construction workers from building a sewer line across the Grand River. The City of Brantford wants to bury the sewer line in a trench under the riverbed and the island.

In the morning, the six faced a hostile construction crew that shouted obscenities at them. The protesters held their ground. When the contractor saw that they wouldn't budge, he stopped work on the project. The six quickly brought in more supplies and reinforcements. They then settled down to hold off the city and wait out the March 1 deadline for completing the river crossing. The protesters have been camped out on that island—in minus-thirty-degree temperatures—for the past thirteen days.

Five of the six original protesters are Indians from Six Nations. The sixth is a non-Indian environmentalist. These protesters have two major reasons for stopping the project. Number one is the fact that the islands in the Grand River were never surrendered in any of the nineteenth-century land swindles, so they still belong—indisputably—to Six Nations. Number two is the fear that the sewer line might break or leak one day. If that happened, the sewer would dump thousands, perhaps millions, of gallons of human sewage and industrial waste into the river. A leak, the protesters fear, would devastate the river's plant, fish and bird life. What's more, the pollution would flow straight into the intake pumps of Brantford's and Ohsweken's water supply.

The six people who led the occupation were not acting on behalf of the band council or the Confederacy, they did it on their own initiative. After construction was halted, though, the Confederacy chiefs voiced support for the protesters, while some band council people muttered that they were renegades. The protesters say they will stay on the island until the police drag them away and arrest them, until the project is cancelled or until the Confederacy tells them to leave.

Although few in number, the protesters made almost everyone on the reserve pay attention to an otherwise routine city construction project. As a result, no one on the reserve, from what I can tell, is clamouring for the city to build a sewer line across *our* island in the middle of *our* river.

It so happens, however, that band chief Steve Williams may already have worked out a deal with the city last December allowing the sewer line to be built. No one knew anything about it until *The Expositor* reported the details of an agreement-in-principle in which the band would allow the sewer line to be built in exchange for $1,000 the band would have to repay if the Six Nations' claim to the island is rejected by the government. The agreement-in-principle wasn't signed by either party and Williams claimed not to know anything about it.

Brantford desperately wants to resume construction on the $2-million project, and even though the delay is costing the city several thousand dollars a day, it doesn't want to arrest the protesters for fear of triggering an even bigger Indian backlash that might not be confined to one little island.

It was against this contentious backdrop that the Mayor of Brantford and the city's chief engineer appeared before tonight's meeting of the Six Nations band council in an attempt to sell the project and get it back on track. What they said, in a nutshell, was that the plans for the sewer line were technically flawless and that nothing would or could go wrong. But several of the protesters and thirty community members were also in the council chamber, and the resulting debate raged for two and a half hours. During the course of the evening I saw the entire band council become briefly gripped by mass hysteria, and I finally discovered what Steve Williams does that makes him so unpopular.

Williams was quoted on the front page of *The Expositor* just four days ago as saying he had "no major problem with the project." At tonight's meeting, Williams watched as the protesters and some band councillors attacked the project before a crowd of angry band members. And by night's end, Williams was saying that he too was "teed off" and "very concerned about this issue."

The trouble is that while he gave the impression that he had changed his mind about the sewer line, Williams never once said, flat out, that he was opposed to it and would try to stop it. Although telling people what they want to hear is the way big-league politics are played, Williams doesn't seem to realize that Ohsweken isn't Ottawa. Around here people like straight-shooters who don't mince words, and they have learned to distrust anyone who sounds like a smooth-talking politician.

Clearly, Williams's brand of politics annoys the people here, but what really angers them is the fact that he often acts against the evident wishes of the community. The sewer line is a case in point. After the community roused itself against the project, Williams did not step back and realize he had little to gain and lots to lose by continuing to support it. Instead of announcing that community opposition had helped him realize his mistake, instead of announcing that he was therefore changing his mind and would take up the fight against the sewer line, Williams played both sides of the street.

The insight that tonight's meeting provided into Steve Williams's character was disturbing enough, but watching the way the band council reacted to the controversy was downright scary. In the course of explaining just how safe the project would be, the city engineer mentioned that there are already other sewer lines crossing the river in other places. They are inspected on a regular basis, he said, and there's never been a problem with any of them. But once he said that, the band councillors seemed to fall under a spell. All of a sudden, they wanted to know a lot more about those other river crossings, and they wanted to examine the inspection reports—all of them, on an ongoing basis—to ensure that all those sewer pipes are structurally sound. By then they were firmly in the grip of an inspection mania, so when Williams said the Six Nations band council had to take on the job of monitoring all the engineering inspection reports of all the sewer line crossings in all the cities up and down the river, everyone nodded their head in agreement.

Unbelievable! No one said, *"Wait a minute. What are we doing? Does anyone around here even know how to read one of those inspection reports? Aren't there other things we should be doing?"*

The meeting ended with the council feeling quite pleased with itself: it had bashed the project and assumed the role of pollution watchdog along the entire river. City officials, who failed to gain the band's support, left the meeting more frustrated than when they came. And I went home shaking my head.

All the players in tonight's little drama went back to their comfortable little homes and tucked themselves into their nice warm beds, including me. All the players, that is, except the ones at the centre of this controversy. Just as they have done for the past two weeks, a handful of Indians settled into their frigid tents and prepared to spend another long and bitterly cold night on a small, nameless island in the middle of the ice-choked Grand River.

Coping with cold

Because Six Nations is located in Ontario's "deep south," I was expecting my first winter here to be little more than a chilly transition between fall and spring. *Ha!*

For the first time in many years, the Big Six is having an arctic winter. It's been colder than a Conservative's heart for nearly a month. The temperature sank to minus-twenty-five degrees three days ago and hasn't moved since. The wind chill is minus-forty. Every day a new low-temperature record is set.

Thankfully, the cold hasn't popped a water pipe, but it's still having a major impact on my lifestyle. Before I go to bed, I stoke up the stove, get a fire blazing and turn down the damper, knowing that by morning the house will be ice cold—literally. When I get up, the first thing I do—even before I go to the bathroom—is start a fire. When I got up today, the digital thermometer on my desk (which is just five feet from the stove) said it was just six degrees in here. It took more than an hour today before the house got warm enough that I didn't see my breath.

The cat's water dish was frozen this morning, just as it has been every morning this week. But it never thawed out today when the rest of the house warmed up, so I had to keep breaking the ice throughout the day so she could have water to drink.

Another part of my daily routine is pouring a pitcher of boiling water into the bathtub to melt the layer of ice on the bottom of the tub so I can take a shower.

For the past three days the pipe that supplies water to the toilet has been frozen so I've had to get a bucket of water and fill the tank every time I want to flush it. The drain in the bathroom sink has frozen again so now I have to shave, brush my teeth and wash my face and hands in the kitchen sink. This is the second time it's happened; the last time it was plugged for two weeks.

And then there's the snow. We got nearly a foot of the stuff the day before yesterday. It was wet and heavy, and since the laneway is fifty yards long, it meant shovelling, literally, a ton of snow. I can't complain because that's what winter's all about. What bothered me, though, was all the shovelling I had to do *inside* the house. When I came downstairs that morning, I found a snowdrift had crept in a drafty window frame, slithered down the wall, settled over the couch and stretched halfway across the living-room rug. There was another snowdrift in the kitchen that buried my shoes and power tools. I looked at my interior snowscape and was instantly grateful, for once, that this old house is so cold that the snow didn't melt and make a real mess.

Tobacco boom spawns
cash and crime

Twenty years ago, Brantford was a comfortable city with a healthy manufacturing industry, anchored by farm machinery giants Massey–Ferguson and White Farm Equipment. For much of this century, in fact, the towns-folk of Brantford surfed a wave of prosperity while the job-less and marginally employed Indians on the reserve were considerably poorer. In those days, just like today, the criminally minded poor stole from the rich. One of the most common thefts occurred on Friday and Saturday nights when young Indian men would get a ride into town, go to a bar and leave at closing time, drunk, with no way to get back home. So they would steal a car, drive it back to the reserve and burn it. From what I hear, the police spent every weekend of the year recovering the burned-out hulks of stolen cars from the reserve's back roads.

How things have changed.

During the late 1980s, Massey–Ferguson and the other big industrial employers went bust and threw an army of skilled workers out on the street. The city's economy was crushed and has never recovered. The city's downtown core is now a basket-case. *The Expositor* reported a month ago—at the height of the Christmas shopping season—

that twenty-three of the forty-six stores on the city's main street were empty, boarded up or burned out. The place is a ghost town.

Over the same period of time, there has been an equally dramatic turnaround on the reserve. Although the community is a long way from full employment, business is booming on the Big Six. There are two hundred small businesses on the territory. More than three hundred people work for the band council, its affiliated agencies and the school system. And then there are the six hundred people who work in the tobacco trade as drivers, retail clerks, distributors, warehouse workers and security guards. It's my guess that the ninety or so smoke huts on this territory are currently making a total profit of more than $1 million a month.

So, with the reserve booming and the city bleeding, our traditional roles and rivalries, in a small way, have been reversed—and so has the nature of interracial crime. Now "poor" white guys from town are driving out to the reserve to rob the "rich" Indians, instead of the other way round. In the past few months there have been three armed robberies—an unheard-of event before this. In all three cases, a carload of white guys robbed a smoke hut at gunpoint. In one incident, they shot the place full of holes. In another, the gun-toting owner fired on the getaway car. (And to think I complained that the worst thing about living next to a smoke hut was the glare of their neon signs.)

Social scientists and casual observers might say that these incidents—white people robbing Indians—demonstrate how times have changed. But the old-timers around here would say it's not new. They would point out that white people began robbing Indians hundreds of years ago. In those days they used a Bible, a keg of rum, a pen and the threat of starvation to do their stealing. And now that some Indians have found a way to enrich themselves by turning Canada's economic system against itself, some white people have started to use guns.

Another effect of the tobacco trade on this community has been a jump in the price of land. Whenever a choice piece of acreage is put up for sale nowadays, it's immediately snapped up by "cigarette people" who pay the asking price with cash, making it that much harder for "ordinary" people to buy land and build a house.

With more disposable income around, many young men are driving their own vehicles nowadays, leading to a corresponding drop in the number of car thefts off the reserve. The evidence is contained in the annual Six Nations police report that was tabled at the band council meeting the other night. The statistics for 1993—the year of the tobacco boom—show a huge drop in the number of cars (from 530 to 482) that were stolen off the reserve and later recovered by the Six Nations police. There was also a decrease in local car thefts, petty mischief and minor assaults. That's the good news.

The bad news is that the number of domestic disturbances went up 50 percent, as did the number of people arrested for drunk driving. Worse, the number of business burglaries, weapons offences and fatal car accidents doubled. In 1992, before the boom, the police did not investigate a single armed robbery; this past year there were three. Similarly, the number of drug investigations went from 0 to 12 in just one year. All together, the Six Nations police laid 662 charges of all kinds last year—a whopping 26 percent increase over 1992.

So, cigarette profits may be up—way up, in fact—but so is the crime rate.

Getting fit
the old-fashioned way

Who would have thought it would be so hard to get fit while living in the country? Not me. I thought that since I was surrounded by the vigour and power of nature, I would somehow be magically transformed into a rugged and robust son of the soil.

Needless to say, it hasn't happened. I realized today, for instance, that I haven't walked anywhere for the past three months, ever since I moved back. Because I live miles from anywhere, I have to drive everywhere. Last fall I occasionally took a walk through the fields behind the house. Because of the snow cover, though, the only walk I take these days is the sixty-four-step trip around the house to fill the bird-feeders.

I need exercise, I know, since the only workouts I've had over the last ten years have come from running off at the mouth. Yes, I could jog or cycle around here—theoretically. It would be hard to do on these roads, but even harder would be finding the will to break my largely sedentary lifestyle.

As for workout videos and exercise classes, I'm hopeless. I just can't co-ordinate my body, arms and legs and keep up with the instructor or the music. There's an exercise class somewhere in the village, but I haven't gone to it. It's partly because I don't want to look clumsy. There's also something about having to drive somewhere to get some exercise that just doesn't make sense.

But it's more than that. I resist exercise for the sake of exercise. It's like sunbathing—by itself it's a boring time-waster. I don't mind getting hot and sweaty if there is a point to it or if it gives me pleasure. The challenge I face, obviously, is to find an activity I need or want to do that will make me more physically fit.

Today, though, I realized that I've been engaged in just such an activity for the past six weeks. Winter has forced me into an exercise routine and I wasn't even aware of it. I give my heart, lungs and muscles a little workout, I get a little sweaty, and I don't embarrass myself. I've stuck to this routine faithfully and I couldn't drop out if I wanted to.

At least five days a week I put on my exercise outfit: work boots, blue jeans, a flannel shirt, a raggedy jacket, leather gloves and a hat. Fully dressed for my twenty-minute workout, I head for the woodpile to begin my "axercises"—splitting wood.

I have developed a routine that seldom varies. To keep from straining or injuring myself, I start with a few warm-ups. I get my bucksaw and grab some of the scrap lumber that's lying around the garage. I make sure it's softwood—spruce, pine or cedar. Softwood is straight-grained, splits easily, burns quickly and is ideal for kindling. With a length of scrap lumber in hand, I saw off a half-dozen pieces a foot long. *Bend, lift, saw, saw, saw. Saw, saw, saw. Saw, saw, saw.*

I then take one of the foot-long pieces and stand it on the end of the chopping block. I hold it steady with one hand while I grab the axe with my other hand just below the head. Then, just like cutting vegetables, I chip off strips of softwood the size of a thick wooden ruler. *Bend, lift, chip, chip, chip. Bend, lift, chip, chip, chip. Bend, lift, chip, chip, chip.*

Moving on to the second stage of the warm-up, I go to the woodpile and pick out a piece of hardwood. But it can't be just any old block of wood. It has to be easy to split—short, straight-grained and without any knots. I lift it and stand it on the chopping block. With one easy two-handed swing of the axe, I split it and the two pieces fall to the ground with a thud. I pick up one of the two pieces, place it on the block and with another easy swing I split it in two once more. This continues, swing after swing, until I have reduced several blocks of wood to a pile of sticks no thicker than a softball bat. These are the pieces I will stack on top of the kindling to get my fire blazing. *Bend, lift, chop, thud. Bend, lift, chop, thud. Bend, lift, chop, thud.*

By now, fully warmed up, I move on to even bigger blocks of wood, pieces that are longer and thicker, with knots and twisted grain. I bend over and lift the piece onto the chopping block. I swing the axe this time with all my strength. I lift it well over my head and drive it into the centre of the block with both hands at the end of the handle. Often, the axehead just buries itself in the block halfway through. But instead of pulling the axe out of the wood and swinging again, I lift the axe, which is buried in the wood, and drive it back down onto the chopping block. The axehead sinks an inch deeper into the grain. Again and again I drive the axe-buried-in-the-wood onto the chopping block until the wood splits in two and flies apart. *Bend, lift, chop. Whack, whack, whack, thud. Bend, lift, chop. Whack, whack, whack, thud. Bend, lift, chop. Whack, whack, whack, thud.*

I'm not paying any attention to the birds now, or to the cold, the snow or the wind. I am in a world of my own. I have fallen into my working rhythm, a rhythm that fuses body, mind and soul. Smoothly, repetitively, methodically, I lift the wood, move my body and swing the axe. I have focused every part of my being towards one simple objective—splitting one piece of wood into two. Swing after swing, the axehead falls. I have become a machine.

By now I'm breathing deeply. My muscles are pumped. The blood is surging through my body and I feel great. I am thoroughly invigorated and I don't feel the least bit tired or sore. As I continue to work I can't help grinning like a fool and laughing out loud. I find myself smiling with sheer joy at the memories I've rekindled of chopping wood for my great-grandmother so long ago. I find myself beaming with immense satisfaction at the change between my new wood-chopping lifestyle and the couch potato existence I led just three months ago.

After working my way through a dozen large blocks, I move on to the next-to-last stage of the workout. I pick out the largest, heaviest block I can find. It is the size of a microwave. The winding, tortured grain is twisted around huge knots. There are branches jutting out at right angles. These blocks are the hardest to split but they will be the ones that will keep the fire burning for hours. I lift the huge chunk of wood onto the chopping block and take a full-bodied swing. The axe barely dents the surface of the twisted grain. I pry the axehead out and swing again. And again, there is just a dent in the surface. I keep attacking the same spot until I have opened a crack that is little wider than a pencil. *Bend, lift, chop, chop, chop.*

I grab a steel splitting wedge and put it in the crack. Then, using the blunt end of the axe, I smash the wedge with all my might. With each swing of the axe, the wedge sinks an inch further into the block. The ringing crash of steel on steel sounds out a half-dozen times before the block is slowly riven in two. *Klang, klang, klang, klang, klang, klang. Thud.*

Even though there is a raw wind whipping in from the north that gives the bitter cold an extra bite and makes my nose run, I don't feel the slightest bit chilly. Instead, I'm so hot I take off my jacket and gloves. I'm breathing hard now and I could use a rest but I'm on a roll and I don't want to stop. So I stand fully erect, arch over backwards as far as I can, take a deep breath, shake my muscles loose, bend over and grab another big block of wood. *Bend, lift, chop, chop, chop. Klang, klang, klang, klang, klang, klang. Thud.*

I stop, take off my hat and wipe the sweat from my forehead, which steams in the cold. I pause long enough to stretch again, shake the fatigue from my arms and take several deep breaths. I'm not grinning any more, except for a half-smile at the sight of the growing pile of split wood, but I still feel good. My earlier exhilaration has made way for a quiet sense of determination and satisfaction.

Finally, I pick out the largest, heaviest, most twisted chunk of wood I can find. With one more deep breath, I summon the strength for the last piece of wood I will split today. *Bend, lift, chop, chop, chop. Klang, klang, klang, klang, klang, klang. Thud.*

After twenty minutes, the chopping block is surrounded by a jumbled heap of freshly split wood. I wipe the sweat from my forehead and, with one last satisfying swing, I drive the axe into the empty face of the chopping block to await my next trip to the woodpile. *Thunk.*

In the fading light at the end of the day, I am sitting at my desk, with a supply of firewood stacked in the corner and a fire roaring in the stove behind my back. As I ready myself for an evening of writing, I feel smug and contented. I am warmed by the fire at my back, by the knowledge that I have cut enough wood to heat my house for another day and by the awareness that I have done my body some good. Since I began cutting wood I have hardened my muscles, toughened the skin on my baby-soft hands and lost ten pounds of ugly fat. I don't get a full-body workout, I know, but it's better than nothing, and I know I have postponed the purchase of an exercise video for another day.

As I pick another stick out of the wood-rack to feed to the flames, I can't help taking a close look at it. It's a piece of oak. The end-grain is dark and weathered. Counting the growth-rings, I can see that this stick came from a tree that was more than sixty years old. A scuffed and dirty strip of bark is still fixed to one side of the wedge-shaped stick. But where the axe has done its work, the bright and gleaming salmon-coloured grain lies exposed. Looking at the sparkling flecks of dried-out sap, I realize that the leaves of this tree had collected the power of the sun for more than three generations and stored it in this grain— just so I could set this stick afire and heat my house. It is a sobering and humbling thought and it reminds me that I must give thanks for this stick of wood, for the tree it came from and for the other blessings of creation that Shonkwaya'tihson has bestowed upon us his children, the Onkwehonwe.

The world's worst
spectator sport

The Iroquois have the distinction of having invented the world's best spectator sport—lacrosse. It's fast and exciting, a supreme test of strength, finesse and strategy. And the Iroquois have the dubious distinction of having also invented the world's worst spectator sport—snowsnake.

For readers who just said "Snow-*what*?," it's a winter game that vaguely resembles a javelin-throwing contest. The "snake" is seven feet long and is hand-carved from one of the close-grained hardwoods—ironwood, hickory or juneberry. The head, which fits through the circle formed by my thumb and forefinger, has a pointed end made of lead to give the snake added weight and to keep the wood from splitting if it hits a rock. There is a small notch at the tip of the "tail" used to throw the snake. The rod-like body of the snake is no thicker than my thumb and is highly polished. (Actually, there are two kinds of snowsnakes, the "longsnakes" and a shorter, stubbier version, the "mudcats.")

Snowsnake is a team sport, with four throwers on a team and several teams competing against each other in a match. The object of the competition couldn't be simpler: whichever team throws its snakes the furthest wins. The contest itself is more than a simple test of strength or athletic ability. A key person on each team is the "shiner." His job is to prepare the snakes using just the right kind of wax, based on his assessment of the weather, snow and track conditions. (Snowsnake, unlike lacrosse, seems to be an exclusively male sport.) Shiners are older men, retired throwers usually. You normally find them waxing a snake while sitting on the back of a pickup parked away from the action, answering questions from the few curious spectators who happen by.

Throwing a snowsnake is a very tricky piece of business. Snowsnakes are thrown not through the air but along a narrow track that is formed by dragging a long thin log through the snow. Unlike the javelin, the snake is not held in the middle and is not heaved willy-nilly in any direction across the thrower's field of vision. First there is the considerable problem of getting the snowsnake onto the track. To minimize this problem, snow is pushed into a waist-high pile and formed into a long sloping ramp called the pitch hole. Cut into the top of the ramp is a wide groove that gradually narrows as the ramp descends to meet the track in the snow.

The thrower grasps the snake in one hand, with his forefinger in the notch at the tip of the tail. Then, trying to keep the long, slender, top-heavy snake balanced, he runs at top speed towards the ramp. As he approaches the high end, he pulls back his arm and fires the snake straight down the ramp and into the track.

It's a lot harder than it sounds. Imagine grabbing a pool cue in one hand, with your forefinger on the small end, running with it at top speed and throwing it with all your might at a groove in the snow that is little bigger than a gutter pipe. Now imagine trying to do that on icy ground, in a snowstorm, in the cold and with the wind blowing, and you have some idea of what it's like to throw a snowsnake.

I've been to a half-dozen different tournaments, and from what I've seen, it looks like a great game to play, but it is decidedly a world-class dud for the people who turn out to watch. Let me count the ways.

First, the weather. Since there has to be snow on the ground, it's always *cold*. What's more, it's usually windy and often snowing.

Second, the seating. There isn't any. Spectators have to stand for the entire match—in the cold, the wind and the snow.

Third, the scoreboard, the big-screen TV, the announcer, the programs and the uniforms. There aren't any. As a result, the casual spectator has no idea who's playing or who's winning.

Fourth, the length of the game. It goes on forever. There is no time-clock and the winner is the first team to score a predetermined number of points, which seems to take all day. (Or maybe because of the cold, it just seems that way.)

Fifth, the boredom. (For an explanation of this, review the last two reasons.)

But maybe I'm being too harsh. Going to a snowsnake tournament isn't that boring—the first time. It's fascinating, in fact, to see the beautiful workmanship of a snowsnake close up, to see the different throwing styles and to see the snake hurtling through the track. But—and I'm exaggerating only a little here—when you've seen one throw, you've basically seen them all.

Finally, the sixth and most important reason why snowsnake is the world's worst spectator sport is the danger, because there is a *small* chance that a casual spectator can receive a nasty little injury. This usually happens when a spectator is standing too close to the throwing ramp. ("Too close" means standing less than fifty yards in front of the ramp. The players constantly warn people to stand back, but accidents do happen.) If the snake is not perfectly aimed down the centre of the groove, it will ricochet off the ramp and off the track at a terrifying speed. The snow-snake, with its pointed, arrow-like head, then becomes a scar-making missile. The unsuspecting spectator is usually speared in the foot or lower leg. Stories abound in the snowsnake fraternity of the number of people who have been speared. One old-timer I met told a particularly grue-some tale. A woman was leaning against a fencepost, he said, when a streaking, seven-foot-long, arrow-headed snowsnake speared her, went through her leg and nailed her to the fencepost. (He swore it was a true story but I didn't ask to hear how the woman got unstuck.)

Okay, so snowsnake may not be entirely spectator-friend-ly, but it does have a number of advantages that big-league sports don't have. It's free, for starters. What's more, there are no crowds to fight and there is always plenty of free parking nearby. As well, you can get close to the players during the game; you can even talk to them and ask them questions. Lastly, you can always get front-row standing room right next to the track, any time you want.

In spite of the fact that its inconveniences seem to out-weigh its blessings, I like snowsnake because it's that rare thing that exists almost nowhere else in the world of ath-letic competition—it is a pure sport. The game is simplici-ty itself and it is played by grown men for sheer joy and little else.

There are none of the trappings associated with any other organized sport. There are no trophies, pennants, gold medals or diamond pinkie rings. There are no play-by-play announcers spouting statistics. There is no league commissioner. There are no mascots, uniforms or fan clubs. There are no player agents. There is no instant replay. There are no judges, umpires or timekeepers. There is no Hall of Fame. There are no salary disputes. There are no bathing-suited bimbos selling beer, cars or cigarettes.

There are no television time-outs. There are no drug tests. There is no all-star game. The players don't get traded and they don't endorse breakfast cereals, toiletries or running shoes.

//

On the last day of January, I went to see the first match of the season. The weather was brutal. There was nearly a foot of snow on the ground, it was brain-paralyzingly cold and it was windy to boot—perfect conditions, I suppose, for a snowsnake tournament.

The throwing ramp was close to the road. The track itself was laid out on an empty field and disappeared into the distance. There were teams from Six Nations and from the Onondaga and Cattaraugus Seneca reservations in the United States.

The players, most of them in their twenties, were dressed alike, more or less. They wore hooded sweatshirts, blue jeans and baseball caps. Only their footwear seemed to differ. Some guys wore construction boots, some wore running shoes and some wore baseball cleats. It was a pleasure to watch them throw, to witness their strength, speed, agility and dignified intensity. It was also a little scary to watch a snake, which wasn't aimed quite right, ricochet wildly off the ramp.

During a break in the action I walked a hundred yards down the track and waited for the next series of throws. A few seconds after the first snake was thrown it whipped by me in a frightening blur. Even though I was a hundred yards away from where it was thrown, I almost got whiplash from snapping my head around to keep the thing in sight. It was like standing next to the track in a subway station when the train screams by without stopping.

I then walked another four hundred yards down the track to see the end of the throws. Looking back at the ramp, more than a quarter-mile away, the throwers were unrecognizable specks in the distance. It must have taken, I figure, something like thirty seconds for a throw to reach me. By the time I saw it, some fifty yards away, the snake was moving slowly, with a gentle side-to-side rocking motion as it slid smoothly over the snow. When it had slowed to a pace that one of the men could keep up with, one of the thrower's teammates would run along next to the track shouting encouragement for the snake to go a little further. *"Come on!"* they yelled. *"Get on up there!"* they bellowed. Eventually, though, the speeding, highly polished hardwood missile would succumb to the forces of friction and gradually slide to a stop. The position of the snake would then be marked and it would be taken out of the track.

The longest throw I witnessed was, by my long-legged pacing, 540 yards (half a kilometre). As remarkable as this throw was, however, it still was far short of the mile-long throws this sport is known for.

After watching for less than an hour, I retreated to a nearby coffee shop to warm up. Looking through the frost-rimmed windowpane, I could just see the distant figures of two dozen men, oblivious to the cold, who continued their waxing, running, throwing, shouting and laughing.

As the last of January's pale light faded in the late afternoon, I sat there wishing I had grown up on the reserve so that I could have been one of the men out there, playing this ancient game and helping to keep another tradition alive. Of course, if I had grown up here, my days as a thrower would be over by now, so I pictured myself instead as one of the overall-suited shiners, perched on the open tailgate of a battered pickup truck, waxing a snake while answering the occasional question from a curious and chilly observer.

I imagined what I would say to the people who had come to see the world's worst spectator sport. I would begin by explaining the rich history, the simple rules and the subtle strategies of the game. I would tell them about the most exciting tournaments in living memory. I would tell them about the mightiest throws ever made by the greatest throwers who ever played the game. And just before the spectators began walking over towards the track, I would stop them, look them right in the eye and, in an ominous tone, I would tell them the story of the woman who was speared through the leg and nailed to a fencepost.

The ground hog was right

It's Valentine's Day and we've been in another minus-twenty-degree cold spell for what seems like weeks now. It's not quite that cold inside the house, thank goodness, but it's close. Every day I wake up seeing my breath, and this morning there was frost on my blanket. I looked at the thermometer and was dismayed to see that it was just four degrees above zero, the lowest indoor temperature this winter. Then I noticed that the water pump was pounding away, trying to keep up the water pressure. Since I had just gotten up and hadn't used the sink, shower or toilet, I took this to be a bad sign.

I walked into the kitchen and discovered, after I did one of those banana-peel spills, that the bathroom and half the kitchen had been transformed into an indoor skating rink. *Ouch.*

From ice-level, where my face landed, I could see water bubbling out of the wall. The water pipe had broken overnight; the water had flooded the kitchen and bathroom and frozen. And the pump, ever so efficient, had kept on pumping and increasing the size of the ice rink.

Not only was it still just four degrees in the house, with no fire going, I was by then sitting on my ice-and-water-covered floor in sopping-wet, ice-cold pajamas.

Just like Boxing Day, I thought, only worse. That day the temperature outside at noon had been somewhere near minus-twenty-five degrees and this same pipe had burst. It wasn't in one of the outside walls, where pipes usually break. No, it was in one of the inside walls dividing the bathroom and kitchen. I'd always thought it was cold in this house, but for a water pipe to break inside an *interior* wall in the middle of the day? That's cold.

On that occasion I'd torn the moulding and panelling off the kitchen wall, stemmed the flood and mopped up the mess. I'd had a general idea of how to repair it, so I'd gathered all the necessary tools and materials, but just as I was about to launch into the job, I thought back to my water pipe fiasco last fall—I thought back to the colossal mess and bother—and decided to call in professional help.

Ken Hill, a local building contractor, came to my rescue—on a holiday—and fixed it beautifully in no time. In fact, he probably could have finished even sooner if I hadn't been "helping" him.

I like Ken. As my late Gramma Thomas would say, he's "good stuff." He's not an old man but I was surprised to find that he did business the old-fashioned way, with me anyway. When he'd finished repairing the pipe I asked him how much I owed him.

"Whatever it's worth to you," he said.

"Well, what's your time and labour worth?" I replied.

He hemmed and he hawed and I fudged and I fiddled and we both fell into step, dancing around the delicate question of money, both of us reluctant to mention a figure, both of us wanting to be fair. Finally, after some more of our awkward two-step, a figure was mentioned and immediately agreed to.

After Ken left I stuffed insulation into the wall near the water pipe, thinking at the time that it would prevent this little mini-disaster from happening again.

Today's calamity showed just how wrong I was. This time, though, having become much more adept at responding to the average household crisis, I moved swiftly and surely into action. I turned off the pump, put on dry clothes, built a fire, mopped up the water and tore the kitchen panelling off the wall again. I went to town, bought a piece of copper pipe, came back and—trying to remember exactly what Ken Hill had done the last time— soldered the pipe myself. Then, holding my breath and saying a little prayer, I turned on the pump.

The water came on and the pipe didn't leak. That was the good news. The bad news was that the pump would not shut off. Although it kept chugging and chugging, it never built up enough pressure to trip the shut-off switch. *Oh, great.* So I looked in the Yellow Pages, called a couple of plumbers and described the symptoms. The diagnosis: a plugged injector—and it's not going to be easy to fix. The injector is at the bottom of the well, for one thing. To fix it, the well cap will have to be taken off, the water lines hauled out, the injector replaced, the lines flushed out, the injector lowered back down and the well cap replaced.

A simple enough job for someone who knows what he's doing. But there's just one small problem: I don't know where the well cap is. It's buried I don't know how far below ground level and it could be almost anywhere in the yard. I asked my next-door neighbour and the previous owner but they didn't know where it was either. The only person who might know, I was told, is over eighty now and has Alzheimer's. *Hmm.*

Since the fix-it guys will charge me fifty dollars an hour, I'll find the well cap myself—but I'm not going to dig up the whole yard looking for it. And even if I knew where it was, I wouldn't try to dig it up now, not with all this snow on top of all this rock-hard frozen ground. This little job will just have to wait until spring. In the meantime, every time I want to use the sink, shower or toilet, I'll have to turn the pump on and turn it off manually.

I finished cleaning up the mess, put the panelling back on the wall and put my tools away. Then I tried to clean myself up. I climbed into the shower and as soon as I was all lathered up, the water stopped running. I had forgotten to turn on the pump. Dripping water and covered with soap, I was barely able to control my irritation as I got out of the tub, walked out of the bathroom, through the kitchen, into the utility room, turned on the pump and headed back to the bathroom. Once back in the shower, I was greatly aggravated to find that the water barely dribbled out of the showerhead. Of course: because the injector is plugged, the pump operates at only half-pressure.

How much longer am I going to have to put up with this?

And then I remembered. Two weeks ago the groundhog saw his shadow and everyone said there would be six more weeks of winter.

Six more weeks? Say it ain't so!

I've never put any stock in this silly folklore before and I hate to do so now, but looking at the way winter has been going so far, with spring nowhere in sight, I think the groundhog may have been right. It will be at least six more weeks before the plumbing in this house returns to normal.

Stirring the ashes

When I was growing up, I had no real religion. My parents are Seventh Day Adventists, and despite all their many efforts, I never accepted their faith and I grew up without any strong religious convictions. I evolved instead into a vaguely spiritual being, but I couldn't identify with Christianity or the little-of-this, little-of-that smorgasbord of "native spirituality" that is so popular in much of the country. I didn't know anything about the Iroquois religion, but as I grew older I began to be attracted to the traditional beliefs of the Rotinonhsyonni because they helped to define my place and my role in the universe.

Because I always lived so far away from the reserve, the Iroquois religion was basically closed to me. Oh, I did go to a few sunrise ceremonies and tobacco-burning rituals, but I knew nothing about the major ceremonies or sacred rituals that take place in the longhouse. Now that I have moved back, I have finally removed the long-distance learning hurdle.

I already know and believe the story of creation. I believe that Shonkwaya'tihson is still in the Skyworld watching over everything He created, and I feel obligated to abide by His instructions. It is because I feel compelled to give thanks as He has decreed, in the proper manner and at the appropriate time, that I went to a Mid-Winter Ceremony today for the first time.

The Mid-Winter Ceremony stems from the time when Shonkwaya'tihson created the Onkwehonwe, the first human beings. He instructed them to offer thanks for the blessings of creation by conducting certain rituals at specific times during the year, but especially at mid-winter, when the maple sap runs, when the strawberries are ripe, at planting time, when the beans are ripe, when the corn is green and at harvest time. The greatest of all the ceremonies that take place during the year is the one that occurs at mid-winter. At the Sour Springs Longhouse, the Mid-Winter Ceremony is eight days long. Today was the second day, a day devoted to stirring the ashes.

Built about 1855, a hundred yards back from the road and nestled in a stand of hardwood, the Sour Springs Longhouse, so named for a nearby sulphur spring, is a steep-gabled building made of squared-off logs. It's large for a log building, probably the size of a four-bedroom, one-storey house. Although it is roughly twice as long as it is wide, there is just one window in each side. A cookhouse and dining room are near the front of the building and separate outhouses for men and women are in the back.

As I walked across the gravelled parking lot towards the longhouse I became increasingly anxious, in spite of my desire and sense of duty. The closer I got, the more nervous I became. When I got to the door, I could hear someone speaking inside and I was seized by doubt. *Is it okay to go in now? Should I wait until he finishes talking?* I stood there worried that someone would confront me when I went in. I was afraid of embarrassing myself and worried about doing the wrong thing. I didn't expect to know many people inside and I knew that none of them had invited me. Although the ceremonies are supposedly open, I've always had the feeling that longhouses were only for those people who had grown up in them, that they're not meant for people like me. But when I realized that my wish to enter the world of the longhouse was greater than my fear of whatever lurked inside, I pushed the door open and walked in. There were nearly two hundred people crammed in there, and it seemed like every one of them was eyeballing me, wondering who I was and what I was doing there.

The longhouse consisted of one long open room with a door near each end. The plain walls and ceiling were painted white. The wooden floor was unpainted. Bare bulbs hung from two light sockets in the ceiling. At each end of the open floor stood a cast-iron stove, with a stovepipe extending through the ceiling overhead. Around the outer edge of the floor there was a ring of high-backed wooden benches, filled with old men and women, obviously the chiefs and clanmothers. Behind them there was a raised platform and a ring of benches against the wall that were filled with younger men, women and children.

All the men sat on one long side of the room, facing all the women sitting on the other. I knew they were also sitting grouped according to their clans but there were no signs indicating which clan sat where. Fortunately, a friend had told me which door to use and where the turtle clan would be so I joined what I assumed was a dozen other turtle clan men standing in one corner. I took off my hat and tried to be inconspicuous.

I could hear an old man speaking but couldn't see him because of the crowd. From my limited language skills I could tell he was speaking Cayuga and was delivering the Thanksgiving Address. But that was all I knew. After a couple more brief speeches in Cayuga (which I didn't understand at all), the bulk of the ceremony was devoted to the stirring of ashes.

In addition to marking the start of the mid-winter doings, the ash-stirring ritual also symbolizes the start of the new year. In the old days, when the Onkwehonwe still lived in longhouses, the people would clean out their firepits and start a new fire at mid-winter.

Nowadays, the ash-stirring is done in the longhouse's wood-burning stoves. Today's ritual began when a young man (one of the faithkeepers) distributed a dozen long wooden paddles to the men and women seated at one end of the longhouse. Those people then went out the door closest to them, walked around the building and came back in the other door and gathered in front of the nearest stove. An old man in the group then made a brief speech in Cayuga and began singing a song. As he did so, he began stirring the ashes in the open door of the stove with his paddle, and the rest of the group joined in the stirring with the paddles they held.

In little more than a minute, the ash-stirring ritual for that group was over. It was then the turn of the clans grouped at the other end of the longhouse. It took almost two hours for everyone to have a turn at stirring the ashes. No one was left out. Not even me. The faithkeeper handed me a paddle and I stirred the ashes just like everyone else.

As I walked back to my spot in the corner, I felt a quiet sense of accomplishment, even though I hadn't really done anything. But, I reminded myself, at least I hadn't embarrassed myself. I hadn't tried to fool myself into thinking I was a "longhouse person" now. Far from it. But I had taken part in a ceremony that had been ordained by the Creator, and even though I didn't understand a word of what was being said, it felt good to be there.

As I waited for everyone to take their turn, I couldn't help noticing that I knew only a handful of people by name. That wasn't surprising since I still don't know all that many people around here. But I was surprised that only one of all the Mohawks I know was there. I realized then that I was seeing evidence of the way that Six Nations is divided, not only along political lines but along religious lines as well.

There is a split, first of all, between the Christians and the "pagans," as they were once called. Many of the people at Six Nations, maybe more than half, are Christians, or profess to be, and avoid the longhouse as they would a mosque. But the "pagans"—the believers in our original religious beliefs—are split as well. Most of these believers attend one of the four longhouses on the reserve—Upper Cayuga (Sour Springs), Lower Cayuga, Seneca or Onondaga. Despite their tribal names, the longhouses have followers from all six Iroquois nations, although the language most commonly spoken in the ceremonies is Cayuga. All the longhouses share the same beliefs and operate in much the same fashion, with only minor variations.

From what I can tell, there is a sizeable community of Mohawk people here who are not Christians and who hold traditional religious beliefs but don't attend any of the longhouse doings. (There was a Mohawk longhouse here a long time ago but it burned down and has never been replaced.) It is this group, a group that could form the nucleus of a distinctly Mohawk longhouse, that is somewhat at odds with the longhouse people.

The way I see it, this religious conflict can be compared to the difference between Catholics and Protestants—one group old and unchanged, the other new and "improved." The Mohawk traditionalists believe only in the religious teachings stemming from the *Kayaneren'tsherakowa* (the Great Law). The traditionalists who attend the various longhouses ("the longhouse people") believe in the *Kayaneren'tsherakowa* just as much, but they also believe in the *Karihwiyo* (literally, the Good Business, popularly known as the Code of Handsome Lake).

Skanyatariyo (Handsome Lake) was a Seneca war chief who began preaching a "new and improved" religion among the Iroquois after he had a vision in 1799. In it, he was met by three angelic beings who said that they had been sent by the Creator to ask Handsome Lake to preach against the sins of drinking, witchcraft and abortions. In later visions, Handsome Lake met Jesus Christ and George Washington and toured the Hell-like domain of the Punisher, a place of eternal torture reserved for sinners who refuse to repent and abide by the *Karihwiyo*. In addition to harsh biblical warnings about Hell and damnation, the code also contains a number of hauntingly beautiful passages that could just as easily have come from the Sermon on the Mount: "The Creator loves poor children and whosoever feeds the poor and unfortunate does right before Him."

Handsome Lake's preaching had a tremendous impact on the Seneca, Cayuga and Onondaga nations in particular, and the people readily accepted almost all of his instructions. They continued to practise all their old ceremonies and rituals, just as they had always done, and they added a few new ones, such as the confession of sins. The one message the longhouse people refused to accept was Skanyatariyo's instruction to disband the "false faces" and other medicine societies.

The longhouse people revere Handsome Lake and have stopped just short of declaring him a saint. When they recite the Thanksgiving Address, for example, they offer thanks for all the blessings of creation, including a special acknowledgment for Skanyatariyo and the *Karihwiyo*.

The Mohawk traditionalists, however, thoroughly loathe Handsome Lake and his code. They sneer contemptuously at the mere mention of his name and call the longhouse people "Lakers." They point out that Handsome Lake had his first vision while he was recovering from an extended drinking binge. They complain also that Handsome Lake was influenced by the Quakers and object to the new religious elements he introduced.

The crazy thing about the tension between the longhouse people and the Mohawk traditionalists, two groups with basically identical religious beliefs, is that when they want to insult one another they haul out the dirtiest word in their vocabulary to spit at each other—but they both use the same word! When they want to ridicule and offend someone from the other side, they call each other a *Christian*.

Today's ceremony finished with two men, one from each end of the longhouse, stirring the ashes one last time. The one from the far end of the longhouse was a husky, grey-haired old man who walked with a pronounced limp. He certainly seemed to know what he was doing and I guessed from his age that he had probably participated in his first Mid-Winter Ceremony during World War I. I wasn't surprised that someone like him—an old man of measured pace and tempered dignity, a man fluent in the language, a man who knew this ceremony intimately—had been selected to perform the closing ritual.

The man who had been selected to represent the turtle clan end, however, could not have been more different. To begin with, he wasn't eighty years old—he was eighteen, if that. His wavy brown hair was tied in a short curly pony-tail, which, combined with his engaging smile and fresh-scrubbed features, made him look as though he'd just stepped out of a milk commercial. He wore running shoes, a Hoyas basketball jacket and a baseball cap. Tall, thin and vaguely athletic, he looked just like any other teenager I've seen hanging around the mall—until he picked up his pad-dle. Instantly, he was the picture of poise and maturity. He strode confidently to the cast-iron stove alongside the old man. Together they walked back and forth between the fires and stirred the ashes. He spoke in his mother tongue without a stutter or trace of hesitation. And then this young man, who looked like he might have been equally comfortable singing the latest song by Madonna or Megadeth, sang the final ash-stirring song with a strong, sure and ringingly pure voice.

Even before the last syllable faded away, I was filled with admiration and the hope that this young man will be blessed with good health so that his voice will be heard singing the songs of the longhouse until well into the second half of the twenty-first century. Watching him, I got a stomach-knotting pang that came from seeing his face superimposed on a teenaged image of myself that I'd dredged up from the cavern of failed dreams in a dark corner of my soul. I flashed lightning-like, back and forth, over three decades of time, the image of his warm ideal and my cold reality mixing into bittersweet fantasy. After wishing I had been just like him when I was young, I realized that I was staring at a past I could never relive. And, just as unrealistically, I couldn't help thinking that I would want my son, if I had one, to be just like him.

I ended my reverie by looking around the crowd of people and realizing that there were dozens of other young men and women in the longhouse who were just as involved in preserving their religion, culture and language. I left the Sour Springs Longhouse hoping that all of these sons and daughters will be cherished by everyone else in this community for what they are—our pride and joy and our hope for the future.

Don't do it again or we'll have to get tough, sir

One of the many things that impressed the Europeans when they first arrived here was the way the Iroquois governed themselves. Being all too familiar with ruthless sheriffs, horrific dungeons and the executioner's blade, the Europeans were amazed to find that the Iroquois had devised a sophisticated form of government that did not require coercive measures of social control. Benjamin Franklin, writing in 1783, was one of the many intellectuals enthralled with the Confederacy: "All their Government is by the Counsel or Advice of the Sages; there is no Force, there are no Prisons, no Officers to compel Obedience, or inflict Punishment."

The glue that held this society of freedom-loving individuals together was the people's belief in the *Kayanaren'tsherakowa* and their commitment to a government based on the principles of reason and open debate. Although the people were free to do as they wished, they were undoubtedly under enormous pressure to compromise their individual wants to arrive at a consensus for the good of all.

The *Kayanaren'tsherakowa* is no longer supreme, unfortunately, and there is little pressure on the people here to reach consensus. To this day, however, there remains an adamantly independent "you-can't-tell-me-what-to-do" streak among the Iroquois, who fiercely resist any infringement on individual freedom.

The collision of traditional Iroquois attitudes and twentieth-century realities takes place most often when the people encounter the police. Many of the people here have a bad attitude towards the police—not because of the colour of the police but because of the colour of the law. A large part of this inborn animosity is, I think, inherited, as though the Iroquois carry within their genetic code a trigger mechanism that causes them to chafe at the slightest whisper of alien authority. What's more, this animosity has been compounded by the history of settlement on Great Turtle Island.

The fairy tale of the North West Mounted Police protecting the Indians from the whiskey traders notwithstanding, the Onkwehonwe know that the police were, in reality, a paramilitary army of occupation that abetted the theft of a continent and then suppressed Indian resistance to the loss of the land. Sitting Bull and Crazy Horse, for example, managed to survive a decade of warfare with the American cavalry only to be killed at the hands of the police after they had surrendered.

The Onkwehonwe burn with resentment knowing that the Government of Canada used the armed might of the police to impose the band council system on this territory in 1924 and again in 1959. The government was even more brutal when it forced the elective system on the people of the Mohawk Territory of Akwesasne in 1899. The police shot and killed an unarmed man, Jacob Ice. As well, they arrested and imprisoned five Mohawk chiefs for a year for resisting band council elections.

And now that the elective system is in place everywhere, the people—especially those who support traditional government—are uneasily aware of the way that some Indian "governments" have used the police to oppress their own people. The best-known and most horrifying example occurred on the Pine Ridge Reservation in South Dakota in the early 1970s. There, a corrupt tribal administration used the police and an armed auxiliary force of self-proclaimed goons to terrorize the traditional chiefs and the people opposed to their rule. The goon squads were blamed for the murders and "accidental" deaths of nearly a hundred people.

The all-Indian police force at Six Nations is overseen by a local police commission. It is meant to be a brown carbon copy of the white system and, by and large, it is. Many officers play a positive and active role in community endeavours while a few, I'm told, adopt an arrogant and needlessly aggressive attitude in dealing with the public. Worse still are the troubling stories that some officers have brutally beaten local men in the process of arresting them.

Clearly, there is an uneasy relationship between the police and many people here, especially the Mohawk nationalists. Many of these people refuse to obey the police. Recently, for example, my eighty-five-year-old uncle, John Maracle, drove up to an intersection on the reserve, saw a Six Nations police cruiser and purposely ignored the stop sign there. The police went after him with siren wailing and lights flashing but my uncle refused to stop until a mile later, when he pulled into his driveway at home. The officer gave him a ticket, which he threw on the ground, saying the Six Nations police had no authority and that the provincial highway traffic act did not apply on this territory. (John was later arrested for refusing to pay the ticket; he will have his day in court this spring.)

A few times in recent years, minor incidents involving the police and some of "the boys" have escalated into tense confrontations with the Six Nations police, backed by reinforcements from the Ontario Provincial Police and the

RCMP on one side and a hastily assembled crowd of armed and angry Indians on the other.

It is against this background that the Six Nations police have to operate. Clearly, they need all the support, goodwill and credibility they can get.

This past January, at midnight on Super Bowl Sunday, police in Brantford stopped a car that was being driven erratically. The driver, who had just left a Super Bowl party, had open beer and liquor in his car and a blood alcohol level of 0.18—more than twice the legal limit. Arrested and charged with drunk driving was Glenn Lickers, the chief of the Six Nations police force.

In court last week, Lickers pleaded guilty, was fined $660 and was prohibited from driving for a year. Two days later, Lickers was on the carpet in front of his "boss," the Six Nations police commission. The commission "fined" Lickers four days' vacation time. (The stiffest penalty the commission could have imposed, according to the newspaper, was the loss of five days' vacation time.)

The sober segment of this community was appalled by the police commission's "penalty." What made it worse was the way the commission chairman stuck up for Lickers instead of the community. At first the chairman pooh-poohed the arrest. "This incident is relatively minor," he said. Later on, the chairman issued a news release that indicated Lickers had received a harsher penalty than other police officers in other jurisdictions receive for the same offence.

I couldn't believe that another jurisdiction would let its chief of police off so easily, so I called the Metro Toronto Police Services Board to see what it would have done. The Toronto board, like any municipality in the province, can impose penalties on the police that include loss of pay, suspension, demotion and firing. The Toronto board member

I spoke to said that he would have been inclined, under similar circumstances, to fire Toronto's chief of police for bringing the entire police force into disrepute.

The final episode of this sorry saga was a news report today saying that the federal government has just granted $126,825 to the Native People's Drinking and Driving Committee of Ohsweken. The committee, I think, is trying to reduce drunk driving through a public awareness program.

I seriously doubt, however, whether all that money will make even the slightest dent in the drunk driving problem around here. What might make a difference—at no extra cost—is a tough-minded local police commission. If the commission had demoted or fired Lickers, it would have hammered home a clear message to the community that drunk driving will not be tolerated, by anyone. And by being tough, the commission also would have brought the police increased respect. As it was, Lickers's punishment amounted to less than a slap on the wrist. It was a non-penalty that didn't cost Lickers anything. What's more, it puts the police here under a bigger, blacker cloud.

I should add that I bear no grudge against Glenn Lickers or any of the Six Nations police officers and I have never had a run-in with any of them. But I think Lickers, at the very least, should have been demoted, for two reasons. The first is simple and straightforward: I believe it would have helped in the fight against drunk driving. The second reason has to do with the fact that the police are part of a foreign justice system that has been imposed on our community. This Eurojustice system is based on expensive penitentiary-based punishment that penalizes innocent taxpayers. The Iroquois, by comparison, based their justice system on the need to maintain peace and harmony within the community by having wrongdoers atone for their misdeeds by compensating the victims of their wrongdoing.

So, given that we'll probably have to put up with a white-oriented police force for some time to come, I think it should be subject to the same kind of discipline as other police forces. The problem is that the local police commission has undermined the concept of discipline and public accountability. As a result, the Six Nations police are becoming more and more like the other parts of the Eurojustice system—a system that is arbitrary and discriminatory, a system that punishes the poor and the meek while protecting the wealthy and powerful.

Close encounters
with a woodstove

Among the things I've learned about using a wood-burning stove this winter are how an airtight stove works, how to erect a chimney and how to buy firewood. I've also learned some very painful lessons. Today, for instance, was the fifth time—the *fifth* time—I've burned my hand on the stove this winter. Once I can understand, maybe even twice, but *five* times?

Today's burn, on the back of my right hand, is the largest of them all and is the size of a taco chip. It's a grotesque shade of blistered purple and it looks as though it's going to make a hideously ugly lifelong scar.

It happened, like all the other times, when I was trying to put another log on the fire. The problem is that the stove's small door gives very little clearance for a large log to fit through, and no matter how careful I am, I can't seem to avoid brushing my hand on the edge of the doorway. I've even tried standing back and tossing the log through the open door but that didn't work because my hand would hit the stove on the follow-through and I'd still get burned.

One of the things I've learned this winter is that I should wear leather gloves when I stuff the stove—that way the glove might get singed but I won't get burned.

Yeah, right. That's if *I* can remember where I left my gloves. Besides, it's such a hassle to put gloves on and take them off a dozen times a day. Surely I've learned my lesson by now. I'll be *extremely* careful when I feed the stove. I mean, I couldn't burn myself again, could I?

I've also discovered that second-degree burns don't hurt at all. Well, at least they don't hurt anywhere near as much as first-degree burns do.

Funny. You would think that the severity of the burn would carry with it a corresponding level of pain. But today's burn—the largest of them all, a second-degree burn with a greater chance of infection—doesn't hurt a bit. I'll be scarred for life but I don't feel a thing. This *should* hurt a heck of a lot more. In a weird way I feel cheated out of my pain.

Whoa! What am I saying? Am I really saying I want to be crippled by excruciating pain for the next couple of days? I must be out of my mind. This winter has been so hard and so long it's made me delirious. What's made it worse is that I didn't get out of the house very often and I didn't see many other people. In fact, all I've done for the past couple of months is chop wood and pound my keyboard. I'm obviously suffering from a bad case of cabin fever, and the only thing that will cure me will be the coming of spring.

Tsi ratiyenthos ne kanen

«//«

When the seeds are planted

Like a bear waking from its winter rest, the sleeping giant that is spring takes a long time to rouse itself and make its mark upon the land.

In fitful spasms the giant yawns and stretches. In its first restless movements, the sun gets higher, the days get longer, the air gets warmer. The snow in the fields wilts and melts. Drop by melted drop, it slides its way ever downward, somersaulting down gullies and ravines to the streams and creeks and, finally, to the river. The ice in the river blackens and crumbles. In the swollen river, beneath the ice chunks tumbling to the sea, the fish fight the surging waters. They lunge into the current, charging their way up the river and up the creeks to spawn in the rippling shallows.

The bare fields and open waters beckon the feathered beings that fled to the south. They soon fill the sky, churning the air with their wingbeats, sweetening the land with their music.

The small four-legged creatures that slept through the winter emerge from their dens and begin their search for food.

In the woods, a river of sap boils up from the ground and surges through the dormant limbs of trees, saplings, shrubs and bushes. The leaf buds soak up the precious fluid and swell with the nubby promise of new life. In the fields and on the forest floor, fresh grass and wildflowers poke through the carpet of dead plant life, covering the dull scabs and fading scars of winter with a cosmetic rainbow.

But spring does not rouse itself in one smooth, even motion. From time to time, the giant stops to rest and gather its strength, allowing icy winds, snow and cold dark skies to cover the land for days on end.

Finally, though, the day does come when spring roars awake and wreaks its frenzied magic on the land. The trees explode, launching bursts of brightly coloured leaves in every direction. They stand like puffy lemon-lime lollipops on a lush carpet of green that covers the earth. Overnight the landscape is green, green, green; the air is hot, hot, hot. The fields and woodlands are quickly speckled with brilliant blossoms of every colour. The air, thick with the smell of flowers and new growth, rings with the music of birdsong.

In this corner of Great Turtle Island, winter is capricious, its severity and length varying from year to year. But the sleeping giant that is spring does not vary. Each year it moves slowly and steadily; creeping, resting, creeping and resting until at last it crushes its feeble human observers with the power of its awesome beauty.

The league of peace

The Onkwehonwe have an extraordinarily high regard for the Confederacy that borders on the religious. And for good reason: the Confederacy was, literally, a divine creation based on sacred principles. To understand why the Confederacy continues to exert such a powerful influence over the people here, it is necessary to understand not only how it operates but how it was founded. So from all that I've heard and read, I've pieced together the following history, a much abbreviated one, of the origins of the Confederacy.

Shonkwaya'tihson, the Creator, made the Onkwehonwe, the first human beings, from a handful of earth. He breathed life into them, taught them how to survive, instructed them to live in peace and to offer thanksgiving to Him. To the Onkwehonwe, peace was not just the absence of war but a state of mind and a way of life. But some time after creation, the Onkwehonwe forgot the Creator's instructions and began warring among themselves. They fought bitter blood feuds that carried on from one generation to the next. One revenge-killing led to another and another. The people's hearts were filled with bitterness and heartache that had no end.

At that time the Iroquois lived in the Mohawk Valley and the Finger Lakes region of what is now known as New York State. Shonkwaya'tihson then caused a man to be born to a virgin mother among the Huron people to the north. It was the Creator's will that this man was to end the blood feuds, cannibalism and warfare among the Iroquois by delivering a special message of peace, power and right-eousness. Today the Onkwehonwe refer to this man, in English, as the Peacemaker.

When he was a young man, the Peacemaker crossed Lake Ontario in a white stone canoe and journeyed to the land of the Mohawks. He told them that he had been sent by the Creator to end their blood feuds and establish a great peace. The Mohawks did not believe him so they decided to test his powers. The Peacemaker climbed to the top of a tall tree that hung over the edge of a high waterfall. The Mohawks then chopped down the tree and watched the Peacemaker disappear into the boiling, rock-filled canyon. If he truly was sent by the Creator, the Mohawks reasoned, he would survive.

The next day, when the Mohawks went back to the site and found the Peacemaker calmly sitting by a campfire, uninjured, they knew that what he had said to them was true. And so it was that the Mohawks were the first of the Iroquois nations to accept the Peacemaker's message.

The Peacemaker then persuaded the Oneida, Cayuga, Seneca and Onondaga nations to also accept his message. As they did so, the Peacemaker designated fifty of their men—nine Mohawks, nine Oneidas, fourteen Onondagas, ten Cayugas and eight Senecas—to be chiefs. As a symbol of office, the Peacemaker decreed, the chiefs were to wear a headdress bearing the antlers of the deer. He also decreed that the chiefs must have skin that is seven spans thick, to protect them from the people's anger and criticism. Their hearts, he said, shall also be full of peace and goodwill and their minds shall be concerned only with the well-being of the people: "Neither anger nor fury shall find lodging in their minds and all their words and actions shall be marked by calm deliberation."

The Peacemaker gave the responsibility for holding the titles of those chiefs to fifty women—the first clanmothers —and gave them strings of wampum to symbolize the titles. It was the duty of the women, the Peacemaker said, to select from the men in their clan a chief who is trustworthy, of good character, of honest disposition and who has proven faithful to his nation.

The Peacemaker then established a great league of peace, known in English as the Iroquois Confederacy and in the Mohawk language as the Rotinonhsyonni. The Mohawks were designated as the Keepers of the Eastern Door, the Senecas became the Keepers of the Western Door, and the Onondagas, who lived in the centre of the Iroquois lands, were designated the Firekeepers—the "hosts" and "chairpersons" of the Confederacy.

At the very founding of the Rotinonhsyonni, when all the chiefs and people were assembled, the Peacemaker uprooted a tree, a towering white pine, which created a great hole in the earth. The warriors then threw their weapons and warclubs into the hole, and a stream at the bottom of the hole carried them away. The Peacemaker then replanted the great white pine we now call the Tree of Peace. The tree, he pointed out, has four great white roots that extend to the corners of the earth. Anyone seeking protection, the Peacemaker said, can trace the white roots back to the tree and take shelter under its leaves. (In the 1720s, the Tuscaroras became the sixth nation to join the league.)

The Confederacy, the Peacemaker decreed, would conduct its affairs by the rules and procedures of the *Kayaneren'tsherakowa*, the Great Law. Under this system of government, the chiefs are spokesmen for their clans, not "leaders." They make their decisions by consensus, therefore there are no votes or elections and there is no such thing as majority rule. Since there are no votes, there are no "winners" and, more importantly, there are no "losers." And since consensus requires everyone's agreement, everyone is united on a single course of action.

The Iroquois benefited enormously from the establishment of the league of peace, which was in existence long before the Arawak people of the Caribbean discovered Christopher Columbus on one of their islands. The nations of the Iroquois stopped their blood feuds and intertribal warfare. Once they became united, they became extremely powerful and dominated a vast stretch of Great Turtle Island, from Quebec to Kentucky.

The Confederacy was mandated to deal with those concerns that affected all Iroquois, primarily warfare and diplomacy. Because it was a government based on reason and consensus, the Confederacy could act only with the consent of the people. With its checks and balances, the Confederacy operated a federal form of government that recognized the powers and prerogatives of each nation and clan and respected the freedom of the individual.

The Europeans who learned about the Confederacy were tremendously impressed by this simple but sophisticated form of government, and it profoundly influenced the thinking of writers and philosophers such as John Locke and Jean-Jacques Rousseau. It also inspired the fathers of modern communism, Friedrich Engels and Karl Marx:

> Everything runs smoothly without soldiers, gendarmes, or police; without nobles, kings, governors, prefects, or judges; prisons, without trials. All quarrels and disputes are settled by the whole body of those concerned...not a bit of our extensive and complicated machinery of

administration is required... There are no poor
and needy... All are free and equal—including
the women.

One of the first colonists to gain a deep-rooted appreciation of the Confederacy (long before Benjamin Franklin
and Thomas Jefferson) was Cadwallader Colden, the lieutenant-governor of New York, who wrote this about the
Confederacy in 1727:

> Each Nation is an absolute Republick by its self,
> govern'd in all Publick Affairs of War and Peace
> by the Sachems or Old Men, whose Authority
> and Power is gain'd by and consists wholly in
> the Opinion the rest of the Nation have of their
> Wisdom and Integrity. They never execute their
> Resolutions by Compulsion or Force upon any
> of their People. Honour and Esteem are their
> Principal Rewards, as Shame & being Despised
> are their Punishments.... Their Generals and
> Captains obtain their Authority likewise by the
> general Opinion of their Courage and Conduct,
> and loose it by a Failure in those Vertues.

Several Europeans and colonists were surprised and
impressed by the fact that the Iroquois had built a society
that didn't require prisons or police. As J. Long, an English
trader and interpreter, explained in 1791, the lack of coercive measures of social control was based on the Iroquois
belief in the supremacy of individual liberty:

> The Iroquois laugh when you talk to them of
> obedience to kings; for they cannot reconcile
> the idea of submission with the dignity of man.
> Each individual is a sovereign in his own mind;

and as he conceives he derives his freedom from
the great Spirit alone, he cannot be induced to
acknowledge any other power.

The truly remarkable thing about the Confederacy—
after five hundred years of war, disease, alcoholism, racism,
broken treaties, residential schools, assimilation and band
councils—is that it is still in business and is still following
the same basic rules and procedures.

//

On this, the fifth day of March, the sun is noticeably
stronger and brighter. A wind is blowing from the south
and the air is warm and fresh. The sap is running, the tree
buds on the maples are swelling with new life, and it is
time for the various longhouses to hold their maple ceremonies. Since this is the first Saturday of the month, it is
also time for the Confederacy to hold its regular monthly
meeting.

I went to the Confederacy meeting today, for the first
time ever. Even though I have long been a supporter of our
traditional government, I had never before seen it at work
so I was naturally curious to see if it would live up to my
expectations.

Like all Confederacy meetings, it was held at the Onondaga longhouse, a long, low building made of peeled logs
that was built four years ago to replace an older building
that had become too small. Unlike the other longhouses
here, it has just one door in the centre of the building.
Inside, though, it's much like the others: it has wood-
burning stoves at either end, with an open floor surrounded
by two tiers of wooden benches.

At the north end sat the Firekeepers, the Onondagas. To
their left, on the east side of the longhouse, sat the
Cayugas and the Oneidas, the "Younger Brothers." Across
from them, on the west side, sat the Mohawks and Senecas,

the "Elder Brothers." The chiefs of the various nations sat in the front row of benches, with their men seated behind them. At the opposite end of the longhouse sat the clan-mothers and the women. Seated at a table in the centre of the floor was the Confederacy's secretary and interpreter.

I took a seat with the Mohawk men and nervously looked around. Everyone chatted quietly while they waited for the meeting to start. Looking at the men sitting on the front benches, it was hard to tell how many chiefs were present. I had never seen half of them before. They weren't wearing name-tags, there were no desk plaques, and no one was wearing a chief's ceremonial deer-antler headdress. I guessed that there were between fifteen and twenty chiefs present. Most of them were middle-aged, a few were elderly. They were casually dressed, many of them in blue jeans, T-shirts and baseball caps.

Eventually, an Onondaga chief stood up and recited the Thanksgiving Address, thanking Shonkwaya'tihson for the gifts of creation and calling on the people to come to one mind. After he finished and sat down, there was a long pause. Finally, one of the Elder Brothers, I don't remember which one, stood up and began speaking. After he had finished and sat down there was another long pause before one of the Younger Brothers stood up and spoke. Back and forth the discussion went, all of it in Cayuga or Mohawk.

Although I recognized a lot of the words they were using, I didn't have a clue what they were talking about. Because I don't understand the language, I wasn't able to appreciate the rich language of Confederacy debate. Almost everything, from what I understand, is expressed in a vivid metaphor that relates to traditional Iroquois life. When one of the Elder Brother chiefs turns the discussion over to the Younger Brothers, he is said to be throwing the matter "across the fire." When an issue is put on the Confederacy's agenda, it is said to be put "in the well."

When the Confederacy adds a section to the Great Law, it is said to be "extending the rafters." If a chief is removed from office (for failing to obey the directions of his clan, among other things), he is no longer entitled to wear the ceremonial deer-antler headdress and is said to be "dehorned."

The discussion today went back and forth across the fire. One by one the chiefs stood, usually with their hands in their pockets, and spoke in the distinctive, breathy, singsong cadence of ceremonial speech while looking at the floor. From time to time all discussion stopped as the chiefs and the men behind them caucused on an issue. It was during these short breaks that observers like me would get a quick rundown from a fluent speaker sitting nearby of what had been said.

I learned that the subject under discussion was a request by the Mohawks of Akwesasne to have their chiefs sit in the Confederacy. During another break I learned that a Cayuga chief had suggested that the Mohawks divide their nine chieftainships among the three largest Mohawk communities—Grand River, Akwesasne and Kahnawake.

After a lunch break, one of the Mohawk chiefs rose to say, in English, that the Mohawks must decide this issue themselves. It was the only time English was spoken all day. After a while, I'm told, the subject changed to the looming conflict over the local school board's plans to take over education on the reserve. The meeting broke up late in the afternoon with no decision being made on the education issue or the Akwesasne request. In the concluding ritual, an Onondaga chief stood and delivered the Closing Address, which once again focused everyone's mind on the Creator and the blessings of all creation.

The Confederacy meeting was a startling contrast to the band council meetings I've attended. The primary reason most people attend band meetings is money. The band councillors are paid $100 to attend. Most of the observers are usually reporters who are also paid to be there. Of the few community members who go to the meetings, the majority are people who are there either because of their jobs, or because they want the council to give them money. And even though the band conducts its meetings in English, the observers often don't understand what the council is talking about because they don't get copies of the documents under discussion.

None of the Confederacy chiefs, by comparison, gets an honorarium for going to the meetings. What's more, very few of the many people who go to the meetings have a financial stake in the discussions because the Confederacy, from what I understand, rarely talks about money. The only reason people attend the meetings, it seems, is loyalty. They go to express their faith in and lend support to a system of government that was given to the Onkwehonwe by the Peacemaker and, ultimately, by the Creator Himself.

There were nearly a hundred observers in the Onondaga longhouse today, and it's my guess that most of them don't understand the language well enough to know exactly what was being said. Yet they sat there all day long. That's the kind of loyalty money can't buy. That's the kind of dedication that will ensure that the Great Law will outlast the Indian Act.

Nearly everyone at Grand River is related in some way, now or in the past, to one of the chiefs or clanmothers. (One of the Mohawk bear clan chiefs is Richard Maracle, my father's second cousin.) But it is more than family ties that has led me to support the Confederacy. I have heard the arguments of those who say that it's time to forget the past and move on. That it's time to accept the blessings of democracy. That it's time to become progressive. That it's time to become realistic. That it's time to become Canadians.

I have considered those arguments and I reject them completely. A representative parliamentary democracy may be the best form of government for a multicultural country like Canada, but the Confederacy is still the best government for the people of the Six Nations. Democracy alone won't solve the problems in this community, and it won't work as long as the Confederacy is still alive.

The most telling difference between the Confederacy and the band council was demonstrated when a man rose from the men's ranks and was given permission to speak. The subject under discussion at the time was education. The man spoke Cayuga and I learned later that he was opposed to the band takeover, that he wanted a group of parents, most of them Cayuga-speaking longhouse people, to run his local school. The middle-aged man was stable, conservative and well respected, but after a few minutes his voice rose, cracked with emotion and he broke into tears.

It was a sobering sight to see a grown man cry so openly in such a circumstance. I can't think of anyone at a band council meeting crying over anything. People there often get angry, yes, but their anger is usually directed at the council or the government. There are no tears at a band council meeting and there are no words of love or thanksgiving because the band council has no heart. It has no soul.

If I don't sell them, someone else will

Imagine the chaos if 100,000 people in Toronto were to lose their jobs overnight—there would be bedlam on Bay Street and pandemonium in Parliament. The whole country would be in a dither.

And yet the equivalent of that is what happened here two weeks ago when Canada and Ontario dropped the tax on cigarettes in an attempt to crush the Indian tobacco trade. At least 300 people lost their jobs, but there was no anguished wailing or outraged howls of protest around here. In fact, there was no public outcry at all. Although hundreds of suddenly unemployed people are now scrambling to pick up the pieces, most others around here, I think, are relieved that the tobacco boom has gone bust.

The shutdown had been coming for months, following last fall's price war and the collapse of the owners' cartel. Then, in early February, Imperial Tobacco announced that it was stopping cigarette exports to the United States, the source of most of the smokes sold here. At the same time, Ottawa said it would order the RCMP to raid the smoke huts and that, in turn, led to threats of armed Indian resistance.

By the middle of February, with the federal and provincial treasuries losing millions of dollars in cigarette taxes every day, the police began trying to shut down the business by going after the non-Indian buyers. They set up roadblocks on the edge of the territory, stopped the people who were leaving and confiscated cigarettes and automobiles. In one day alone, I'm told, the provincial police here seized eight cars.

A week later, Canada and Ontario cut their taxes so that the price of a carton of cigarettes in a Brantford convenience store plunged from $41 to $23, just $3 more than the price on the reserve. Instantly, the market for Indian smokes evaporated and half the smoke huts here closed up faster than a government office on a Friday afternoon.

At the band council meeting last week, with the largest employer on the reserve in tatters and 300 people newly out of work, the subject wasn't even mentioned.

Two weeks after the tax cut, fewer than half the ninety smoke hut owners are still in business, grimly trying to hang on. One of them is a nephew of mine, Kyle Skinner.

I went to visit him today at his smoke hut, a shiny Atco trailer perched on a neatly gravelled parking lot under a big sign reading "Mohawk Tobacco." Inside there were some cigarette cartons on a shelf, a display case containing some Indian crafts, a few pieces of Indian artwork on the walls, a TV set, a few chairs and no customers. When I entered, Kyle was hunched over behind the cash register, his arms resting on the counter. He wore a faded sweatshirt and a Cheshire cat grin with flashing white teeth. Around his neck he wore a gold chain as thick as a pencil. There was a chunky gold ring on one of his beefy fingers. Kyle is twenty-two years old.

Having already laid off all six of his employees, he was minding the store himself and having a bad day. By six in the evening he had made just $200 in sales. "Last year," he said, "a bad day was ten times that much."

His best day ever, he says, was last fall when he sold

$8,500 worth. (By comparison, another guy I know was averaging $13,000 in daily sales a month before the crash.)

Kyle, who dropped out of school in grade eleven, started working in a relative's smoke hut two years ago and, after getting a firsthand look at the profits being made, decided to go into business for himself. He managed to borrow $15,000 from local "investors" and opened for business last July. With four full-time and two part-time staff, he was open from nine in the morning till nine at night, seven days a week. In no time he was averaging over $100,000 in gross sales a month and taking home 10 percent of that in profit. Under the terms of his loan he was required to pay back the entire $15,000 and an extra $10,000 in interest within six months. He did.

His customers came from all over southern Ontario, including several who would buy two or three thousand dollars' worth at a time. Business was at its best, he said, in the first few days of the month after people received various kinds of government cheques. "You don't have to be particularly intelligent to make this work," he said, "but location is everything."

Kyle, ironically, doesn't smoke. He considers it a dirty habit. I asked him if it bothered him to sell a product that caused cancer and killed people. "I've never given a lot of thought to that aspect of it. People are going to smoke anyway," he laughed, "and they gotta buy 'em from someplace so it may as well be me."

In the nine months he's been in the business, he's watched prices slide and profit margins drop so that now he makes only $2 a carton. "You could survive at these prices but the volume's just not there," he said.

Kyle has to sell twenty-five cartons a day just to pay the lease on his trailer site. By dinnertime, though, he had sold only ten cartons. "This isn't over," he said. "The taxes are going to go back up again. There's no question about that, it's only a question of when."

Still, Kyle said he had no regrets and was happy with the way things turned out. "I learned *lots* about business," he said—everything from the basics of making his business premises look clean and inviting to the complexities of market saturation and the psychology of a price war.

Although he will walk away from the tobacco business with roughly $20,000 and a late-model Oldsmobile, Kyle says he doesn't know what he will do next. His first priority, no doubt, will be to sell off his inventory. He's sitting on $30,000 worth of cigarettes and is selling them at the rate of just $300 a day. "So," he said with a laugh, "it's going to take a while."

A smell of a time

As a rule, people like some smells much more than others because the smells are usually linked to a childhood memory. A lot of older people, for instance, especially love the smell of freshly baked bread because it reminds them of the home-baked bread their mother used to make in the family kitchen. Or they love the smell of freshly cut hay because it evokes nostalgic memories of life on the farm.

I wonder, though, what kinds of smells young people these days will be remembering fondly fifty years from now. Given their upbringing and lifestyle, I expect that they might get weepy-eyed at the smell of things like Kentucky Fried Chicken or a brand-new pair of Nike Air Jordans.

As for me, the one smell I love more than any other is the scent of smouldering cedar. When I smell it nowadays, I am instantly transported back to the time when I was a little boy and my family lived with my great-grandmother, Sarah Thomas. Gramma would go outside to one of the four big cedar trees in front of the house, tear off one of the fan-shaped fronds, bring it inside and put a fresh sprig on top of our wood-burning stove. In seconds, the heat from the stove would liberate the scent trapped beneath the dull, green, stippled surface. The sprig would turn a bright shiny green, then dark green, then brown and finally black. As the sprig got hotter and hotter, the sap would start to crackle, boil and burn and the essence of the cedar's lifeblood would rise in lazy spirals of thick white smoke. The sharp, pungent smell would drift through that old house; it would freshen the air, clear out my sinuses and soothe my mind. Gramma used to burn cedar all the time and the top of her stove would always be littered with the black, brittle, dried-out skeletons of cedar fronds.

I've tried to burn cedar in my city apartments but it's never worked out very well. For one thing, there was always the problem of supply—there were never any cedar trees in my neighbourhood. For another, I had to make do with an electric stove. If I set it on high and put the cedar sprig directly on the burner it worked okay, but it just didn't seem to have the same soothing effect. There was also the messy problem of trying to clean up the little black cedar bits that fell down through the burners and inside the stove.

This past winter, with a wood-burning stove at hand and my own little cedar tree in the front yard, I've burned cedar nearly every day, although I've cut back somewhat because I don't want to strip the tree bare.

As much as I like the fragrance of smouldering cedar, though, I couldn't wait for the smell of spring. At the end of March, I took the plastic off the windows, opened them and let fresh air blow through the house for the first time in months. (Of course, fresh air blew in through cracks in the house all winter, but it wasn't quite the same thing.)

The plastic has been off the windows for more than a month now. The trees are in bud and the grass is green again. With the windows open I can feel the invigorating warmth and freshness of spring. But when I got up today, I lit a fire in the stove and started burning cedar at a furious rate. I couldn't haved cared less about the fate of my little cedar tree. Sprig after sprig, sometimes two or three at a time, I kept the smoke billowing off the stove. After a while there was so much smoke in the house that I'm sure the walls and windows were bulging outwards. The house must have looked like an inflated balloon that was ready to burst, but still I kept laying the cedar on the stove.

I wasn't madly trying to recapture my lost youth with my frenzied burn-athon. Nor was I trying to see if cedar's therapeutic vapours could somehow clean my walls, windows and furniture. No. What I was trying to do was fill this house with cedar incense so that I wouldn't be able to smell the sickening stench that had invaded the house overnight. The smell was so nauseating it woke me up before dawn. I tried to go back to sleep but the smell made it impossible to sleep, or even to breathe. *What the hell stinks? Did somebody dump a dead whale in my living room, or what?* Coughing and gagging, I stumbled through the house searching for the source, but the smell was everywhere. Despite the chilly temperature, I went outside in my pajamas and slippers to escape the smell and get some fresh air. Once outside I took a deep breath but the smell was there, too, and it burned its way into my lungs. I tried to cough it back out but it just slithered down my throat and the sickening odour in my mouth made me gag. I almost threw up.

And then I figured it out. The stench that woke me up, nearly poisoned me and fouled the air for miles around was unmistakable. It was the smell of shit.

I'm not talking about the smell of your cat's litterbox or the smell of your baby's diaper pail. No. What I'm talking about is the smell you'd get from standing on an island of shit in an ocean of diarrhea. *That's* the rotten stench I'm talking about. The kind of smell that makes you hold your nose and breathe through your mouth—and worse. The kind that is so bad it makes you get in your car and get out of town.

The wind was blowing from the north this morning and it was repulsively obvious that the shit-smell I was breathing was coming from the farm directly across the river. It's just about planting time around here, and it smells as though the farmer over there has decided to fertilize his fields by covering them with shit. Lots of it. From the way it was stinging my eyes and blistering the paint on my car, I'd say he must have laid it on about ten feet thick. The shit-stink is so hideously rotten I am beginning to think that maybe chemical fertilizers aren't so bad after all. Sure, they poison the water, they kill fish, insects, reptiles and birds, they alter human DNA, they cause cancer and birth defects, but at least they don't smell like *this*.

My neighbour Shelly says it smells like pig shit. She should know—she keeps a horse, a cow, goats, chickens, ducks, and she just sold the family pig. Of them all, she says pig shit is the worst. (Maybe that's why they sold their pig?) Her husband Bill says that, judging from the truck traffic he's seen on the other side of the river, he thinks the farmers over there may be using human shit on their fields. *So that's what companies that pump out septic tanks do with the stuff!*

There is no escaping the smell because the fumes just seep under the doors, come down the chimney and wiggle in through the many cracks in the walls and windows of this leaky old house. I have a lot of writing to do today and I won't let myself get driven out. I won't run away. So my only defence is to keep burning the cedar. It's a good thing it's chilly today and I need to burn wood to heat the house. I'd hate to think what I'd do if it were too warm for a fire.

Oh well, it can't last forever. In a day or two the shit-cloud will disappear and the air will be fresh and clean again. In the meantime, even though I'm not one to call on divine intervention in times of stress, I'm tempted to pray for a south wind to start blowing so the farmer across the river will get a taste of his own fertilizer.

While I'm waiting for the wind to change, I just have to keep reminding myself of one thing. It might smell bad here for two days a year, but for the millions of people who live near pulp mills, oil refineries and chemical plants, who live in a toxic fog of automobile exhaust, every day of the year is a smelly day.

Ah, the rural life! Isn't it great to get away from the stink of the city and be able to breathe all this (*cough*) fresh (*gag*) country (*wheeze*) air!

Turtles are sceptical

The foundation of traditional Iroquois society is the super-extended family known as the clan. As I understand it, all of the people of all the Iroquois nations are members of just nine main clans, nine super-families. The clans are named for their original associations with various creatures: wolf, bear, deer, eel, beaver, turtle, heron, snipe and hawk. The people of the Mohawk Nation belong to one of three clans: turtle, bear or wolf.

The Iroquois are a matrilineal people—children belong to their mother's clan and nation. Because all the members of a clan are said to be descended from a common female ancestor, they are all theoretically related. A turtle clan Mohawk, therefore, is considered to be more closely related to a turtle clan member of any other Iroquois nation than to a Mohawk member of the bear or wolf clan.

The Great Law forbids men and women of the same clan from marrying one another because they are considered brother and sister. Since they are then forced to marry someone from another clan, the Iroquois not only avoid the diseases and birth defects caused by inbreeding, they also strengthen the social structure by creating a web of interlocking inter-clan alliances.

One major difference between Iroquois clan-based culture and Euro-Canadian society involves the role and defi-
nition of fatherhood. Under the clan system, children are
considered to be much more closely related to their mater-
nal uncle than their father. This is because a child, the
child's mother and the mother's brother are all members
of the same clan. Because a child's father belongs to a different clan, the father is technically not related to the
child. In traditional Iroquois culture, the father was
regarded simply as a child's mother's husband. The real
father-figure in a child's life was his or her mother's brother. A man was a "father," then, not to his own children but
to his sister's children.

Tom Porter, a well-known Mohawk cultural leader, says
that each clan has its own distinctive personality, presumably because the members of a clan are all related and
share common character traits. Porter has devised an
Iroquois "clanoscope" that includes comments like these:

> Turtle clan people are like their namesake—
> slow but consistent. They are skeptical and
> afraid of change. They avoid committing them-
> selves to doing anything right away. Once turtle
> clan people understand an issue fully, they will
> not change their mind and they will persevere at
> what they are doing. They are slow to forgive-
> and-forget. Turtle clan people make good teach-
> ers.
> Wolf clan people are not shy. They're aggressive
> and they'll bite. They are good debaters and love
> to argue just for the fun of it. They may argue
> and fight but they don't hold a grudge. They are
> bold and are not diplomatic. Wolf clan people
> are doers. If you want something done, they're
> the people to see—if your feelings don't get

hurt easily. Wolf clan people make good warriors.

Bear clan people are lazy. They are very diplo-
matic and they will skirt an issue just to make
friends and keep from offending someone. Bear
clan people are easygoing and happy-go-lucky
but when you push them to the limit, they will
fight with anyone. Afterward, they hold a grudge
for a long time. They get along very well with
kids. Members of the bear clan make good medicine people.

The clan system, unfortunately, has grown progressively
weaker over the last two hundred years. By the middle of
the eighteenth century, the Iroquois had largely adopted
the colonial custom of living in single-family log homes.
Once people stopped living in longhouses, the communal,
clan-based lifestyle began to wither. As the Iroquois came
under the increasing influence of churches and missionaries, the clans and the matriarchy grew weaker still. When
couples got married in church, the woman and the ensuing
children were assigned the man's last name, accelerating
the establishment of patriarchy among the traditionally
matrilineal Iroquois.

The federal government also attacked Iroquois matriarchy and undermined the clan system. In 1868, Canada
placed Indian people under the federal Indian Act. Ottawa
began calling each local grouping of Indian people a
"band." It did not use the word "tribe," let alone "nation,"
because it did not want to admit that Indian governments
were equal to their own.

To put its bureaucratic stamp on Indian existence,
Ottawa compiled a list of the Onkwehonwe in each Indian
community across the country. These were the first "band
lists." The Department of Indian Affairs maintained the

lists, so it was the government—not the Indians—who decided if someone was entitled to be "an Indian." And since names could be added to or taken off the list, people could become "an Indian," or cease to be one, at the stroke of a pen. Until the 1980s, this happened to a thousand people every year.

In keeping the Six Nations band list, the government imposed its European-based patrilineal social structure on the Iroquois. When a Mohawk man married a Cayuga woman, for example, the ensuing children were automatically placed on the (Mohawk) man's band list. But Canada's cultural imperialism went even further. Because Canadians at that time considered women to be their husbands' property, the government also took the woman off the Cayuga rolls and put her on the Mohawk band list.

Worse yet, when a Cayuga woman married a white man, she was taken off her (father's) band list and declared, in effect, to be a white woman. She lost all her Indian rights—even if she divorced him later—and she could be prohibited from living on the reserve and from being buried there. But when a Mohawk man married a white woman, he stayed on the band list and retained all his rights. His wife was placed on his band list and became "a Mohawk Indian," entitled to the full exercise of aboriginal rights and the provision of all government services, such as they were.

The blatant discrimination against Indian women stayed in place for more than a century until it was finally outlawed in 1985. This one government regulation, section 12(1)(b) of the Indian Act, shredded the fabric of Indian families, communities and nations. Although the government has tried to correct the effects of its legislated discrimination with the reinstatement provisions of Bill C-31, the damage is extensive, and Indian people will suffer the wounds and bear the scars for generations to come.

My family was among the thousands victimized by Indian Act discrimination. My father's father was a member of the Bay of Quinte Mohawk band, but he gave up his Indian status and signed himself off the band list in the 1920s so that he could legally buy alcohol and possess it without being arrested. My father, as a result, was never registered on the band list. And when my father married my mother, she was taken off the band list and none of their children were registered. My family and I did not become registered Indians until the late 1980s, after Bill C-31 came into effect.

Today, after centuries of being attacked from without and being compromised from within, the Iroquois clan system—the heart of our traditional form of government—is in terrible shape. Although some clans are relatively active, several clans have ceased to function at all and exist in name only. A few clans, I'm told, have died out completely.

Although the taboo that prohibits marriage between clan members is often ignored, a bigger problem for the clan system is the fact that, by my estimate, at least a thousand people in this territory are "clanless" because of intermarriage. When an Indian man marries a white woman, the children do not belong to their father's clan, or to any clan, unless they are formally adopted into one. In the old days, there was a place in the clan system for everyone and everyone had a place. When outsiders became part of the community, whether it was a white person or an Indian from another nation, they were routinely adopted by one of the clans. To leave people out of the clan system was to invite dissension and discord into the community. Although the Great Law spells out how people are to be adopted, the clans rarely adopt anyone these days and clanless individuals rarely ask to be adopted.

A bigger problem yet is clan confusion. In the old days, the Mohawks had nine clans. There were three distinct

turtle clans, three distinct bear clans and three distinct
wolf clans, each with its own chief and clanmother. Over
time, however, the distinction between the individual turtle, bear and wolf clans has blurred. Consequently, most
Mohawks today may know themselves to be a member of
the turtle clan, for example, but they don't know exactly
which one. As a result, most people in this territory don't
know who their clanmother is or who their chief is. Since
the people don't know who their clan leaders are, they cannot possibly give them direction. And since the clan leaders
are not getting direction, they are not truly representing
their clan.

The aforementioned problems are daunting enough in
isolation, but the problems are greatly compounded by the
fact that the people, clans and nations of the Iroquois have
been fractured and dispersed for more than two hundred
years. The Mohawks are the most widely scattered; they
live in six established territories (Kahnawake, Kanesatake,
Akwesasne, Tyendinaga, Wahta and Grand River) and two
new settlements (Kanienkeh and Kanatsohareke).

Although the U.S. and Canadian governments keep separate band lists for each reserve, the Mohawks themselves
have yet to establish a central registry listing all the members of each clan. Until that is done, until the people know
who their fellow clan members, clanmothers and chiefs
are, nothing can be done to sort out the confusion.

And is there ever a lot of confusion to straighten out. For
instance, there are just nine Mohawk chieftainships so
there should be just nine Mohawk clanmothers. But the
most telling sign of the splintered state of the clans is a
survey that one of my cousins made of all the Mohawk territories a few years ago. She found more than seventy
women claiming to be Mohawk clanmothers!

//

Many people here are totally lost and confused when it

comes to the clans, and I am one of them. When people used to ask me what clan or nation I was, I told them that I was a turtle clan Mohawk. But it was only this week, after a long conversation with my grandmother about her matrilineal ancestry, that I learned the truth about who I am.

My mother's mother is Martha (Lickers) Hill. Her father, Elijah Lickers, fathered seventeen children with an Indian woman before the turn of the century. Elijah then left his Indian wife and eloped with Ellen Harriet Owens, a white woman. They had seven children, including Gramma Martha. She's eighty-nine years old now and lives in a seniors' home in Brantford and is the only one of the twenty-four children still living.

My grandmother was raised in Brantford and never lived on the reserve. Elijah died while Martha was still a small girl so she doesn't know much about him. She doesn't know, for example, if he is the same Elijah Lickers who is identified in Confederacy records as an Onondaga chief who was dehorned because he eloped with a white woman.

But if he *was* that chief, it is extremely unlikely that Ellen Harriet Owens was ever adopted into a clan. And since Gramma Martha never lived on the reserve, it is also extremely unlikely that she was ever adopted. Although my mother lived with an aunt on the reserve while she was growing up, she says she was never adopted into a clan.

What all this means is that because my mother's mother's mother was white, my Gramma Martha, my mother, all of my mother's brothers and sisters, all of my brothers and sisters, all of my sisters' children—and I—do not have a clan and we do not belong to any Iroquois nation.

What a realization.

I didn't know that my mother's mother's mother was white until I talked with Gramma Martha. I never questioned my ancestry because so many of my ancestors— thirteen out of my sixteen great-great-grandparents—were "full-blooded Indians." Now, though, I know that I am not, in strict traditional terms, a Mohawk, a Cayuga, an Onondaga or anything else.

I still feel, nevertheless, that I'm a Mohawk, and this comes from the fact that my upbringing was almost entirely focused on my father's side of the family—all of them Mohawks.

Even though my family left the reserve when I was five years old, I felt as though I grew up in a Mohawk environment. The language I heard as a boy was Mohawk and, twenty years ago, that was the language I started trying to learn myself. When I was growing up, my family always returned to stay on the upper end, the Mohawk end, of the reserve with my Gramma Sarah Thomas. We were forever visiting and socializing with my father's Mohawk relatives. From the time I was eight years old, when I began working for my father's carpenter business, I worked with all-Indian crews, most of them Mohawks. In fact, almost all the Indians in my life while I was growing up were Mohawks. It's no wonder I absorbed a large measure of the Mohawk mind-set—the blunt, tough-talking, chip-on-the-shoulder, don't-back-down attitude that is so prevalent in Mohawk country.

Despite my adopted Mohawk identity, I have a plastic card from the Department of Indian Affairs in my wallet that says I am a member of the Upper Cayuga band. I got it as a result of Bill C-31. My father was added to his mother's band (Upper Mohawk) and my mother was added to her father's band (Upper Cayuga). I could have been added to either one and I ended up on the Upper Cayuga list. That didn't trouble me in the least because the government's registration system has nothing to do with who we really are. Some people here may believe that they are the kind of Indian the government says they are, but I don't. Being added to one of the government's band lists was just the price I had to pay to be registered as an Indian so that I could, in turn, buy a house and return to live on the reserve.

(Being on the Upper Cayuga band list, incidentally, entitles me to collect American treaty money, compensation for the loss of the Cayuga lands in what is now New York State. In the seven years since I've been on the list, however, I have never collected because I don't consider myself a Cayuga. But then my refusal, based on a high-minded point of principle, isn't much of a financial sacrifice. The treaty payments are $2.50 a year.)

When people ask me now about my clan or nation, I'll have to tell them that I have no clan and that, in spite of my upbringing and orientation, I am not, technically speaking, a Mohawk. I won't like having to make such an admission but I know I can't manufacture my family history, I have to accept what it is and what it means.

It's profoundly unsettling to have come to this realization because I know by announcing it I am, in a way, shutting myself out in the cold, setting myself apart from the people I consider *my* people. For someone who cares about Iroquois tradition, it's extremely disturbing to realize that I have no tradition. The irony is that I wouldn't have arrived at this point if I hadn't been trying to pinpoint my roots.

There is a solution to my predicament, however, one that is perfectly in keeping with Iroquois tradition—adoption. One widely published version of the Great Law says that anyone can apply to the chiefs of a nation to be adopted into one of their clans. It also says that any member of the five original nations of the Confederacy can adopt an individual or family into their clan and the chiefs of the nation have to confirm the adoption. The chiefs then have to address the people of their nation with these words:

> Now you of our nation, be informed that (such a
> person, such a family or such families) have

ceased forever to bear their birth nation's name
and have buried it in the depths of the earth.
Henceforth let no one of our nation ever mention the original name or nation of their birth.
To do so will be to hasten the end of our peace.

The Big Smoke

One of the elements of maturity is the ability to recognize and admit one's mistakes. Well, after attending tonight's band council meeting, I've realized that, as a non-smoker who struggles to avoid breathing second-hand smoke, I have been looking at this smoking thing all wrong.

In the seven months since I've moved home, I've become increasingly annoyed with the local attitude towards smoking in public. In fact, this attitude is one of the things that sets Six Nations (and many other native communities) apart from the outside world. Here, people pull out an ever-present pack of cigarettes, light up, suck in and exhale with a grand flourish. They perform this ritual with the calm self-assurance that comes from knowing that smoking—almost anywhere—is not only a right but is something approaching an obligation. Few smokers ever bother to ask their non-smoking companions or the people nearby, "Do you mind if I smoke?"

Smokers have the upper hand here, I think, because there are so many of them. A recent band survey found that 42 percent of the students in grades seven through twelve are smokers, a figure nearly twice the provincial average. And if 42 percent of the teenagers here smoke, it's likely, then, that more than half the adults smoke. (By comparison, less than one-third of the adults in Canada smoke.)

With the exception of the local school board meetings, every public function I've attended here has been conducted under a grey-blue cloud of second-hand smoke. At the band council, five of the twelve councillors (and many of the spectators) smoke their way through the meetings. And people light up just as freely at Confederacy meetings as well.

At the restaurants and cafés I've been in here, there's no such thing as a non-smoking section. At the hockey and lacrosse games I've attended in the Ohsweken arena, the "No Smoking" signs were ignored by spectators and game officials alike.

The non-smoking movement may be winning the battle for clean air in the rest of Canada, but its success stops at the edge of the reserve. That's partly because of the live-and-let-live attitude of many Indian people and their reluctance to tell other people what to do. But a lot of it probably also has to do with the fact that this, after all, is tobacco country. The farms that grow almost all of Canada's tobacco are just a few miles away, and many Indians here work on them, priming and picking the plant. Until the government slashed tobacco taxes, the reserve was the largest cigarette market in southern Ontario. In the last couple of months, some local tobacco tycoons have even built their own cigarette factory. At its height, then, the tobacco trade employed, by my estimate, more than three times as many people as the band council's bureaucratic empire.

Despite the crash at the retail end of the business, Six Nations still has a huge stake in the tobacco trade. Could this be the reason why no one speaks out against the lack of protection for non-smokers here? Could it be that to raise a whimper of complaint against the economic engine that drives a huge portion of the local economy would be to invite the community's wrath and retribution? *Hmm*.

So, with these thoughts gnawing at the back of my mind, there I was tonight, choking and coughing my way through another band council meeting. With increasing cynicism I sat in a nicotine fog as the chief and council discussed plans to improve community health. But when they began discussing their plans for economic development, I was hit by a blinding revelation. I realized then just how selfish I'd been. Here I was all this time thinking only of myself. I hadn't given a single thought to the economic well-being of the entire community. Financial salvation and economic prosperity, I realized just then, lie in marrying our needs to our strengths. We already have a lot of people here who pick tobacco, make cigarettes and sell them. But why stop there?

Instead of simply tolerating the business of selling tobacco, Six Nations should get into the business of selling *smoking*. This community should build on its links to the tobacco industry by creating a supportive and nurturing pro-smoking environment. We should advertise the Big Six as a place where smokers can smoke wherever and whenever they want. If we do that, the smokers will surely come, and when they do, they will bring money—lots of it. Just think of it. There are millions of desperate smokers within a two-hour drive of here who have no place to smoke in public. The Big Six could become known as the Big Smoke—the smoking capital of Great Turtle Island. We could all become rich. Here I had been glaring at second-hand smoke all this time while completely ignoring the wealthy smoker attached to the cigarette. Holy tar and nicotine! Why didn't I think of this before? Of course, this would mean that people like me would have to stop grumbling and start supporting the business of smoking—but I know now that it would be worth it.

We could start by tearing down the "No Smoking" signs in the arena and putting up signs at the edge of the territory saying "WELCOME SMOKERS." Smoking would be permitted, of course, in every store and office on Six Nations territory. We already have smoky restaurants, we'd just have to build a few more and tell the world that cigar smoking is permitted in all of them.

We could build a hotel and convention centre and give all those frustrated smokers a place to smoke without having to go outside, a place where they could meet, talk and smoke to their hearts' content. All the rooms in the hotel, of course, would be smoking rooms with a raft of safety features—fireproof furniture, asbestos sheets and state-of-the-art sprinkler systems.

We could build a movie theatre where smokers could enjoy a movie and a cigarette at the same time. The back of each fireproof seat could have a cup holder, an ashtray and one of those push-in cigarette lighters that automobiles have. There would be huge fans on the ceiling to blow the smoke *down* and more fans on the walls that would silently pull the smoke out of the theatre *sideways* so the smoke wouldn't block out the movie.

We could become a world-class tourist destination if we just built the proper attractions and facilities. We could, for example, build a museum devoted to the history and development of tobacco and smoking. It could be filled with high-tech exhibits to educate and entertain smokers from around the world. There could even be a hands-on display for the kiddies that would show them how to prime tobacco, how to cure it and how to blend it with chemical additives. It could even teach them survival skills, like learning to hand-roll their own cigarettes. Think of it! The school tours alone would pay for the cost of the building.

Next to the museum, we could build a Hall of Fame and

hold an annual induction ceremony that would honour the greatest smokers of all time. Thousands would show up just to get a glimpse of the athletes, movie stars and celebrities being inducted. There would be an unending stream of visitors wanting to see the displays and memorabilia. We could show them Albert Einstein's pipe-cleaners, Marlene Dietrich's cigarette-holder, Winston Churchill's cigar-cutter, David Letterman's ashtray and the Marlboro Man's last lung x-ray.

Because there aren't any tall buildings on Six Nations, there aren't any elevators here, but we could build one ten storeys high and I'm positive that smokers would drive for hours just so they could smoke in one. Come to think of it, the smoking elevator could be the main attraction in a smoking-related amusement park for the kiddies.

And that's not all. We could hold a Smokers' Olympics, the first of its kind. There could be a 100-millimetre dash, with smokers racing to see who could finish one of those long cigarettes first. There could be a marathon, with smokers competing to see who would be the first to smoke their way through an entire carton. And there could be a figure skating or gymnastics-type event that would focus on the beauty of smoking. The contestants would have to perform compulsory exercises—like lighting up and blowing smoke rings—and they would also be judged on a five-minute freestyle routine that would be choreographed to music. The possibilities are endless.

Once the people from Player's, du Maurier, Camel and Salem find out what's going on here, they will be begging us to take their money. They'll be putting up billboards all over the place. They'll buy up all the advertising time on CKRZ-FM, the reserve's radio station. They'll fill the *Tekawennake* with full-page ads. They'll be fighting over the privilege of sponsoring all the minor hockey, lacrosse and softball teams.

The big tobacco companies will be eating out of our hand. We could get the highest bidder to build a swimming pool here in exchange for letting them name it. Since we already have something called the Red Indian Mini-Mart here, a swimming pool called the Red Man Chewing Tobacco Aquatic Centre would not sound out of place at all.

We could, I'm sure, convince the tobacco companies to invest in a scientific research and development centre that would put Six Nations at the leading edge of smoking technology. We could find ways to recycle cigarette butts and empty cigarette packs into useful and environmentally friendly consumer products. We could invent special filters to create flavoured cigarettes—imagine how sales would skyrocket, especially in the teenage market, if we could come up with a pizza-flavoured cigarette. We might even find a way of adding nutrients to tobacco so that they could be absorbed through the lungs. And then we could advertise that smoking a pack a day provides all the required vitamins and minerals for a balanced diet.

And if, for some reason, a lot of smokers start getting lung cancer, strokes or emphysema, we could then build a special clinic to take care of them. And like everything else here, smoking would be permitted in the clinic because everyone—cancer patients included—should have the right to smoke wherever they want. No one, especially someone hooked up to an IV unit or an oxygen tank, should be forced to go outside to have a cigarette. If we allowed patients to smoke in their rooms, we'd have so many smokers with all kinds of medical problems coming here that we might be forced to treat only the millionaires.

Needless to say, the staff at the clinic, theme park, museum, hotel, convention centre and Hall of Fame would all be smokers. They would have to be, if only to provide the proper pro-smoking environment. What's more, I think there would be other advantages to having an all-smoking staff. For starters, they could smoke on the job anytime they wanted—whether they were serving breakfast, pumping gas or giving injections. And because there would be no need for time-consuming smoke breaks or expensive smoking rooms, all of the businesses here would become that much more productive and profitable. Everybody would be happy if the Big Six became the Big Smoke—customers, employees and businesses. But the real winner would be the future generations of Six Nations, because their economic well-being would be guaranteed in perpetuity.

All it would take for my little idea to become a reality is a little leadership and a lot of public support. There's no reason why this idea wouldn't work. If everyone here got behind it, we would become an economic superpower that would be the envy of every city on the planet.

The more I think about this idea the more I realize that we *have* to follow through on it because that's what the Creator wants. Why, after all, just *why* did the Creator give our ancestors the gift of tobacco in the first place if He didn't intend for us to use it so that we could become *rich, rich, rich*?

The power of
the good mind

The *Tekawennake* published the latest broadside today in the continuing feud between two local men who have battled it out in the letters-to-the-editor page for the past month. The feud started when one of them wrote a letter, signed with the name Gawitrha, that criticized some Confederacy people, including some chiefs, for being "elitist." That triggered a response, signed "Arenho:ktha, a strong Confederacy supporter," that defended the chiefs and jeered at Gawitrha as someone who was relegated "to sit against the wall" (whatever that means). Gawitrha replied the week after that with an accounting of his pro-Confederacy credentials stretching back forty years and a denunciation of Arenho:ktha as a clanless person with no consequent affiliation to the Confederacy. Arenho:ktha blasted back last week, just as Gawitrha did today, each one attacking the other and insisting that their view of the Confederacy is right.

Although I've never met either man and don't know who they are, I think I'd probably like them both if I ever met them because they are both Confederacy supporters and, presumably, they (and I) are working towards the same goals. At the same time, though, it was dismaying to see two Confederacy supporters wage such a bitter, public and personal battle over something like the Great Law. I now realize, however, that my dismay only shows how naive I am and how much I have to learn. If this little feud taught me anything, it is that I, a newly discovered clanless person, should keep my mouth shut and keep my thoughts about the Confederacy to myself if I don't want to get my family and upbringing slagged in the press.

The Gawitrha–Arenho:ktha feud also got me thinking about how quick so many of our people are to judge and condemn others. I've noticed that many Onkwehonwe cannot criticize the actions of others without bad-mouthing them in a personal manner. Around here it's not "So-and-so said one thing and did another," it's "So-and-so is a lying, (bleep)ing, no-good (bleep)er." (And, yes, occasionally I too am guilty of bad-mouthing others instead of simply criticizing their actions.)

Clearly, we have come a long way from the old saying, "If you can't say something good about someone, don't say anything at all." That quaint piece of advice might have originated with a (white) Victorian-era grandmother, but it is a sentiment I think the Onkwehonwe must have lived by as well in the old, old days. That's because, as I understand it, our people used to live by the principle of "the good mind." In those days, our entire society and way of life was centred on maintaining harmony and preserving the Great Peace. And since calling one another down would create disharmony and disrupt the peace, bad-mouthing people could not have been part of our cultural tradition. In fact, the most frequently voiced element of our cultural tradition today is the Thanksgiving Address, which calls on its listeners to come to one mind, a mind focused on gratitude, humility and peace.

For a long time I didn't know how our people came to be so judgmental and disparaging. One reason, I think now, is that we learned what we were taught by missionaries, schoolteachers and government agents a long time ago. It was the nature of those people to be judgmental and disparaging so they called our ancestors dirty and dumb, they called them savages. From this beginning our ancestors learned to bad-mouth others and this non-Onkwehonwe cultural trait has been passed down to us.

There is as well, I think, another reason that *is* rooted in our tradition. We instantly make harsh judgments of other people's actions because we carry a very highly developed sense of right and wrong, of good and evil, that comes from our teachings. The instructions that the Creator and the Peacemaker passed down to us are clear and explicit and they allow the people who know them to be very certain and very confident about their judgments. (The problem, however, is that most of the time we're certain that *we* are right, because, in effect, the Creator or the Peacemaker says so.)

So, when you combine that degree of inborn moral certainty with the learned habit of being judgmental and disparaging, you get, I realize, what we are right now: a very pleasant and easygoing people—as long as you see and do things exactly the way we do.

Our teachings also hold the key, I think, to understanding another facet of our character, namely, the fact that so many people here see conspiracies, plots and sinister omens everywhere. I can't count the number of people I know who blame some incident or misfortune on the dark and secret doings of their personal bogeyman. Otherwise intelligent people blame a bizarre roster of evil forces—among them the Trilateral Commission, the Freemasons, the CIA and the Free Trade Agreement—for the most far-fetched problems. People who are less well-read simply blame the band council, the government, the police or the white man. All of these people, I find, believe that something evil and sinister is responsible for everything they don't like or understand.

For them, there is no such thing as a simple or innocent explanation. It's always some conspiracy.

For hundreds of years our people have been suspicious in our dealings with white people and government—for good reason. Our massive distrust of the white man, therefore, is not paranoia, it's simply a finely honed instinct for self-preservation, and we have exercised a heightened sense of vigilance accordingly.

But being hyper-vigilant still doesn't explain all the outlandish things I see and hear, things that never made sense until Bob Jamieson said something to me that made everything fall into place. Bob is a jovial old-timer, a widower, the interpreter for the Confederacy and a much-practised storyteller. During one of our conversations, Bob told me that he had almost never argued with his wife when she was alive. And the few times he did, he said, he could feel the Punisher's tail, flicking him, inciting him to keep arguing, goading him to say something hurtful.

And then it hit me. The Punisher—the Left-Handed Twin—*He's* the one responsible for all these bogeymen and conspiracy theories.

To understand who the Punisher is, it's necessary to backtrack to the dawn of creation. Supernatural twins were born at that time to the woman who became Mother Earth. One twin was right-handed and had a good mind; the other was left-handed and had a mischievous, evil mind. The Right-Handed Twin created the plants and animals on the earth. The Left-Handed Twin then followed and tried to undo the work of his brother by creating thorns, weeds and poisonous plants. When the Right-Handed Twin made the deer, the Left-Handed Twin created wolves to eat the deer. When the Right-Handed Twin created the sun to shine over the earth, the Left-Handed Twin caused it to fall from the sky and stay hidden all night. Eventually, the Right-Handed Twin won the battle for control of the earth and we know

Him now as Shonkwaya'tihson, our Creator. When He lost
the battle for control of the earth, the Left-Handed Twin
was banished to the underworld. And every night since,
and only at night, the Left-Handed Twin has exited the
underworld and roamed the earth to continue working his
mischief against the Onkwehonwe.

Nowadays, some older Onkwehonwe regard the Left-
Handed Twin as an undisputed reality. In the preachings of
Handsome Lake, He is described as a Devil-like being
called the Punisher. Whatever his name, the Left-Handed
Twin plays a major role in Rotinonhsyonni tradition and
culture. For instance, it was to avoid giving the Left-
Handed Twin a chance to cause harm or mischief that the
Peacemaker, in the Great Law, prohibited the chiefs of the
Confederacy from meeting after sundown.

So, if you believe the story of creation, it makes perfect
sense to accept the belief that miscellaneous misfortunes
are the work of the Left-Handed Twin. Even though most of
the people here have probably not discussed or considered
the Left-Handed Twin as an element of daily life for at least
a generation, He is still a reality in their everyday lives.
That's because the long-standing belief in the Left-Handed
Twin—and the long-standing precautions—have affected
the psychology of the Onkwehonwe personality. Over thousands of years, the Onkwehonwe have come to regard the
night as a time to be wary and cautious. Furthermore, they
have come to regard the world as a place where evil and sinister forces are lurking about, ready to do them harm. This
way of thinking has carried over to the present day. Even
though most people don't speak an Onkwehonwe language
any more or talk about the Punisher, the Left-Handed Twin
is just as real to the people today as He was a few hundred
years ago. It's just that they now call Him the Free Trade
Agreement or the Six Nations band council instead.

Anyway, that's my theory.

The cancer of complacency

"Familiarity breeds contempt," the old saying goes. But when it comes to meetings of the Confederacy, I would have to say that familiarity breeds sadness and disappointment.

The first meeting I went to was in March, where I was excited by the Confederacy's vigour and enchanted by its traditions. I then went to the meeting in April, and now that I've been to the May meeting, I have to say, sadly, that the thrill is gone. I haven't given up on the Confederacy— I'm still a supporter—but I'm now a lot less starry-eyed and a lot more realistic.

In the past few months, as I've learned more about the Confederacy, I have heard many people in this territory direct a common complaint at some of the chiefs and clan-mothers: they do not consult with their people and they act as though they were the Pope, President and Prime Minister rolled into one. These complainants are angry over the way some clanmothers ignore their clans and automatically select their son to be chief or their daughter to be the next clanmother, while some of the chiefs ignore their clans and do or say whatever they wish.

When I was in the Confederacy meetings, it was hard for a newcomer like me to tell just how many chiefs were there. The Peacemaker appointed fifty chiefs when he founded the Confederacy, but I don't know how many active chiefs there are now. In fact, I don't know if anyone knows. I have never seen a list of the chiefs and their clan-mothers but I know that some titles are vacant, either because the chief died and hasn't been replaced, or because the clan itself has died out. As well, some of the titles, I'm told, are held by chiefs who live in the United States and belong to the *other* Confederacy council, headquartered on the Onondaga Territory in New York State. (The conflict between the councils at Grand River and Onondaga as to which one is the "real" Confederacy could be the subject of a book in itself.)

It didn't look as though any of the nations had their full complement of chiefs in attendance at the meetings when I was present. Ordinarily, that's not a problem for the Confederacy, except when it's the Mohawk chiefs who don't show up. Although one widely published version of the Great Law says that all nine of the Mohawk chiefs have to be present for the Confederacy to deal with matters of major importance, they probably haven't all been there in decades.

I know who four of the Mohawk chiefs are. Two of them go to the meetings and the other two, from what I am told, purposely stay away. I don't know exactly why but apparently there's a century-old grudge against the chiefs from the other four nations. The Mohawks I sit with at the meetings tell me that the boycotting chiefs are angry over what they say is constant Confederacy interference in Mohawk business. They also complain that the other nations ridicule the Mohawks because they can't speak the Mohawk language.

In the meetings I attended, I had an admittedly brief and blurry glimpse of the Confederacy in action, but I was troubled by what I saw. For one thing, the chiefs didn't ever seem to get anything accomplished. Although my understanding of what they said and did was limited by the fluency of the people sitting next to me, it seemed that they would discuss a subject for a while and move onto something else without ever coming to a decision.

What was especially disillusioning was seeing how little they focused attention on their real enemies and how much they fought amongst themselves. One Mohawk chief, Richard Maracle, was the subject of most of the conflict. A Cayuga chief attacked him in council for appointing a Mohawk man in Kanesatake a faithkeeper and for selling $1,500 licences to local men authorizing them to sell tax-free tobacco on the territory. In both cases, the Cayuga chief said, Richard was acting outside his authority. (The Mohawks I was sitting with, however, said Richard was simply conducting Mohawk business and had every right to do what he did.)

Things got really wild today when a group of sixteen local people made their second attempt in two months to dehorn Richard. They interrupted a discussion on education, stood in front of the chiefs, accused Richard of some kind of wrongdoing and tried to take away his chieftainship. While the other chiefs may have wanted to see Richard dehorned, they managed to defuse the situation and get the group to leave by telling them that they were not following the proper procedure to remove a chief.

Richard Maracle wasn't the only chief being censured by the people. A group of Confederacy-supporting parents denounced one of the Cayuga chiefs for working against them by siding with the band council's school board.

I was surprised by a general lack of respect during the proceedings I witnessed. One middle-aged chief all but accused another elderly chief of being senile. People barged in and interrupted the chiefs. A chief bluntly told the interpreter to shut up and sit down. A Mohawk man, not a chief, berated a Cayuga chief and an Oneida chief by their first names and was then cut off by an Onondaga chief.

I have read a lot of old-time writing about the Confederacy and I suppose I've become disillusioned because I naively thought that nothing had changed since Benjamin Franklin wrote these words:

Having frequent Occasions to hold public Councils, they have acquired great Order and Decency in conducting them. He that would speak rises. The rest observe a profound Silence. When he has finished and sits down, they leave him five or six Minutes to recollect, that if he has omitted any thing he intended to say, or has any thing to add, he may rise again and deliver it. To interrupt another, even in Common conversation, is reckoned highly indecent.

There have been forty observers at the last two meetings, fewer than the one in March, but the turnout is still ten times higher than the number of people the band council attracts. Ironically, one of the Cayuga chiefs complained last month that there aren't more people attending Confederacy meetings. I couldn't help thinking that if the chiefs really wanted more people to come to their meetings, they could easily do something about it. The way things are now, none of the Confederacy meetings are advertised and the chiefs seem to like it that way. In fact, I'm told, a few years back the reserve's radio station did announce the date of upcoming Confederacy meetings on its community bulletin board but stopped after some chiefs and Confederacy people complained.

Although I haven't been impressed by what I've seen of their meetings, the Confederacy is still capable of mighty deeds once it makes up its mind to do something. Two weeks ago, for instance, former band council chief Bill Montour went before the band council and announced that he was ready to start building a $15-million tire recycling plant on the reserve—with or without band council support. He was going to use experimental and supposedly non-polluting technology to melt the tires and recycle the leftovers, and he'd create twenty-five jobs in the process. The trouble is that the people here remember all too well the 13 million tires that went up in smoke in nearby Hagersville just four years ago. The Confederacy, clearly worried about the environmental threat posed by Montour's plan to burn 15,000 tires a day, met the very next day and decided to stop the project. A delegation of Confederacy protesters showed up on the job site the next morning and Montour ordered work to be halted. When Montour was unable to convince the chiefs a few days later to change their minds, he said he would take the project to another reserve.

Faced with what it saw as an imminent threat, the Confederacy stopped a multi-million-dollar high-tech project dead in its tracks in no time at all. What made it happen, I think, was the immediacy of the danger. Because the Confederacy does not face imminent peril on any other front right now, there is nothing forcing the chiefs to work together and that, I think, is why they fight among themselves instead.

I'm tempted to agree with one chief who says the reason the Confederacy can't accomplish anything is because the Onkwehonwe have it too good, that things are too easy. The only threat the Confederacy faces now is the cancer of complacency that is slowly eating away at the heart and soul of the people.

Bread and Cheese Day

The closest thing Six Nations has to a national holiday is known unofficially as Bread and Cheese Day and it is celebrated on the Monday of the long weekend in May—Victoria Day. Like *Noyah*, Bread and Cheese Day is a home-grown institution that is unique to Six Nations. But unlike the widely dispersed home-based festivities of *Noyah*, all the Bread and Cheese Day doings take place at the fairgrounds in Ohsweken. Thousands of people from across the territory, Christians and longhouse people alike—together with hundreds more who drive in from Brantford, Buffalo and elsewhere—come together on this one day to take part in an enormous give-away and spring party that celebrates tradition, family and good clean fun. Except perhaps for the annual pow-wow, it's the largest gathering of the year. (Canada Day, by comparison, is just the opposite—it's known as The Big Snore because *nothing* happens. Maybe it's because few people here consider themselves Canadian.)

The origins of Bread and Cheese Day are somewhat murky, but from what I've read, it started in the early 1860s when Queen Victoria ordered bread and cheese to be distributed to sick and needy Indians on her birthday, May

24. Within a few years, a simple handout became a formal occasion sandwiched into an all-day party. The chiefs and visiting dignitaries usually made speeches that recounted the role of Iroquois warriors in the American War of Independence and the War of 1812. Consequently, Bread and Cheese Day evolved into a celebration of the historic ties between the Six Nations and the British Crown. In addition to the formal speeches, the festivities also included footraces, softball games, bicycle races, archery contests, concerts and dances.

When Queen Victoria died in 1901, the distribution of bread and cheese ceased. But soon after the elected band council was imposed on the Grand River Territory in 1924, it voted to resume the distribution at council expense. (As I see it, an unpopular but shrewd band council realized it could buy goodwill in the community by reviving a popular tradition.) If the meaning of the Victoria Day holiday was a little hazy in 1924, it's even foggier now because in 1982 the band council voted to name it Independence Day. It did so to protest the British government's refusal to honour its obligations to the Onkwehonwe when Britain approved the patriation of Canada's constitution in the early 1980s.

The day, whatever it's called, usually begins with a brass band leading a parade through Ohsweken to the fairgrounds. At noon the bread and cheese is distributed with a minimum of speechmaking and the rest of the day is given over to fun and games. In recent years these have included lacrosse games, horse races, bike-decorating contests, picnic games, tug-of-war matches and pretty-baby contests. It all takes place in a county fair atmosphere complete with cotton candy and amusement rides.

I've been to the doings here a half-dozen times over the years but today was the first time I ever went through the actual bread and cheese experience. My daughter Zoe was spending the weekend with me and we timed our arrival to be an hour late so that we would miss the long line-ups. But when we got to the arena, there were still a couple of hundred people in line, with more people showing up all the time. Inside there were several rows of tables staffed by band employees, band councillors, the band chief and Miss Six Nations, the band beauty queen. Behind the tables were dozens of boxes filled with pieces of bread and cheese. (This year the volunteers cut up and distributed 2,000 loaves of bread and 3,200 pounds of cheese.) When I finally reached the head of the line, one of the band councillors smiled and handed me a piece of bread thick enough to cut into four slices and a chunk of cheese the size of my fist.

Although the focal point of the day is bread and cheese, what makes Bread and Cheese Day great are the thousands of people. Moving through the crowd, I was constantly bumping into one friend or relative after another. I was especially delighted to meet a few people I hadn't seen in more than ten years. Even though I might have seen some friends and relatives just the day before, I was caught up in the spirit of the day and I stopped and exchanged gossip, pleasantries, stories and laughs with almost everyone I met. We chatted about many things—the weather, our jobs, our health and our gardens—but the number-one topic of conversation was catching up on the latest doings and whereabouts of all the members of our respective families. As I left the fairgrounds, after two hours of concentrated visiting with people I like, love and respect, I was fairly glowing with peace and goodwill.

I had a great time, but I'd still like Bread and Cheese Day even if I didn't know anyone, because I like being surrounded by thousands of Onkwehonwe. After spending forty years in (white) mainstream society, in which I was always singled out for being different, it was very comforting to be part of a great commonality, to be, literally, just part of the crowd. Gone is the tension that comes from being made to feel different. In its place is the serenity that comes from knowing that in that crowd, in that place, I was in a world in which my traditions and beliefs were shared by everyone around me.

As I left the fairgrounds, I couldn't help thinking that only at Six Nations could two non-traditional foods, a carnival midway and the memory of a long-dead queen be celebrated under a banner declaring independence from Great Britain. Yes, Independence Day does have a murky history, questionable political significance and a dumb name, but so what? It will always be Bread and Cheese Day for me and for almost everyone else on the Big Six. And whatever it's called, it's still a very special day because it's the first chance that people have following the end of a long, hard winter to stage a mass celebration of three of the great things in life—food, family and fun.

Why Iroquois women are so tough

In the old days, Iroquois women wielded enormous political power. They owned the land and they selected the chiefs. They dominated their families and clans and ruled every longhouse in every village. When a couple married, the woman stayed put and the man moved into his wife's longhouse. When a man entered marriage, therefore, he was moving into a home that was owned by women, in a society whose descent was determined by the female line, whose chiefs were selected and deposed by women. And because he lived under the same roof as his wife's mother and all of her sisters and her unmarried brothers—who were all members of the same clan, different from his—I'm positive that wife-beating would have been non-existent.

Iroquois villages were light-years ahead of surrounding white settlements when it came to "women's rights" and there are several instances in which white women lived among the "savages" and refused to leave. One of them involved a servant woman who ran away to live with the Oneidas. Some years later, when she was asked why she didn't return home, she replied, "Here I have no master, I am the equal of all the women in the tribe, I do what I please without anyone saying anything about it, I work

215

only for myself—I shall marry if I wish and be unmarried again when I wish. Is there a single woman as independent as I in your cities?

From what I've been told, the Iroquois stopped living in communal longhouses about the year 1750. But by the middle of the nineteenth century, after a hundred years of living in single-family log houses, Iroquois women still wielded enormous clout on the homefront, according to missionary Asher Wright, who lived among the Seneca in western New York:

> Usually the females ruled the house. The stores were in common, but woe to the luckless husband or lover who was too shiftless to do his share of the providing. No matter how many children, or whatever goods he might have in the house, he might at any time be ordered to pick up his blanket and budge; and after such an order it would not be healthful for him to attempt to disobey. The house would be too hot for him, and unless saved by the intercession of some aunt or grandmother he must retreat to his own clan, or go and start a new matrimonial alliance with some other.

Over the past five hundred years, however, Iroquois women have lost much of their political power. These days, Iroquois country is much more of a man's world. Although they are now much weaker politically than they used to be, Iroquois women are still strong—mentally, emotionally and spiritually. They have an abundance of vitality, guts and determination. They are spunky, impassioned and tenacious. They confront adversity with courage and resilience. Iroquois women are, in the word I like to use to describe them, *tough*.

The evidence is everywhere. Go to any meeting in Iroquois country and you will see dynamic women in leadership positions. And they don't sit there silently—they speak up and take action. In emergencies and times of crisis you see Iroquois women leaping to the forefront, fully involved in shaping the outcome of the situation at hand.

The fact that Iroquois women are still so tough after losing most of their political power is, I think, another one of those genetic things. Just as Iroquois women seem to be born with a robust sense of humour, they also carry within their genetic code a chromosome that makes them strong.

I never knew why until now. I didn't know if they were tough because they were matriarchs, or if they were matriarchs because they were tough. Today, however, I finally figured out the answer to this chicken-and-egg mystery.

For the past three days I've been busy putting in my garden, so I've had a lot of time to think while my body's been occupied. Boy, has it been occupied. I worked up the soil, chopping big clods into small ones. I picked weeds, dug up rocks and tossed them aside. I dug furrows and mounded hills. I planted row after row of plants and seeds, covering them carefully. Lastly, I hauled buckets and buckets of water and lovingly watered my planting.

My garden includes a dozen rows planted with corn, beans and squash. Many Iroquois call them the Three Sisters because they were said to be the first foods to spring from the bosom of Mother Earth at the time of creation. For thousands of years the Three Sisters nourished and sustained the Iroquois. Two-thirds of our traditional diet, for instance, consisted of corn. To this day, the Three Sisters continue to be grown and cherished by the Iroquois.

In addition to the Three Sisters and a row of Indian tobacco, I also planted a dozen rows of tomatoes, beets, broccoli, cantaloupe, carrots, cucumbers, potatoes, peas, peppers, pumpkin and watermelon. By the time I'd finished late this afternoon, I was dirty, sweaty, tired, sore and covered with bug bites. And after three days of hard work, I had planted a garden the size of a basketball court.

It was while I was doing all this gardening that I realized just why Iroquois women are so tough. This understanding is not based on scientific study, anthropological research or New Age psycho-social babble. As I see it, *Iro-fem* toughness is not explained by the fact that women give birth and raise children. Nor does it have anything to do with the political power that Iroquois women used to exercise. After three days of sweating in my garden, I figured it out: Iroquois women are tough because in the old days the men did the hunting and the women did all the gardening—and gardening, the old-fashioned way, makes you *tough*.

To begin with, the word *gardening*—with its modern connotation of a casual hobby—doesn't do justice to the difficulty or the amount of work that Iroquois women did. All told, Iroquois women grew seventeen varieties of corn, eight types of squash and sixty kinds of beans. They gathered eleven varieties of nuts, twelve types of edible roots and thirty-four kinds of wild fruit. In fact, more than 80 percent of the food in the family cooking pot was put there by the women.

What's really astonishing is the fact that they produced all that food with nothing more than a sharp stick. They didn't have a chain saw, axes, stumpers or chippers to clear the land. They didn't have a tractor to plow the ground. They didn't have a tempered steel hoe, rake or cultivator. They didn't get their water from a rubber hose attached to a well and a pump. They didn't have scientifically engineered high-yield pest-resistant seed stocks. They didn't have chemical fertilizers, pesticides, herbicides or insect-repellents.

All they had was a sharp stick, knowledge and perseverance. Gardening under those conditions for thousands of years, with their family's well-being and survival at stake, instilled in the genetic essence of Iroquois women a strength, confidence and serenity that can still be observed in their descendants today.

But Iroquois women stopped doing all the family gardening two hundred years ago, sometime after the move to the Grand River Territory. At that time, European missionaries and government agents were trying to persuade the Iroquois to change their lifestyle. They wanted the men to stop being hunters and warriors and become commercial farmers, and they wanted the women to make the switch from full-time gardeners to full-time housewives. The Europeans thought that the Iroquois would quickly switch from subsistence gardening to commercial farming once they saw how new technology (oxen, plows and steel tools) would increase their crop yields. But the Iroquois—men and women alike—resisted this social revolution for many years.

According to a Quaker who travelled in Seneca country in the first decade of the nineteenth century, the men regarded farming as an occupation fit only for sissies. This, according to the Quaker, was an opinion that was also shared by the women, who mercilessly ridiculed the manhood of any hunter-warrior who tried to farm: "If a Man took hold of a Hoe to use it the Women would get down his gun by way of derision & would laugh & say such a Warrior is a timid woman."

Once the Iroquois made the change, however, and saw the results of the new technology—corn that was planted in ground broken by a plow, for instance, grew a foot taller, with larger cobs, than corn that was planted using a wooden hoe—they never went back to the old way.

Nowadays, it seems to me, most of the vegetable gardening around here is done by the men. And that, thank goodness, means a guy like me can put in a garden without every Pam, Jill and Mary calling my manhood into question. The women, however, can still ridicule me for being a poor gardener, and I'll be the first to admit that I'm just a beginner.

I go by what I hear and see around me, and local tradition has it that tomatoes don't get planted until the twenty-fourth of May, the Queen's Birthday. So there I was at a large local garden store last week, buying a raft of plants and seeds. Once inside, I was surprised to see how much space the store devoted to growing flowers, shrubs and ornamental plants and how little was devoted to growing food. In fact, when I asked one clerk where the seed potatoes were, he was genuinely puzzled, as if he'd never heard of them.

This is a garden store? I thought. *Hmmph.* Gardening, to my overly practical and traditional mind, means just one thing—growing food. If I can't eat it, I won't plant it. As I compared my purchases to the people who were buying only flowers and shrubs, it was obvious that when it comes to gardening, I am way out of the mainstream—but, then, what else is new?

Last week, I asked my neighbour to plow up the small flat area down by the creek. The flat is just a few feet above river level and it gets flooded every few years so the soil is thick and rich. It sure grew a great crop of weeds last year. They formed a thick jungle more than seven feet high.

While I was planting the garden, my thoughts turned to the Iroquois women of yesteryear and the kind of gardening they had to do then. Even though I was using a steel hoe, I realized after just one day of hoeing and stooping that I was sorely lacking in *Iro-fem* toughness. By the time I had finished, my respect and admiration for those old-time gardeners had increased a thousandfold. And when I was done, despite the fact that I was wearing mosquito netting and insect-repellent, I was covered with a layer of swollen welts caused by dozens of mosquito and black-fly bites. The clouds of flying bloodsuckers nearly drove me crazy, but in the end I found a small measure of comfort in the realization that they are just like me: they are compelled by their nature to suck blood just as I am compelled by my traditions to plant the Three Sisters. We do what we do because we are compelled to fulfil our obligations in the Great Circle of Life.

A band council report card

The auditors handed out the reserve's financial report card for the past fiscal year the other day. The band passed—not with top marks, but it passed. That in itself is quite an achievement. In 1991, the band was $1.6 million in debt. Last year, the council hired a new band manager who promptly reported that the band's spending and management practices were out of control. They're still not much better.

The band received $39 million last year to operate all its programs and services. But in keeping track of that money, the band kept thirty-eight different sets of books using different computer systems and accounting packages. Trying to get an overall picture of the band's finances under these circumstances is, to say the least, extremely difficult. Nevertheless, the band did not overspend last year and was able to reduce its debt to $600,000.

The band may have passed its financial audit but it failed my political audit. I have watched the band council's well-intentioned bumbling for the past five months now and it's obvious to me that it has no clear idea just what its job is or what it should be doing. In spite of their oft-repeated claim to be *the* governing body on this territory, the chief and council spend little time enacting "laws" or dealing with major issues. Instead, they spend most of their time dealing with administrative and financial trivia. For example, the band said nothing this year about the multi-million-dollar tobacco trade. At the same time, however, no financial matter was too small to deserve the attention of the chief and council.

Judging by the way it operates, the council likes to play Santa Claus. At the beginning of each general council meeting, local groups and individual band members show up asking for money, often with plaintive, doe-eyed children in tow. For instance, I watched a teenager ask for $375 to go to a summer space camp and a teacher ask for $5,000 to take a group of students and parents on a road trip to a pow-wow in New Mexico. After being told that the applicants had raised some money themselves, council voted to give them exactly what they requested. Financial need, or, for that matter, the merit of the request, seemed to have no bearing on the council's decisions. A well-known local couple whose combined annual income is in the neighbourhood of $75,000 wrote a letter to council asking for $195 to pay their sixteen-year-old son's fees at a hockey camp. They got the money, no questions asked.

This willy-nilly approach to giving away money is not limited to the council. A committee of two employees gives grants of up to $3,000 to band members who have, or want to start, a small business. Applicants are not required to supply a financial statement or business plan. The committee has no criteria for evaluating applications and the band doesn't follow up on how the money was spent. This year forty-five people applied to the slush fund, twenty-eight were funded and one of the seventeen "losers" spent twenty minutes of the band council's time complaining that the band played favourites in handing out the money. Although the band manager called the program and its evident problems "a headache," the band council did nothing.

In addition to being a source of easy money for many people, the band council is also the largest local source of high-paying jobs. It is, as well, the largest single employer on the territory, by far, with more than two hundred workers on the payroll. With a general shortage of jobs elsewhere, the matter of just who gets a job with the council is closely scrutinized by many people because of the band council's reputation for nepotism and cronyism.

In January, however, the council voted to adopt a new policy that put hiring in the hands of senior administrators and diminished the role of the band council. This was done, as elected chief Williams explained at the time, to counter complaints that "you had to have voted in band elections or be a member of a certain family to get a job."

The council's biggest failing, though, is its often total lack of political judgment and common sense. Even people who are staunch supporters of the elective system would agree.

The latest incident involves the band's attempt to enforce its residency by-law, which says that only band members can live on the reserve. The by-law was intended to keep white people, primarily non-Indian spouses, off the reserve. The irony is that there are already plenty of white women living on the reserve, but they are "status Indians" and are therefore exempt from the by-law. Another irony is the fact that the Great Law provides for the adoption of outsiders and allows anyone to take shelter under the leaves of the Tree of Peace. Nevertheless, earlier this year the band began trying to evict Pamela Henderson, the non-Indian spouse of a man who lives on the reserve. But when the band cited its by-law and ordered her to leave, she refused.

The band then asked a top Toronto law firm for a legal opinion on the validity of the by-law. The firm reported, basically, that the by-law wouldn't stand up in court because it was badly worded. (The by-law's preamble said, for instance, that its purpose was to protect band members *and their families*.) The lawyers also advised the band to rewrite the by-law before going to court to get an eviction order. The council, most of whom never finished high school, decided it knew better. It hired a law firm *in Vancouver* to take the woman to court.

The case is doomed. What's aggravating is that the air fares, not to mention the legal fees, are going to be enormous.

A more common weakness, though, is the council's reluctance and refusal to do anything about the problems it sees. Faced with a problem demanding a solution, the council, more often than not, hears out the complaint and does nothing. I'm not saying that this is true of *all* the councillors. One or two of them try to make changes and get things done. There are some councillors, though, whose ashtrays and coffee cups get a bigger workout at the meetings than their microphones.

The band council has been in place for seventy years now and it has evolved its own way of doing things. One particularly flabbergasting idiosyncrasy is the way in which the elected council has perverted democratic voting procedures. When a councillor abstains on a vote, the abstention is counted as a vote in favour of the motion, as in "silence means consent." If I hadn't seen it myself, I wouldn't have believed it.

The crazy thing is that in Indian country silence, traditionally, often does not mean consent, it means just the opposite. When people are opposed to something, and they don't want to create a conflict, they say nothing. Benjamin Franklin recognized this Iroquois character trait more than two hundred years ago:

The Politeness of these Savages in Conversation is

> indeed carried to excess, since it does not permit
> them to contradict, or deny the Truth of what is
> asserted in their Presence. By this means they
> indeed avoid Disputes, but then it becomes diffi-
> cult to know their Minds, or what Impression you
> make upon them.

Indian tradition to the contrary, the government used the Indian Act to impose the "silence means consent" rule on the way band councils conduct their affairs. And even though it tries to say every once in a while that it does not follow the Indian Act, the Six Nations band council still hangs on to this bizarre, anti-democratic voting procedure in the head-shaking belief, I think, that the rest of the world does the same thing.

Another of the council's infuriating traits is its practice of banning the press from some of its meetings. The council is regularly bashed by the *Tekawennake*, which makes little distinction between news and editorials, but that's no excuse for banning the press; that only demonstrates con-tempt for the community. "Knowledge is power," and it's clear that the council intends to keep the information—and the power—to itself.

By not sharing information with the people here, the council also fails to *empower* this community. The princi-ples of modern-day journalism—openness, fairness, hon-esty and balance—are not new to Onkwehonwe. They are the very same principles on which our traditional society was based. Every aspect of our lives used to be governed by the principle of consensus, but in order for everyone to come to one mind, everyone had to know what everyone else knew—and that required communication and the free flow of information. Our ancestors would never have achieved all the glorious things they did if they'd based their lives on keeping secrets and hoarding information.

Despite my distaste for an elected chief and council, I have nevertheless developed a little sympathy for them—a *little*. It has to do business, after all, with the Department of Indian Affairs, and getting the department to do even the smallest things can be extraordinarily time-consuming and frustrating. Trying to get something "medium-sized" accomplished, like getting money for a new school, is an undertaking of colossal proportions. And trying to do something big, like settling the Six Nations land claims, has proven to be impossible.

Dealing with the department can be unbearably frustrating. For example, when Parliament passed Bill C-31 in 1985, the department was obligated to give the band more money to provide for additional housing, education and other services caused by the increase in band population. In the past nine years, band membership has doubled, to about 18,000 people. The trouble is that the department refuses to tell the band how much of the increase is due to Bill C-31. To identify the people who were added to the band list because of the legislation, the department says, would be an invasion of their privacy. As a result, the band has no way of comparing the population increase with the amount of money it gets. It has to take the department's word that it is not being shortchanged—not a wise thing to do, given the history of government–Indian relations.

I'm also a *teensy* bit empathetic about the exasperation the elected council must feel over the constant obstructions from the traditionalists. In the conflict between the Confederacy and the elected council, it should be understood, the Confederacy rarely speaks out. Most of the opposition comes from individuals, who relentlessly pressure the band council at every opportunity. As a result of constantly having to contend with Confederacy-based opposition, the band council's plans are always being delayed or stymied. The opposition has crippled the band's ability to act on several major issues.

And there are many times, I must admit, when the band council does the right thing. For example, I watched the council vote down a half-baked plan for a new housing subdivision that didn't include adequate recreation space or proper access roads. And at the same meeting the council also voted not to pay some of its long-term employees for vacations they didn't take fifteen years ago. But hey, the fabled law of averages says the council can't make a bone-headed decision every time.

And there's one last admission I have to make. From what I've seen over the past five months, the chief and council appear, for the most part, to be motivated by a sincere and selfless desire to help others. I'm positive that they honestly believe they are working in the best interests of the community. And are they ever dedicated. I am amazed by the great gobs of time they devote to their responsibilities. They attend hours upon hours of meetings every week at a cost to their personal, social and family life that most people don't fully appreciate.

But.

Hard work and good intentions are not enough. The problems of this community will not be solved by a bigger band council with more money, more employees and more programs. We don't need more of the same. The people who run the elected system are not the problem either. They are basically good people who have been sucked into an oppressive, destructive and alien system that will never meet the needs or wishes of the people here.

Although the problem is the system itself, the elected council can still break the impasse with the Confederacy, and it can help to begin to solve the real problems in this community.

But that's another story.

Tsi yawenta'tarihen

•//•

When the days are hot

Thick. *It is all so overwhelmingly thick. Everything in creation is swollen with the fullness of life that reaches its peak during the moon that follows the longest day of the year.*

The bush is a dense and impenetrable mass of exploding foliage—limbs and leaves shooting out in all directions. Rooted smugly in forbidding lushness, the hulking forest, dense and green, defies trespass, its summer secrets locked away. Fuelled by blazing sun and soothing rain, the bush grows—upwards, outwards and inwards. It inches its way across the fields, filling in the open spaces and making itself ever more dense.

The fields are choked with a thickly matted thatch of grass and weeds, their thin stalks tightly bunched, their chest-high feathered heads spiked and lacy. The meadow's rippling green carpet, speckled with white, yellow, blue and purple, dances in the breeze, rocking and rolling to the rhythms of the wind.

In the rich bottomlands, a towering jungle of weeds erupts from the earth's floor. But these weeds are not slender, delicate straws that wave in the wind. They are firmly rooted, beefy plants coated with barbs and topped with flowered heads. Crammed together, they push relentlessly upward, all the while shooting out broad bulky leaves, as they try to outmuscle one another for a place in the sun.

There is no escaping the thickness of it all. Even the air in summer is thick. Especially the air. It is so saturated with moisture that birds trail wakes through the sky. The scorching heat transforms the clammy atmosphere into a scalding steam-bath. The sweltering fog hangs heavy, bearing down on everything.

The air is also thick with the raucous clamour and clatter of the two-legged, four-legged and six-legged beings. From every direction the sky is filled with the chirping, cooing, trilling and warbling of birdsong; the whining, buzzing siren of insects; the bass notes of bullfrogs and the soprano of peepers that all blend together to create summer's symphony.

And at the centre of all this, here I am, surrounded. It's as though all the life-forms on earth have grown, expanded and pushed their way into my physical space and conscious being. But I don't shrink back because I too have been strengthened by the summer sun. I can feel the friction as I squeeze my way into this overloaded environment. I can feel the energizing tension of all these life-forms crowding together at the peak growing point of the year, suffusing the air and filling my being with the excitement and energy of the fullness of life.

Roasting the media

The federal and provincial governments dropped the tax on tobacco ninety-five days ago, and it's been ninety-four days now since the news media dropped the cigarette-smuggling story. For months before the taxes were lowered, the media ran a steadily increasing barrage of stories about the Indian cigarette trade. The bulk of the news coverage can be divided into three kinds of stories: 1) Indians are smuggling cigarettes; 2) Indians are illegally selling contraband cigarettes; and 3) Indians are damaging Canada's economy.

When tobacco taxes were lowered, the cigarette trade in Indian country dried up overnight. By the next day, the media had designated some other issue as the crisis of the moment demanding everyone's attention. But, then, that's the way the news media operate—if an issue affects the rich and powerful, it's news; if an issue affects only the poor and the powerless, nine times out of ten it's not.

Ordinarily, the only one who gets to hear my tirades about the media's anti-Indian bias and fleeting attention span is my cat. But this weekend I was able to take my complaints right to the source. The CBC held a think tank and navel-gazing exercise in Ottawa this weekend and I was invited to be one of the speakers. One of the sessions was organized to discuss how CBC-TV News covered the story of the Indian tobacco trade. The session began with the screening of ten news items showing how the story was covered on five different days by the English- and French-language TV networks.

The French coverage singled out the Mohawks and demonized them, making it look as though they alone were destroying Quebec's economy and threatening its sovereignty. The English coverage, by contrast, mentioned smuggling, contraband and shrinking government tax revenues but rarely, if ever, mentioned Indians or the Mohawks. However, although the difference in coverage was often so striking it led me to wonder if the reporters were covering the same story, I didn't see any fundamental differences between the French and English media. Nor do I see any fundamental differences in the way they report on casinos, teenage suicides or other so-called "native issues."

The ten stories dealt with only one symptom of the fundamental problem that underlies the relationship between the Onkwehonwe and the people of Canada: namely, Canada's continuing refusal to enter into nation-to-nation negotiations aimed at establishing a peaceful and prosperous co-existence between our two peoples based on the principles of equality and mutual respect.

Although there isn't a major difference between the way French and English media see Indian people, there is a fundamental difference in the way the mainstream media and Indian people look at life.

It's necessary, for starters, to understand that the Onkwehonwe don't see Canada as being composed of two founding nations, nor do we see it as a confederation of ten equal provinces. The way we see it, there are only two kinds of people on Great Turtle Island—there are Indians and there are immigrants.

It has often been suggested that reporters should "stick to the facts" in covering a story rather than writing about their opinions or feelings. But what are these so-called facts? When the media deals with Indian people, sticking to the facts is not as clear-cut or black-and-white as one might think. No matter which language is being used, reporters have to use words to describe the events they have witnessed, and the words they use often have positive or negative connotations. I'm sure that most reporters have the best of intentions when they set out to cover Indian issues. They think they can produce fair and balanced reports, and they think they can do justice to both Canada and the Onkwehonwe by sticking to the facts. But some of the words they used in the stories about the Indian tobacco trade included "illegal," "contraband," "criminal" and "smuggling."

These are value-laden words the government uses to slander Indians. They are not the words that the Onkwehonwe use to describe what they are doing. If reporters think they can do justice to both Canada and the Onkwehonwe by using words like "smuggling" and "criminal," they probably also believe that the camera never lies.

Reporters should also be aware that they reveal the deep-rooted bias against Indian people that exists in this country in the language they use, even when the story they're working on doesn't have anything to do with Indian people. This goes for both the French- and the English-language media. This is not a matter of ill-will. In fact, most reporters are not even aware how they reinforce that bias every day.

For example, the Euro-Canadian media glorify democracy based on the principle of one person, one vote. Implicit in that glorification is the belief that people like the Iroquois, who reject democracy and select their leaders in a different way—in our case, through the clanmothers— are uncivilized.

The Euro-Canadian media sanctify the concept of government by majority rule. And part-and-parcel of that philosophy is the view that people like the Iroquois, who reject majority rule and who try to make their decisions by consensus, are quaint or backward.

The Euro-Canadian media are in love with the supremacy of individual rights and freedoms as expressed in the Canadian Charter. But implicit in that love affair is the judgment that people like the Iroquois, who believe that the wishes of the community are more important than the wishes of one individual, are savages.

Another example: the Euro-Canadian media are annoyingly self-righteous in praising the virtue of the "rule of law." What's more, they denounce people who think otherwise and call them barbaric. But what the media fail to point out is that "the law" is *Canadian* law that was shoved down the throat of the Onkwehonwe, even though people like the Iroquois have their own law—the *Kayaneren'tsherakowa*.

Even on such a seemingly trivial matter as the weather, the media routinely say that sunny weather is good and rainy weather is bad. But people who put food on the table by growing it themselves, who provide for their families by living in accordance with the natural rhythms and forces of Mother Earth—these people know that to talk of weather in terms like these is simply air-conditioned nonsense.

The last example of inherent bias is that the Euro-Canadian media worship at the altar of economic growth. The media cheer when the stock market goes up and cry when the gross domestic product goes down. But people who strive to live in balance with Mother Earth know that the world economy, the production of goods and services, is entirely dependent on this planet's natural resources— resources that are being used up. And the people who have this awareness know that basing a global economy on the principle of unlimited growth, in a world of limited resources, is madness.

I've done these how-the-media-handle-native-issues seminars before and I've said many of the same things, but what made me feel good about this presentation was the feeling that this time I was much more convincing. The only difference between then and now is that this time I am speaking as an Indian who lives on a reserve. My new address, I'm certain, gave me a little extra credibility with the non-native audience. Moreover, it allowed me to speak with more passion and greater confidence because I was speaking from within the circle of our existence. More important than that, however, is the fact that living on a reserve has broadened and deepened my knowledge, it has brought my view of the world into sharper focus and it has strengthened my convictions. I left the think tank in a very buoyant mood, not so much because of my performance but because of the realization that moving to the reserve has had the unintended benefit of making me and my preaching a little more effective.

The glow of self-satisfaction didn't last very long, however. The next morning's newspaper carried a 250-word article showing that not everyone got the message. The article highlighted the previous day's events under the headline "Native Accuses Media of Bias." What I thought was a brilliant argument packed with pearls of wisdom ended up being distilled into two dry sentences that "stuck to the facts" and missed the point.

"Journalists covering native issues are inherently biased against Indians, a CBC media seminar was told Saturday," the article began. "Mohawk journalist Brian Maracle said that Eurocolonialism pervades Canadian media and consequently there is no balanced reporting of the native side of stories."

Instead of detailing the clash of world views I presented,

the article depicted me, I feel, as one more whining Indian tilting at windmills. The article was "factual." I just wish it had captured my main point—that the media are so thoroughly steeped in Euro-Canadian values that they are incapable of recognizing just how biased they are. They are blind to the fact that they are wedded to ideas they consider proper and noble and, consequently, they are inherently biased against people who don't share those ideas. What annoys me is not that the media are biased (I'd be surprised if they weren't) but that they claim to be neutral, fair and objective purveyors of the truth. I don't expect the media to change their bias, but I would like them to be a little more honest and up-front about it. I'd like them to admit that, because of their shared bias, they are partners with government in seeking to assimilate the Onkwehonwe and turn us all into little brown Canadians.

People of the flint

One thing I've noticed in the past nine months is that it is politically correct, in a very small circle, to use our "real" names. Five hundred years ago, when Columbus thought he had found India, he called us Indians. (And, as the old joke goes, we Indians thank the Creator every day that he wasn't looking for Turkey.) Forty years after Columbus, when the first French explorers came calling, they met the Algonquins, who said that their enemies to the south, the people of the Five Nations, were "*Irinakhoiw*"—"real snakes." They also said that the enemies who lived closest to them, a people who practised ritual cannibalism, were "*Mohawik*"—"cannibals."

So, thanks to the Algonquins, we have been called Iroquois and Mohawks ever since. But if the French had asked *us*, we would have told them that our name for the aboriginal people of Great Turtle Island is not Indian, it's Onkwehonwe—first/real/original people. We would have told them that our name for the people of the Five Nations is not Iroquois, it's Rotinonhsyonni—the people of the longhouse. And we would have told them that our name for the people who lived in the wooded hills east of the Finger Lakes is not Mohawk, it's Kanyen'kehaka—the

239

people of the flint. Because they had to guard against attackers coming from the east, the Mohawks—excuse me, the Kanyen'kehaka—were also known as the Keepers of the Eastern Door. Nowadays, though, most of the Kanyen'kehaka living in the Grand River Territory use the English–French–Algonquin name—the "M" word—to describe themselves. And such is the state of cultural decay that many of them don't even know their true name.

Although many people are doing what they can to revive and strengthen Kanyen'kehaka traditions on an individual basis, there are few organized efforts to do so. The largest, by far, is a group that meets every week in the second-floor offices of Mohawk Auto Supplies. The group usually includes at least a half-dozen chiefs and clanmothers and another two dozen "ordinary" Kanyen'kehaka. It's the closest thing to a meeting of the Kanyen'kehaka Nation that there is in this territory.

Some people in the community, however, scoff at the meetings because they are held at "Warrior headquarters." (Mohawk Auto Supplies is owned by Richard "Dick" Hill, said to be the leader of the Mohawk Warrior Society at Grand River.) A distinctive red flag, with an Indian head superimposed on a sunburst, flies on top of the building. It was designed by Louis Hall, the godfather of the modern Warrior movement, who named it "the unity flag." Ever since the 1990 Oka crisis, however, the red Indian-head banner has been known, thanks to the media, as the "Warrior flag." Except for the red flags flying over Mohawk Auto Supplies and a dozen homes across the Grand River Territory, the Warriors are, from everything I can see, invisible and inactive. Despite their low profile, the Warriors' confrontational reputation looms over "the Nation meetings," as they're called, but it hasn't kept many of the chiefs, clanmothers and dozens of non-Warrior Kanyen'kehaka from attending at one time or other.

I went to my first Nation meeting two months ago; I was intrigued from the start and I have been back every week since. Even though I knew very few people there and few people knew me, I was personally welcomed and handed the minutes of the last meeting. I was also given copies of the various documents under discussion. I was routinely asked for my opinion on the topic at hand (being grossly ignorant of much of what was being discussed, I always declined to speak). And on my way out of the meeting, having done little more than take up space, I was always asked to come back. I couldn't help comparing this experience with band council and Confederacy meetings, where visitors don't get handed any paperwork, are not asked for their opinions and are neither welcomed nor invited back.

I've found the people to be sincere and zealously dedicated to the cause of reviving the Kanyen'kehaka Nation and strengthening Kanyen'kehaka traditions. In this way, they are Kanyen'kehaka nationalists. (The other peoples at Grand River—the Cayugas, Onondagas, Oneidas, Senecas and Tuscaroras—for some reason I don't fully understand, don't exhibit the same degree of nationalism.)

The first task they have set for themselves is to clear up the clan confusion and resolve the disputes involving various clanmotherships and chieftainships. Only when the Nation is back in working order, the Kanyen'kehaka say, will they return to take their place alongside the other nations in the Rotinonhsyonni Grand Council.

The meetings, which often last until midnight, take a typically hard-edged Kanyen'kehaka attitude to everything, an attitude that is rooted in the paradoxically twinned concepts of individual freedom and commitment to the Great Law. These Kanyen'kehaka bristle at the idea, popular in some quarters, that the chiefs are the decision-makers and the leaders. They believe instead, based on Rotinonhsyonni tradition, that the chiefs are simply spokespersons for the clans and for the nation, that the power remains with the people. Because we share the same goals and attitudes, I have developed an affinity with these Kanyen'kehaka and I think, at long last, I have found my political home.

The Kanyen'kehaka nationalists are afflicted with more than a few growing pains, not the least of them caused by the fact that, while they want to operate traditionally, the clans are far from ready to do their part. In the meantime, the people continue to meet as "a nation" and try to strengthen the traditional system until it can operate as it once did. So now, when certain decisions have to be made, rather than breaking into individual clans the meeting divides in two. The men stay where they are and talk about hockey and fishing while the women go off to another room and talk about the issue at hand. Eventually the women return, announce their decision and the matter is settled. When it comes to decision-making among the Kanyen'kehaka (these ones anyway), the women are still in charge. The men who attend these meetings, and half the people there are men, seem to be entirely comfortable with this arrangement and are utterly confident in the women's competence and ability to do the right thing. As one of the men said one night, "It takes a lot of manpower to do some jobs but not much womanpower."

A few times over the past two months, the Kanyen'kehaka have spent a fair bit of time discussing how to deal with the news media. They wanted someone from the group to relay a particular statement or decision to the media— and nothing else. They didn't want that person to answer any questions or provide any personal opinions because they didn't want to give the media the opportunity to misinterpret any off-the-cuff remarks. Everyone emphasized the enormous responsibility and the need to get the Kanyen'kehaka message to the public as accurately as possible, so someone suggested selecting a media spokesperson.

Someone else suggested getting the chiefs to represent the Nation. There was another suggestion that a man and woman from each clan form a committee to deal with the media. Each suggestion seemed to have a drawback, however, and was discarded.

Then someone wondered aloud if there were any volunteers. Everyone scanned the room, looking to see if someone would come forward. Before anyone could move, though, an older man who hadn't spoken all night leaned forward and said in a booming voice, "The old people always used to say that the best thing to do for this kind of job is to get the dumbest person in the room to do it." There was an awkward pause in the room until the man explained why. "They're too dumb to do anything more than what you tell them, and they're too dumb to argue."

No one volunteered to be known as the dumbest person in the room so the women decided that no one would speak for the Nation, that the words of the people in a written press statement would speak for themselves.

In addition to absorbing various facts about the clan system while silently sitting through the meetings, I also saved a lot of money by keeping my mouth shut. That's because there was a "cuss can" in the middle of the room, and anyone who said the forbidden word had to put in a dollar. That word, surprisingly, did not refer to sex or a bodily function. It was the "R" word—reserve. A reserve, the nationalists point out, is land the Canadian government has set aside for Indians under the terms of the Indian Act. The land at Six Nations, they remind everyone, was purchased from the Mississauga Nation in 1784 and given under the Haldimand Deed to the "Mohawk Nation and such others of the Six Nations Indians." Despite Canada's claim to the contrary, the Kanyen'kehaka insist that all of the Grand River lands are still Kanyen'kehaka territory.

And it is over the future of the Grand River territory that the Kanyen'kehaka nationalists are on a collision course with the rest of the Six Nations. There is a feeling among these Kanyen'kehaka that the Grand River Territory should be governed by the Kanyen'kehaka Nation and not by the band council or the Rotinonhsyonni. These people point to the fact that only the Kanyen'kehaka are mentioned by name in the Haldimand Deed—and that they still have the original deed—as proof that the land was intended to be theirs. But given that the Rotinonhsyonni governed the territory for more than a century before the band council was imposed in 1924, I expect that it will vigorously object to any effort by the Kanyen'kehaka to take over.

I'm not taking sides in this argument because as a clanless person I have no voice, and if I ever do get adopted into a clan it will be the women in my clan who will be making this decision anyway. What's more, I am positive that the women, guided by the Great Law, will make a decision that is best for the people and the coming generations.

But it doesn't matter right now which side has the more convincing argument, because neither the Kanyen'kehaka nor the Rotinonhsyonni are anywhere near ready to govern this territory. If the Kanyen'kehaka are ever going to get their act together and start flexing their political muscles, they clearly have a lot of work to do. The good news is, at least they have started.

Insects rule

Recently, *The Toronto Star* devoted a full-page article to the pests of summer and ways to combat them. The article said there are more than one hundred species of black-flies and seventy-seven species of mosquitoes in Canada. Mosquitoes, the article said, don't bite people wearing light-coloured clothes standing in short grass at midday in bright sunlight. *Ha!* Either I've got a species of mosquito that scientists don't know about or the mosquitoes here don't read *The Toronto Star.*

But my problem isn't just mosquitoes. Ever since the end of winter, I have been waging a steadily intensifying war against the entire insect world. I have been battling black-flies, deer-flies, horseflies, houseflies, moths, gnats, ladybugs, ants, earwigs, bumblebees, hornets, wasps and woodticks. They have taken over every inch of the landscape, invaded my house and occupied most of my waking thoughts and attention. Although this old log house is roomy enough and I've got nearly two acres of land, this place just isn't big enough for a hundred billion of them and me. So the war is on.

I should add here that I don't hate the six-legged critters, because I know they each have a place and purpose in life's grand design. But as far as I'm concerned, that place and purpose does not include crawling on my food or sucking my blood. And since I don't intend to be a hostage all summer, trapped inside my house by the clouds of stinging, biting, blood-sucking beasts swarming outside, I'm fighting back.

I don't spray the bushes or ditches with pesticides because I'm not trying to exterminate every bug in sight. While I'm in the garden I take defensive measures only. Even on the hottest days, I wear heavy pants tucked into thick socks worn inside work boots. On top, I wear a homemade hooded mosquito jacket that covers my torso, neck, face and head. I wear fingerless gloves so that only the tips of my fingers are exposed. I look like a cross between a beekeeper and a bag lady. Too bad the outfit doesn't work.

No matter how carefully I adjusted the jacket's netting the first half-dozen times I used it, I still came out of the garden swollen and blistered. The scars from the black-fly bites are only now starting to fade. So now, when I want to work in the garden, I put on the same outfit but I also douse myself thoroughly with the strongest chemical insect-repellent money can buy, the kind that is so potent it causes birth defects retroactively. Needless to say, working in the garden in this get-up and under these circumstances has not provided the carefree pleasure I thought it would.

The garden is a fair distance from the house and is surrounded by a thick patch of weeds. (Could that be why there are so many mosquitoes in the garden?) The house itself is surrounded by lawn. A lot of lawn. A lawn the size of the outfield in Yankee Stadium (but nowhere near as green, flat or free of weeds).

When I lived in the city I couldn't have cared less what my dinky little lawn looked like. If the grass got a little

long, so what? I had better things to do. When I couldn't
put it off any longer, I borrowed my neighbour's electric
mower and did the dirty deed in ten minutes. (Now that I
think about it, I never bought my own lawn-mower, I just
borrowed my neighbour's, every time I needed to cut the
grass, every summer for thirteen years. You were a great
neighbour, Art Williamson. Bless you and thank you again.)

But here lawn care is another story. Unlike Ottawa, this
territory doesn't have a spraying program to control the
mosquito, black-fly and woodtick population. Since I had
no intention of being breakfast, lunch and dinner for those
leeches, I bought a riding lawn-mower this spring and
went on the offensive. Every week since I have been out
there on that mower, keeping the grass short and doing my
best to make those bloodsuckers homeless. The trouble is
that it's not a ten-minute job any more. Even though my
mower cuts a swath as wide as the back end of a southern
sheriff, it still takes me nearly three hours to finish the job.
And to think I used to snort contemptuously at the cityfolk
I saw who spent all their spare time obsessively manicuring
their lawns. Just look at me now—I'm the very picture of
suburbia, perched on my riding lawn-mower every week,
going in circles to keep the grass from reaching my ankles.

With the lawn neatly trimmed at least I can enjoy the
outdoors—during the day. When dusk comes, though, I
have to retreat to the house. But there is no refuge because
I am fighting—and losing—the battle against my six-
legged enemies inside the house as well.

Although there are screens in all the windows, my house
is still full of flying pests. I write with a bucket of citronella
burning next to me, but I still slap ten mosquitoes a night.
The other day I woke up at 4:30 a.m., turned on the lights,
grabbed a fly-swatter and nailed five of the blood-filled par-
asites. *How do they get in here?* It's bad enough having to
slather myself with insect-repellent to work in the garden

but I refuse to use the stuff inside the house. That would be admitting defeat, and I refuse to give in to those needle-nosed vermin, so I'll keep on slapping and itching instead.

Besides, I don't think insect-repellent works against the wasps and hornets in here. At least once a week I have to do battle with one of those stinging creatures. The scariest thing, though, is having to duel with bumblebees the size of hummingbirds.

At night the moths appear. The only species I have been able to keep outside are the pale-green moths the size of robins that keep banging against the windowpane trying to get in. All the rest are already inside. There are tan-coloured ones smaller than raisins. There are chartreuse-coloured ones with transparent, lacy wings the size of my thumbnail. There are looney-sized ones that have velvet-black wings, iridescent blue bodies, bright-orange heads and fluffy antennae. Once in a while one of them will buzz my head and get stuck in my hair. It's annoying when that happens, but especially so when I'm in bed and almost asleep.

I've given up trying to kill all the moths. Now I kill only the ones ◁ that insist on crawling ⌒across my computer screen ◁ while I'm trying to write ✕ and hope the rest of them will just go away.

And there are gnats—dozens of them that crawl over the TV screen while I'm watching the news and dozens more that swarm me while I'm reading in bed.

As for the creepy crawlers, they are, by comparison, hardly any trouble at all. On the few occasions when I have seen one of those grotesquely repulsive earwigs, I am the last thing they see. Similarly, there was an army of ants that used to march across my kitchen counter a couple of times a day, but I set out some poisoned bait and they disappeared.

The ants, gnats, moths, earwigs, wasps, hornets, bumblebees and mosquitoes are bad enough, but they are just an occasional nuisance. What really drives me into an insect-killing frenzy are the flies. They're everywhere.

I've hung up those curling strips of sticky flypaper in every room. I vacuum them up on the window ledges and swat dozens more every day. I've let the spiders build bigger and bigger webs in the corners. I've tried nearly everything but I still can't get rid of them. *How do all these creatures get in here?* I think it probably has a lot to do with this house. I guess if I want to continue to live in a crumbling 150-year-old log house, I'll just have to get used to living with insects. It's a package deal.

The Good Tidings of Peace, Power and Righteousness

During a recent Kanyen'kehaka "nation meeting," someone, I can't remember who, was trying to make a point by saying, as many people do around here, "According to the Great Law..."

At this, one of the older men leaned forward, halfway out of his chair and, clearly irritated and frustrated, bellowed across the room, "*Which* Great Law? There's twenty of them!"

His booming interruption squelched discussion momentarily as everyone else in the room silently contemplated a spot on the wall or the floor between their feet. *It's true*, I thought, as I examined the ceiling. *There probably are twenty different versions of the Great Law. I've got eight of them at home myself.*

The Great Law, the *Kayaneren'tsherakowa*, explains many things—the number and title of the chiefs assigned to each nation, the role of the clans, the duties of a clan-mother, how Confederacy meetings are to be conducted, adoption laws, funeral speeches and the use of wampum, to name just some of its provisions. The eight published versions I have are consistent regarding most of the elements, and I think that probably holds true for all "twenty" versions. The problem is in all the minor, and not-so-minor, differences.

Perhaps the best-known version was written by Seth Newhouse, a Six Nations Kanyen'kehaka, who began writing the Great Law in English in the early 1880s. In his 1897 version, Newhouse said that the Peacemaker designated the Kanyen'kehaka as the leaders of the Confederacy and granted them a veto so that no measure could be passed without their approval. The Peacemaker also decreed, according to Newhouse, that no business of major importance could be conducted unless all nine Kanyen'kehaka chiefs were present.

In 1900, however, a committee of ten Six Nations chiefs wrote their own version of the Great Law because, reportedly, the Newhouse version was "faulty and erroneous." The chiefs' 1900 version makes no mention of any special powers for the Kanyen'kehaka. Neither does a version by Onondaga chief John Arthur Gibson that was dictated in 1912 and translated just two years ago. These different versions have aggravated the conflict between many Kanyen'kehaka, who say the Peacemaker gave them special powers, and the other Confederacy chiefs, who say, "Not so."

In some ways this situation is similar to the disputes that various Christian denominations have about the meaning of certain passages in the Bible. But at least they are arguing over the same printed words. We can't agree on a common printed version of what the Great Law says, let alone what it means. And what makes it even harder to reach a common understanding is that some chiefs say the "real" Great Law is not on paper—it's the oral one, the one recited in one of the Onkwehonwe languages. That means, I guess, that the only people who can talk about the *Kayaneren'tsherakowa* or say what it means are the ones who can recite it in one of our mother tongues. And although there are very few people left who can do that, some of them, I'm told, disagree about some of its provisions.

One of the people who can still recite the Great Law the old way is Jacob Thomas, a seventy-three-year-old Cayuga chief. Jake, as he prefers to be called, has made a career of teaching and preserving the culture and traditions of the Rotinonhsyonni. This summer he has once again taken on the task of publicly reciting the entire *Kayaner-en'tsherakowa* in English, and he has scheduled twelve days to do it. Today, July 3, was the ninth day of the recitation, and I went to listen.

The grand event took place on Jake's property at the Jake Thomas Learning Centre. It was held under an open-air tent the size of a basketball court, with another equally large tent set aside as a dining area. The first time I attended one of Jake's recitals, about four years ago at the community hall in Ohsweken, there were nearly three hundred people there on the first day. Today, three recitations and four years later, under the big top on a Sunday afternoon, there were just thirty people. Most of them were non-Indians, from as far away as Washington, D.C., and Edmonton, Alberta. There were fewer than a dozen Onkwehonwe in the crowd and most of them don't live here.

Two other chiefs and a clanmother were on stage to help answer questions, but most of the actual recitation was left to Jake. Among the sections of the Great Law he explained today were those dealing with the creation of a Pine Tree Chief and the "dehorning" of a chief. Much of what he had to say was not the actual wording of the law but his explanation and interpretation. Some things, he said, were very clear. Under the Great Law, he said, "Men don't tell women what to do. It's the other way round. Clanmothers and women in general tell men what to do." He also explained that some things, such as day-care centres and seniors' homes, "go against the Great Law," even though they're not specifically mentioned, because each clan should take care of its own children and elders; it shouldn't be left to the band or a non-profit organization.

Jake can be a funny speaker. At one recitation, he matter-of-factly told the audience about the first meeting between the Peacemaker and the Kanyen'kehaka. The Kanyen'kehaka, he said, had ordered the Peacemaker to climb a tall tree overhanging a high waterfall. And then, he said, one of the Kanyen'kehaka pulled out a chain saw and cut down the tree. Jake paused for a second, waiting for the joke to register, and the crowd exploded in laughter. Jake laughed too and said he was "just checking to see if you're paying attention." The crowd laughed even more.

Today, though, Jake made very few jokes. Despite the uplifting and positive nature of the message he was reciting—"the Good Tidings of Peace, Power and Righteousness"—the tone of Jake's delivery was angry and bitter. He spent much of the day delivering a cranky, finger-wagging denunciation of all the people who don't obey the Great Law and all the people who don't know their language and culture. Looking around the tent it was easy to understand why he was upset. He and a number of volunteers had gone to great lengths to organize an extraordinary event and his own people hadn't shown up. Perhaps it was the eight-dollar daily admission fee that kept some people away. But the low turnout could also be a measure of Jake's success in having recited the Great Law to hundreds of local people already.

Despite the enormous and praiseworthy effort that Jake has put into the recitation, it won't settle all the arguments about what the Great Law says, especially with some Kanyen'kehaka, because they insist that the "pro-Kanyen'kehaka" Newhouse version is correct. In fact, the way the Kanyen'kehaka and the rest of the Confederacy are arguing about the Great Law makes me think that the

Rotinonhsyonni are becoming more and more like communist organizations and fundamentalist churches—quarrelling over doctrine, splitting into smaller and smaller factions, each one convinced they are right; all of them professing to be the *real* communists, the *real* church, the *real* traditionalists.

When the Onkwehonwe first came to the Grand River in 1784, they were already a diverse people. In addition to the Kanyen'kehaka, Oneidas, Onondagas, Cayugas, Senecas and Tuscaroras, there were Delawares, Tutelos, Nanticokes, Creeks and Cherokees. But in spite of our diversity we were united by the Great Law and there was little conflict. For the past century, though, the people who continue to believe in our traditional government have somehow become divided over the *Kayaneren'tsherakowa*, and this has made it easier for the elected system to have its way.

The Grand River territory, in fact, is now the Bosnia of Great Turtle Island. When I read the news these days from the British Isles and from the Middle East—when I read that the Israelis and the Palestinians are talking peace; when I read that the Catholics and Protestants of Northern Ireland are talking peace—then, I ask, why can't we Rotinonhsyonni talk peace?

Stove polish: a cleaning product, linguistic dinosaur and parlour game

Although there are very few fluent Kanyen'kehaka speakers on the Grand River Territory—only eighty-seven at last count and only seven of them less than forty years old—there is one Kanyen'kehaka word that most people know and use on a regular basis. It is *shekon*, pronounced "SHAY-go." People usually voice it in a gregarious and friendly manner and they use it to mean "hi" or "hello." Many people, including me, use it to answer the telephone. There's such a good feeling associated with the word, in fact, that the local cigarette factory has cashed in by marketing a brand of cigarettes named "Sago."

The curious thing is that *shekon* doesn't literally mean "hi" or "hello." By itself, it means "still," "yet" or "again," and as part of the term *shekon oya*, it means "some more." Very few people around here know that it comes from an old traditional greeting: *Shekon oya Onkyara'seha tontahontaweya'te'*. This cumbersome mouthful stems from the time when the Kanyen'kehaka were still living in longhouses in the Mohawk Valley and it was the expression people used when visitors arrived at their door. It literally means, "Some more cousins are coming into the house." Over time, *Shekon oya Onkyara'seha tontahontaweya'te'*

255

was abbreviated to just *shekon,* and in the process, it
evolved into our own distinctive way of saying "hello."

The Kanyen'kehaka equivalent of "How are you?" is
Skennenkowa ken, which enquires about a person's men-
tal, emotional and spiritual well-being. By itself, the word
skennen means "peace" and is sometimes used as a greeting instead of *shekon.* Loosely translated, then, the question "How are you?" means "Are you at peace?"

Although I have used *shekon* as a greeting for years, I
didn't know until just a month ago exactly what it meant
or where it came from. My parents were never taught the
language by their parents, so they couldn't pass it on to
me, and even though I began to study the language more
than twenty years ago, I never learned anything more than
a few expressions and a little of the vocabulary. In mid-
July, though, I began taking an intensive Kanyen'kehaka
language course—four hours a day of classroom instruction, four days a week. I've been following it up with two
hours a day of homework every day of the week.

Kanyen'kehaka, like almost all the other aboriginal languages of Great Turtle Island, is what linguists call a poly-
synthetic language. This makes it completely different
from almost all the other languages on earth. The way I
understand this difference is that sentences are not made
up of individual words, as in English, Russian or Japanese.
Instead, pieces of words are assembled to make super-
words that are sentences in themselves. That's because
most people rarely talk about objects in isolation—a hat,
for example. They talk instead about a hat in a particular
context. Either the hat is big, new, black or expensive. Or
it's mine, yours, his or hers. Or someone has bought a hat,
or owns a hat or is wearing a hat.

In Kanyen'kehaka, people assemble the different charac-
teristics of a particular hat into one word. For example, the
prefix indicating a female individual (*yako*-), the root word

for hat (-*nonhwarore*-), a joining syllable (-'*tshera*-) and the stem of the verb "to buy" (-*hninonh*) mean nothing by themselves. But when they are assembled in the proper manner—*yakononhwarore'tsherahninonh*—a single word has been constructed that means "She bought a hat."

One of the complicating things about Kanyen'kehaka is its tendency to be extremely specific about explaining just who is doing something. English speakers get by with eight active pronouns: I, you, he, she, it, we, you and they. Kanyenkehaka, by comparison, uses fifteen pronouns: I, you, he, she, it; you and I, he/she and I, you (two), they (two males), they (two females); all of you and I, they and I, all of you, they (males) and they (females). What makes it even more complicated is the fact that there are ten different sets of pronouns. Depending on the verb being used, for instance, the prefix for the pronoun "I" can be either *ka-*, *k-*, *ki-*, *ken-*, *kon-*, *waka-*, *wak-*, *waki-*, *waken-* or *wakon-*.

And there's more. There's another set of thirty-seven prefixes dealing with verbs in which one person performs an action in relation to someone else. For example, some of the prefixes for the verb "to tell" are: I tell you (*kon-*), you tell him (*etshe-*), he tells us (*shonkwa-*), etc. Incidentally, the Kanyen'kehaka word for the Creator uses the prefix *shonkwa-*, meaning "he" performed an action on "us." The other elements of the word are -*ya't*- (the root word for the human body) and -*ihson* (a verb form meaning "finished making"). The literal translation of *Shonkwaya'tihson*, then, is something like "He has finished making our bodies."

And if these 187 prefixes aren't enough, it should be noted that they deal only with the present tense; there are 90 more dealing with past, future and conditional verb tenses.

Although Kanyen'kehaka grammar appears to be tremendously complex, the Kanyen'kehaka alphabet is extraordinarily simple. There are just six vowels—*a, e, i, o,* *en* and *on*—and eight consonants—*h, k, n, r, s, t, w* and *y.* (And since there are no *b*s, *p*s, or *m*s in this alphabet, it means that any Kanyen'kehaka speaker could easily become a master ventriloquist.) Although these letters are few in number, they spell endless trouble when it comes to pronunciation. After just a few minutes practising some Kanyen'kehaka tongue-twisters—with my English-speaking mouth forced to move in ways it's never had to before—all the muscles in my face are throbbing with fatigue.

The other basic and distinctive element of the spoken language is breath control. An apostrophe in a word tells the speaker to cut off the sound at the end of the preceding vowel, while an *h* often has to be pronounced with a soft puff of air. The breath control needed to make all the stops, starts and breathy eruptions in the middle of a chain of tongue-twisting syllables, I'm certain, would challenge any opera singer.

The longest word in the Kanyen'kehaka language also has the reputation of being the hardest one to pronounce. In English, the word means "stove polish," the substance people once used to make their old black wood-burning stoves shine like new. In Kanyen'kehaka it's *yenonhsa'tariha'tahkwatsherahon'tsihstakwa'tsherahstarathe'tahkwa* and its literal meaning is something like "what is used to shine the black thing that heats the house."

Once the people here stopped polishing their stoves and stopped using *yenonhsa'tariha'tahkwatsherahon'tsihstakwa'tsherahstarathe'tahkwa* in everyday conversation, the word became a linguistic dinosaur. But it didn't disappear entirely. It gained new life instead as the centrepiece of an informal little game that tests memory and oral dexterity, a game that has been played ever since I can remember. It usually goes something like this. A boy who doesn't speak

Kanyen'kehaka will be talking to an old man, a fluent speaker, about something having to do with the language when the boy will suddenly demand, "Quick! Say stove polish." And with that command, the game begins and the fun is on. Everyone in the immediate vicinity will jerk their heads around and watch in amusement as the old man struggles to remember how to assemble all the parts of the word in the right order. They will smile and watch the expression on his face as he cocks his head, opens his mouth and rolls his eyes upward searching for the word. They will smile and listen as he tries to say *yenonhsa'tariha'tahkwatsherahon'tsihstakwa'tsherahstarathe'tahkwa* without stumbling. If he makes a mistake, everyone will laugh, including the old man who, more often than not, will immediately try to say the word again. And if he makes another mistake, everyone will laugh all the more. And everyone will keep on laughing until the old man finally gets it right or until he stops trying.

But, if the old man can say the word instantly, smoothly and flawlessly, the listeners are always surprised and impressed. Their eyebrows shoot up, their eyes open wide, their mouths form little "o"s and they give a little "oh-ho-ho" laugh before they shower the old man with praise and congratulations. The stove polish game usually ends when the old man has the last laugh: "Now it's your turn," he'll say. "Let's hear how you say it."

Ah, stove polish. It's such a great game. It's fun for the whole family and batteries are not required. There's even a version of the game, I'm told, in which fluent speakers delight in taking turns saying the word aloud for no other reason than the sheer joy of being able to pronounce it. In this way, *yenonhsa'tariha'tahkwatsherahon'tsihstakwa'-tsherahstarathe'tahkwa* reminds me of "supercalifragilisticexpialidocious." It has become a feel-good word, a missing link in the evolution of our language that has been reborn as a vocal toy that takes speaker and listener alike on a tongue-twisting, rib-tickling, roller coaster ride that loop-de-loops its way over and under the playground of human speech.

What thrills and intrigues me about learning the language is the insight it provides into Kanyen'kehaka culture and psychology. Learning the language is helping me to learn more about my own people and why, in a small way, I am the way I am.

I have made these discoveries because of the way the instructor, Tawit (David) Kanatawakhon-Maracle, is teaching the course. Tawit, a Kanyen'kehaka from Tyendinaga who teaches a Kanyen'kehaka language and culture course at the University of Western Ontario, has devised his own curriculum to break down the complexities of the language into manageable, bite-size pieces. Tawit has published two Mohawk–English dictionaries, a dozen short stories and is working on a CD-ROM version of the textbook. He is, in effect, a one-man language revival factory.

When he uses a word, *kanonhsa* for example, he does not say that it means its English equivalent—"house," in this case. Rather, he breaks the word into syllables and explains what each one means literally. In the case of *kanonhsa*, the *ka-* indicates that whatever is being spoken of is man-made; the *-non-* indicates an arch shape; the *-hs-* indicates that it has depth; and the *-a* at the end shows that it exists. The literal meaning of *kanonhsa*, therefore, is "a long arch-shaped man-made thing." And that, not coincidentally, is a pretty accurate description of the traditional Iroquois dwelling, the longhouse.

Similarly, I have learned that the literal translation of *anonwarore* is not a "hat" but something that covers the top of the head, an *atekhwara* is not a "table" but something that food is put on, and so on.

Kanyen'kehaka, and other aboriginal languages, still assemble word parts to come up with descriptive new names for various elements of modern technology. The word we use for television, for example, *kaya'tarha*, refers to the images of people on the video screen. *Kaya'tarha* contains the root word for the human body (*-ya't-*) and a form of the verb "to hang something up" (*-arha*), so the literal translation, then, is not "television" but "a man-made hanging body thing." Likewise, the word for computer, *kawennarha*, literally means "a man-made hanging word thing."

Judging by the way they name things, the Kanyen'kehaka are a very practical people. For example, if they don't have a use for something, they don't give it a name. They gave specific names to flowers with medicinal properties—the bloodroot and the jack-in-the-pulpit, for example—but not to hollyhocks or buttercups, because they didn't use them for anything. They just called them *Otsitsya*, flowers.

In addition to being practical, I think the Kanyen'kehaka must have been modest as well, at least in the old days, given the way introductions are handled in the language. Kanyen'kehaka speakers, for instance, don't say "My name is so-and-so." They say instead, "They call me so-and-so." Similarly, they do not ask bluntly, "What's your name?" Rather, they ask, "What do they call you?"

The Kanyen'kehaka are a matrilineal people and our language, appropriately, is governed by a female bias. In describing the weather, for example, the female, not the male, verb prefixes are always used.

Another example. When the gender of a person being spoken about is unknown—as in the question "Who bought that house?"—the female verb prefix is always used. So even though the resulting question will literally mean "Who (is the female person who) bought that house?" everyone will know that the scope of the question includes women and men.

A related quirk in the language has to do with naming aunts and uncles. *"Rakenoha'a* Thomas" means "my Uncle Thomas." But if I want to say "Aunt Helen," I have to say *"Ista'a* Helen," even though *Ista'a* is the short form of *Ake'nihstenha* which means "my mother." The word for mother is used, followed by the aunt's name, because there is no one specific word for "aunt." This stems, I think, from the fact that the Iroquois used to live in longhouses that were ruled by a tightly knit circle of women. And not just any women. The typical longhouse contained at least one grandmother and all of her daughters, along with the daughters' husbands and their children. Most of the adult women in the longhouse were sisters. And since a woman lived across the firepit from one of her sisters, they undoubtedly looked after one another's children from time to time. Given the fact that sisters were so closely bound by ties of blood, sweat and, in all likelihood, a few tears, it makes perfect sense to me that children would call their mother's sister their mother too.

A clue to the way Kanyen'kehaka think about the world can be gleaned from examining the way sentences are constructed. The usual sentence structure in English is "subject, verb, object," as in the sentence "John carefully paddled his canoe through the rapids yesterday." But sentence structure in Kanyen'kehaka, when nothing particular is being emphasized, is just the opposite. In Kanyen'kehaka that sentence would be expressed something like this: "(yesterday) (through the rapids) (his canoe) (carefully) (he paddled) (John)."

Now, even though both the English and the Kanyen'kehaka sentence contain essentially the same words, I don't think they say the same thing. I may be completely off-base linguistically, psychologically and otherwise, but it seems to me that the way in which these two sentences are constructed illustrates one of the fundamental differences between the Kanyen'kehaka and English-speaking people.

I think of the difference in visual terms, as though the speaker of each language were making a mini-movie with words. The first thing that an English speaker does with the camera of speech is focus on the subject of the sentence, the individual. Using the canoe-paddling example, the English speaker's movie begins with John's face filling the screen. Then gradually the camera pulls back to show that John is paddling a canoe. The camera then pulls back even further to show that John is paddling through a set of rapids.

Contrast that with the Kanyen'kehaka speaker's mini-movie. It begins with a set of rapids. Then we see the front of a canoe plowing through the rapids. We then see that a man is paddling the canoe through the rapids. And finally we see that the man paddling the canoe through the rapids is John.

These two different movies represent two drastically different ways of looking at life. It is irritating to watch a movie in which every scene begins with a close-up of the hero as the camera pulls back to reveal the action and the background. Yet that is the way most English sentence-movies are made. Visually, it makes much more sense to start with a panoramic view and then zoom in on the action and the hero's face, as Kanyen'kehaka sentence-movies do. The way that the English-speaking world structures its sentences explains to me, in a small way, why western society is so self-centred and narcissistic, why it is so fixated on the cult of the individual and why it is so obsessed with celebrities. And western society is precisely that way because the individual—politically and grammatically — always comes first.

In Kanyen'kehaka, by comparison, context takes first priority. Only when the action is placed in context does the individual appear, and this, to me, reflects in a small way why Indian societies are the way they are: why they are egalitarian, why the people are modest and why the environment is revered.

Kanyen'kehaka sentence structure, it might be said, reflects one of the major principles of old-time life—the freedom of the individual—because individual words are not bound to one another in the sense that the subject of the sentence dictates the way the sentence is constructed. Any part of the sentence can come first, depending on what the speaker wants to emphasize. But the gender, number and tense of all nouns, pronouns and verbs must be consistent and agree with one another because agreement, consensus and unity are fundamental principles of traditional Kanyen'kehaka life.

When some Kanyen'kehaka speakers want to emphasize something, they make it the first word in the sentence. English speakers, on the other hand, emphasize something by stressing it or saying it more loudly. The following examples show how different words are emphasized in English and Kanyen'kehaka:

My father *is fishing*.
Rarhyokawines ne Rake'niha. (He's fishing) (my father).

My father is fishing.
Rake'niha rarhyokawines. (My father) (he's fishing).

This feature of the language should illustrate another of the differences between the Kanyen'kehaka and English-speaking people, but I'm not sure just what it is. Could it be that English relies on force and emotion to confer meaning while Kanyen'kehaka relies on logic and reason? *Hmm*.

Whatever its meaning, this difference tells me, in a small way, why Onkwehonwe old-timers speak in such a calm, level tone of voice—what often sounds like a monotone to non-native listeners. It also explains why I get so annoyed by the verbal histrionics of some English speakers who want to make a point.

A related matter has to do with volume, because I get irritated by the braying and squawking that seems to be a major characteristic of English and other languages. Kanyen'kehaka doesn't sound as loud—even when it's spoken at full volume—so it isn't as aggravating. The reason, I think, has to do with the fact that half the words in the language contain sounds that are little more than puffs of air. It's impossible to shout when you are constantly voicing soft, breathy half-vowels. It's like trying to shout with a mouthful of cotton candy. You can't do it.

The one telling thing I learned about myself in this course has to do with the Kanyen'kehaka sense of future time. According to Tawit, there are two ways to talk about doing something in the future. In statements like "John said he will go canoeing tomorrow," the verb "will go" in Kanyen'kehaka indicates only an intention to go at the time it is said. Another, more definite future verb form is used when it is known that something actually *will* happen. It seems, however, that in most conversations the casual form of the future verb is used most of the time. So, when John says he will go canoeing tomorrow, it means he *intends* to do so *unless* something else happens in the meantime—he gets in an accident, say, or he gets busy doing something else or he simply changes his mind. A lot of Indian people I know still have a fluid sense of future time. Many times I have waited and waited and waited for some Indian to do something that he or she said they were going to do and never did. When that happens to me, I usually just shrug it off and forget it because I know I have made other people wait in vain for me many times. The trouble is that not all of the people who waited for me shrugged it off. A lot of people, non-Indian people especially, regard a statement of intent as a binding contract and this, needless to say, leads to more than a little friction between the races.

The curious thing about this aspect of the Onkwehonwe character is that most of the people I know who have an extremely casual attitude towards future time don't speak their native language. And while it might seem that they don't have a legitimate, language-based reason for having this attitude, it should be understood that this is more than just a matter of verb tenses and vocabulary. The problem is that the English word "will" does not adequately express the lack of concern and ambiguity that exists in the Onkwehonwe mind about the future. This mind-set has been passed down from mother to daughter and father to son, and the change to another language has obviously not changed some of our behaviours. Just because we started speaking English doesn't mean we also started playing cricket and eating kippers. No, we still play lacrosse and eat corn soup and we still have an attitude regarding the future that is hard to pin down.

One of the problems I have in trying to learn Kanyen'kehaka is the fact that there is no standard method of writing, spelling and teaching the language, so the teachers in each community, judging by what happens here, just do their own thing. What's more, few teachers are trained in the grammar, etymology or linguistics of Kanyen'kehaka. We desperately need more teacher training if we are ever going to stop the practice of hiring fluent speakers as teachers in the belief that just because they can speak the language they automatically know how to teach it.

We also need to stop the practice of hiring teachers just because they are educated. There are a number of instances of people being hired to teach Kanyen'kehaka in area schools though they have just a smattering of the language. I know, because I've been approached to teach Kanyen'kehaka as a second language as a substitute teacher this fall after just a month in this program. Although it was flattering to realize that my effort to learn the language has been noticed, I declined the offer because I have little conversational ability and I still have a lot to learn. Surely, I figure, there is someone better qualified than *me* around here. In an odd way, the offer reminded me of my days as a carpenter when we used to say that a good plumber was someone who could connect piping and fixtures so fast that he (they were all men in those days) could connect two lengths of pipe to the main line, turn on the tap and keep ahead of the water. I would have been in exactly that situation if I had accepted that teaching offer, and I'm not sure I'd be able to stay ahead of the kids.

The last major problem facing adult language students is the lack of programs that bring together a well-planned curriculum, ample materials and a fully-qualified teacher in a concentrated course. But that's exactly what the program I'm in now is like, and when the chance to take it came along, I pounced on it like a televangelist on a ten-dollar bill.

One of the things I have learned in this class is a word that is used all the time in situations like this. It is based on *e'tho*, which means "so," "there" or "enough." As part of the expression *ta ne'tho* it means, "That's it. That's all. The end."

Ta ne'tho.

Summer nights, summer lights

The days are getting shorter now. It's only a little after nine o'clock and already the darkness is rising out of the ground. Since I have been writing all day, I am only partly conscious of the gathering dusk. I am mesmerized instead by my computer's keyboard and screen, hypnotized by the images and feelings I am struggling to put into words. Suddenly my fingers stop and my eyes are drawn out the window by a flash of light. I look at the bird-feeder. *A reflection? A bird? No. Nothing.*

My eyes fall back to resume the dance they have been doing all day. Up and down they two-step, from keyboard to screen to keyboard to screen. They watch my fingers stagger across the keys and they leap to watch the words creep across the screen. And then a light, another one out the window. My head snaps up and my eyes search for the source of the flash. I look at the driveway. *A headlight? No. Nothing. At least I can't see anything.*

My eyes drop back to their rutted dance path. My fingers resume their staggering, the words continue creeping and my eyes keep leaping. And then another flash. My eyes strain at the window and scour the lawn, the hedge, the trees and the road for the brightness. I study the horizon.

Lightning? No. But there was a light. There was something there.

I stop typing, turn to the window, look into the dusk and finally see what is making the light.

Fireflies!

Dozens of them! Hundreds of them!

The lawn is a riot of dancing, flickering sparks. Blinking, twinkling, sparkling flashes of light.

Yellow. No, green. No, yellow. Green. Yellow. Green.

There's one. There's another. And another. And another!

Near. Now far. High. Then low.

They're everywhere!

I dash to every window in the house and eagerly look outside. *Yes! Yes! Yes!* The fireflies have me surrounded. Everywhere I look they are blinking at me. Glittering in the twilight, the dancing diamonds speak to me.

"Come!" the sparkles say.

"Take your eyes from your work."

"Let your eyes play with us."

"Dance with us."

"Dance with me."

"No, me!"

"Look at me."

"Over here!"

"No, me!"

"Look at *me*."

I am giddy with excitement and my face is a jumbled map of joy and amazement. My eyes are beaming and my mouth is gaping. I haven't seen a firefly in years! Instantly, I am transported to a world of wonder and joy, awash in the memories of every time and every place I've seen these magic creatures. One by one, the vivid scenes roll over me, images of carefree summer evenings spent playing, dancing and running in a glittering cloud. It's all I can do right now to keep from running outside, to keep from standing in the middle of the flashing sparkles, to keep from spinning around and around and making myself the centre of a twinkling tornado of light.

My eyes leap from one glowburst to another in a frantic and futile effort to see just one firefly. I want to follow its path as it flies, dips, hovers and turns. I want to see it light up its corner of the darkness. I want to see it transform itself from a nearly invisible insect into a flying ball of light. I want to see its gleam go on and off, on and off. I want to watch the dance of a single firefly. But I can't. Because as one firefly switches off and another goes on, my eyes zigzag from one lightspot to another and another. Quickly exhausted from countless ricochets across my field of vision, my eyes slump and pull back, content simply to wallow in the dazzling spectacle of hundreds of yellow-green sparkles that veil this house with a pulsating glow.

As the evening wears on, I go to the window again and again to watch their cheerful blinking in the shadowy gloom. By midnight's cool blackness, though, they are gone.

I can't wait for dusk to come tomorrow night because I'll be at the window, waiting, waiting and looking for the magic little creature that can lighten a grown man's heart.

The politics of language

In the nine months since I've moved back, the *Tekawennake* has carried ads for at least one hundred jobs with the band council and its related agencies. Being jobless, I have read the ads with more than passing interest, even though I have no intention of ever working for the band council, just as I never intend to work for that other notorious mob, the Department of Indian Affairs.

Every time I pick up the paper and read those ads, though, I get more and more angry. The ads consistently ask for people with the highest possible qualifications— university degrees, computer skills and years of experience. Even a labourer on the new school construction project is expected to have a grade twelve education. But what really angers me about the council's ads is the fact that the one skill missing from the list of requirements considered necessary to work here—in an Indian community with Indian people—is fluency in an Indian language. I suppose there's nothing wrong in asking for the moon. Apparently, though, the thought has never occurred to anyone in the band office that one of the qualifications they could ask for is an ability to speak Kanyen'kehaka or Cayuga. Even the school board's ad for teachers in the

271

native language program did not absolutely require it.

Apart from the school board ad, the only other agency that even mentioned native languages was the band tourism office, which advertised an eight-week summer job as a tour guide for $6.70 an hour. "Knowledge of a native language an asset," the ad said.

Just when I thought things couldn't get any worse, I found an ad in this week's paper that has me seething with fury. It's for a "home support worker," a $21,315-a-year job with the Home Support for the Elderly program. Among other things, the person hired will be required to "deliver high quality home support services to community seniors." The ad lists seven mandatory job requirements, including a grade twelve education, a class "G" driver's licence and a willingness to take specialized training. Like most of the other band council ads, it says "the successful applicant will be Native in preference to other applicants." But the ad does not require applicants to speak a native language, even though the people they are to work with, the elderly, are just about the only ones left around here who still do. The ad doesn't even say that someone speaking a native language will get preference over other applicants. If anyone on this territory should be required to speak a native language as a condition of employment (apart from a language teacher), it should be a home support worker for the elderly. For the band council to send employees who don't speak the language into the homes of the old people is, I think, inconsiderate and disrespectful in the extreme.

I don't want to think that the band council has deliberately adopted this policy so that it will have a workforce that doesn't speak the language. I also don't want to think that the council figures that the languages are so far gone that they aren't worth saving. Those thoughts are just too infuriating to contemplate. But what other explanation can there be? Why doesn't the band ask or require its job applicants to speak one of the languages? I don't know. I can only give the council the benefit of the doubt and call those one hundred ads an honest mistake, an accidental oversight by a careless or unthinking white-oriented administration to whom the preservation of our languages means little or nothing at all.

The languages are in deep trouble at Six Nations. Less than 3 percent of the people living on this territory speak Kanyen'kehaka or Cayuga, and the band council is doing nothing about it. What kind of encouragement or incentive does the band's hiring policy give to the hundreds of kids and dozens of grown-ups enrolled in the various language programs around here? There are better reasons for learning the language than money, heaven knows, but some people might look at those ads and think that it isn't worth all the effort if the only employment it will help them get is a $6.70-an-hour summer job as a tour guide.

One of the reasons why the band has done nothing to save the languages is that the band thinks that it isn't its job. "That's the job of the schools," the band will say, "or the parents or the longhouse."

But even if it felt some responsibility to help save the languages, the band wouldn't do anything anyway because it is afflicted with the grant mentality: unless it gets a grant, it can't do anything.

Wrong. There are plenty of practical, symbolic and important things the band could do—things that don't cost any money—if saving the languages really meant something to the band council. For instance, the band could insist that band employees answer all of its telephones with a greeting in Kanyen'kehaka or Cayuga. It could change the names of the rest rooms from "Men" and "Women" to *"Ronkwe"* and *"Yakonkwe."* It could put up road signs and stop signs in Kanyen'kehaka or Cayuga. It could start calling the Grand River by its original name,

Ose Kahyonhowanen (Willow River). And if the band really wanted to do something to help save the language, it could adopt a policy requiring anyone applying for a job with the band council to speak one of the Iroquois languages, beginning in the year 2000.

All of these things—and many more—could be done at no cost if the band council truly felt that saving the language was important. For that matter, the members on the council could make it a personal priority and set an example by learning the language themselves and using it.

My dream is to see Kanyen'kehaka and Cayuga strengthened here to the point that they become the primary language that people use at home, on the job and at play. It may take a lifetime to reach that point, I know, and it certainly won't be easy—but it can be done. For example, Hebrew and Icelandic were on the edge of extinction a hundred years ago, as I understand it, but they were revived and today they are vibrant, living languages.

There are a number of things that stand in the way of a revival of the Onkwehonwe languages, not the least of them being the lack of an established, tried-and-true teaching system for adults. Another barrier, curiously enough, is the attitude of some of the old people. There are, I'm told, a number of fluent speakers here who believe the language should not be written down. Their mother tongue, they say, is an oral language and was never intended to be put on paper. As a result, they decline to help in the production of dictionaries and teaching materials.

A few of them also have a hyper-critical and self-righteous demeanour that doesn't help or encourage people like me to learn the language. I have heard a couple of fluent speakers harshly criticize an audience of local people for not being able to speak the language, which to my mind is just blaming the victim. If anyone is to blame for the present unilingual generation, it is the old-timers, most of them now dead, who didn't teach or didn't insist that their children speak the language. And if I didn't know any better, I'd say that one or two of these old-timers are purposely cantankerous, uncooperative and hard to get along with so that they can savour the perverse satisfaction of being able to say that when they die, the language will die with them.

But there is one thing that all of the old-timers say about the language that I agree with wholeheartedly. They are absolutely right when they say that the language is the key to our culture. Without the language, our ceremonies, songs and dances will cease. Without the language, we will be unable to recite the Creation Story, the Thanksgiving Address and the Great Law the way they were intended. Without the language, the clanmothers will be unable to "raise" a chief and the Confederacy will cease to function. Without the language, the people will be unable to receive an Indian name and the names themselves will lose their meaning. Without the language, we will lose our traditional way of thinking and our distinctive view of the world. And, perhaps worst of all, without the language, we will lose touch with Shonkwaya'tihson, our Creator.

The chain of cause and effect is very clear. Once we lose our language, we lose our culture. And once we lose everything that sets us apart from mainstream society, we will surely lose the little land we have left.

In addition to being angered by the ad for the home support worker, I was saddened today because it happened to be the last day of the intensive, daily Kanyen'kehaka language program with Tawit Kanatawakhon-Maracle. I learned a tremendous amount in that class and I wish it didn't have to end. But in another two weeks, just after Labour Day, Tawit will be back teaching a night class once a week, and I'll be there.

Despite all the studying I've done over the years, my Kanyen'kehaka is still not as good as my beginner's French, and I'm afraid sometimes that it might take me another twenty years to achieve a small degree of fluency. But I'm not discouraged. I'm making progress and I'll keep at it until I achieve my goals. After I develop some basic conversational ability, I want to learn the Thanksgiving Address so that I can recite it and know what I'm saying. My long-term goal is to write in the language—short stories, newspaper articles, who knows, maybe even a novel.

Eventually, I'd like to see the language revived in all the Kanyen'kehaka territories so that our preservation as a people will be assured. There are, thank goodness, three hundred schoolchildren enrolled in Kanyen'kehaka and Cayuga immersion programs here, and there are dozens of adults who are working hard to develop fluency themselves. But the biggest problem we face is the fact that most of the people here don't care enough about the language to put the hard work into learning it. They might agree that the death of the language will mean the death of our culture and the loss of the land, but they're not particularly worried about it because it isn't an immediate threat. That is something that will happen to someone else—to the coming faces, the people who haven't been born yet. And because these terrible things won't be happening to them, the people don't feel any need to do something now to prevent it. Like the band council, the people feel that saving the language is someone else's job.

The people just don't have any incentive to learn or use the language, but they would be motivated to learn if language preservation were tied to something they really cared about. And if there's one thing that people here revere more than anything else, it's their tax exemptions. So, if the people could somehow be required to speak the language if they wanted to remain tax-exempt, hundreds and thousands of people would stampede to sign up for classes, and the preservation of our mother tongue would be assured. It's a crude and sad commentary on the state of the language here, but *tokenhske' na' ne'e*—it's true.

The education crisis implodes

The dust has settled, for now, on a senseless, infuriating and stomach-churning chapter in the history of Six Nations education. For the past three months this community has been torn apart by a crisis over who will control and administer the schools on this territory—the Department of Indian Affairs or a self-appointed committee of Six Nations people backed by the elected band council.

For the past twenty years there has been a growing movement by Indian bands across the country to take over the operation of their schools from the Department of Indian Affairs. Six Nations is one of the last, and is certainly the largest, Indian community to have its schools still controlled and administered by the department. But it's not because the people here like the way the department runs the schools. Rather, it's probably because, for more than a century, most of the teachers, principals and administrators here have been Six Nations people. And although the people are not happy with the department's control, the problem exists as to just who will take over the schools, because virtually no one wants the band council to run them.

The crisis began to build just before Christmas when the

band council anointed the Six Nations Education Board (SNEB) as the body to take over the schools here. When the news got out, though, there were no champagne corks popping in the community, because SNEB was seen as a self-appointed body with no support or credibility. Nor was there much in the way of public or vocal opposition—just occasional coffee shop grumbling.

Then, in March, councillor Dave Johns tried to stop the takeover by filing a lawsuit against SNEB and the Six Nations band council. His statement of claim said, among other things, that the band council doesn't have the power to give control of the schools to SNEB because that power is held by the Minister of Indian Affairs.

Once the lawsuit hit the fan, the band council and SNEB dug in their heels and the community's opposition began to crystallize. The parents of children in the Kanyen'kehaka and Cayuga immersion programs complained loudly when SNEB refused to say that Onkwehonwe culture and language would be "a top priority" in band-controlled schools. (SNEB tried to say that *everything* was a priority.)

Much of the community's growing anger came to be focused squarely on Rebecca Jamieson, the brains behind SNEB and the driving force behind the takeover plans for the past six years. Jamieson, known throughout the community simply as "Becky," is a forty-two-year-old Tuscarora with a Master's degree in education. Despite her little-girl nickname, Jamieson is cool and tough, an Iron Lady who was determined to push the takeover through no matter what. Although she claims to be a simple administrator who just does what she's told, Jamieson is clearly the brains behind SNEB. Because of the uproar, I went to a meeting of the Six Nations Education Board to see for myself and found Jamieson handling the major issues and controversies while the board buried itself with niggling trivialities.

When she appeared before the band council in April, Jamieson brazenly stonewalled the council about the progress of the funding negotiations with the government. Although she had just finished meeting with the Minister of Indian Affairs, Jamieson flatly refused to tell the council what the Minister had said. The band council didn't raise a peep of protest.

In May, a group of retired schoolteachers showed up at a band council meeting to complain that SNEB was creating a second-rate school system. The *Tekawennake* followed that up with a blistering anti-SNEB editorial. The following month, SNEB's own negotiating team reported at a public meeting that talks with the government were going poorly and that, because of the anti-SNEB protests, the negotiators were unsure of their mandate.

By the end of July I couldn't hold my tongue any longer. I lost it at a special clear-the-air meeting of SNEB and the elected council. The SNEB chairperson began by saying that the department was dragging its feet in negotiations. The band council began to worry openly if the takeover, then just five weeks away, would ever take place. A few councillors, though, were fed up. They attacked SNEB and said they had made a mistake empowering the education board because it had "created chaos and confusion."

With that, I couldn't keep quiet any longer. Although I had lived here for nine months by then and had gone to more than two dozen public meetings of all sorts, I had never spoken a word at any of them. What I saw at that very moment, though, was a golden opportunity to share my insights into the crisis, insights that I had gleaned through many hours of independent observation. I was sure that once I explained what was wrong and how to fix it, the council would be blinded by my logic and would act instantly on my suggestions.

I began by applauding SNEB for its intentions and its

efforts, but to keep the community from being ripped apart, I added, the only sensible thing to do was for SNEB to step back, regroup, and let the department continue running the schools in September.

None of the councillors applauded. They just went on to other business as though I had been talking about the weather. That didn't bother me, though, because as I was sitting down I realized just what I had said and I went into shock. It was quite a telling moment, actually, because I realized then that I had used my public speaking debut to say that I wanted the Department of Indian Affairs—the very agency that has oppressed the Onkwehonwe for 127 years—to run the schools instead of our own people.

What an admission! I still can't believe those words came out of my mouth. I rationalized my remarks, though, by thinking that letting the department run the schools was the lesser of two evils. But I also took a cold hard look at the situation and concluded that, after six years and more than a million dollars spent in consultations and planning, the people here are not ready to run their own schools yet.

With less than a month to go before the September 1 takeover deadline, the negotiations over a financing agreement between SNEB and the department broke down. SNEB insisted that the department commit itself to financing the Six Nations school system. When the department refused to do so, despite its obligations under the Canadian constitution, the department was forced to announce that it would continue operating the schools after all.

Looking back on it all, the department displayed nothing but contempt for the community throughout the negotiations. Clearly, it had no intention of living up to its legal and moral obligations and it hoped that SNEB would be too stupid to recognize a bad deal.

The announcement that the department would continue operating the schools did not end the crisis because both sides continued trying to strike a last-minute deal. And so, through the month of August there was a flurry of increasingly angry meetings, eight of them by my count, in which the community bellowed in protest while the band council lamely defended its increasingly discredited education board. A three-hundred-name anti-SNEB petition gathered by the Kanyen'kehaka was pooh-poohed by the band council at one meeting. A speaker at another meeting likened the SNEB negotiators to the Indian scouts employed by the U.S. Cavalry to hunt down Geronimo.

By the end of the month, the opposition to the Six Nations Education Board was total. There were no supportive letters to the editor. There were no pro-SNEB petitions. There were no groups of teachers, parents or community groups demonstrating in favour of the education board. Nothing.

Month after month the crisis built as the deadline drew nearer. The arguments multiplied. The rhetoric escalated. The stress and strain intensified. Finally, with the start of school just hours away, at yet another packed meeting, there was one last showdown. At the time, a group of parents were preparing to occupy the SNEB offices the next day and force it out of business. That was averted only at the last minute when Jamieson announced she was leaving her job. The crisis evaporated and tempers cooled.

This month, with the kids back in school, with the department in charge for another year, with SNEB thoroughly disgraced, there was the final indignity, the last crazy turn of events. The band council, confronted with unrelenting and massive community opposition, finally ordered SNEB to be restructured. But who ended up getting the job of overhauling the Six Nations Education Board? You guessed it—the Six Nations Education Board.

It's starting all over again.

We're number one

I've never been much of an athlete, or even a sports fan, but the one sport I do take an active interest in is, appropriately enough, an Iroquois game—lacrosse. This summer, for example, I saw a dozen lacrosse games; that's more than all the pro hockey, football, baseball and basketball games I've ever seen put together. As a fan, my team is the Six Nations Chiefs, and tonight, in the Brantford Civic Arena, before a national television audience, the Chiefs beat the perennial champions of western Canada, the New Westminster Salmonbellies, to win it all: a national championship and a solid-gold trophy, the Mann Cup.

On a comparable night in any other sport there would have been standing-room-only crowds. In the semi-pro lacrosse league that operates in the United States, for example, the Buffalo Bandits played before a sell-out crowd of 16,284 in their championship game this past April. That, sadly, was not the case here. Tonight, in the deciding game of the playoffs, there were just 2,459 people in the stands to witness the triumphant, in-your-face comeback of Indian lacrosse.

It wasn't always like this.

When the Europeans first came here they were awed by

the chaotic vigour of the game and the enormity of its size and importance. They marvelled at the sight of teams composed of dozens of players battling one another for days on end before entire villages.

There is a detailed report of a lacrosse game played on the Grand River Territory in 1797 that illustrates just how big the sport was then. The Senecas who lived in western New York challenged the Kanyen'kehaka living in villages along the Grand River to a grudge match to settle a feud that had itself been triggered by a bloody lacrosse game three years before, in which a Mohawk had viciously and deliberately clubbed a Seneca in the head. The game was arranged by the Kanyen'kehaka leader Joseph Brant and the Seneca chiefs Red Jacket and Cornplanter. According to an eyewitness account, there were six hundred players on each team, but "only" sixty men from each side played at one time. After every twenty minutes or so the men, wearing only breechcloths, would come off the field and be replaced by another sixty-member squad. In addition to the players, more than a thousand Senecas travelled to the Grand River to camp out and watch their men play, with even more Kanyen'kehaka gathered on the other side of the field. The game was played, reportedly, on a hundred-acre open field—an area the size of fifty football fields. After three days of fierce play, the Senecas won. Now *that* was a lacrosse game!

By the 1840s the first white teams began playing lacrosse against teams of nearby Indians. Despite their lack of success, the number of white men playing the game increased steadily. On July 1, 1867—the day of Canada's birth—the National Lacrosse Association was established under a banner that proclaimed, without a hint of irony, "Our Country and Our Game." In the wake of all the Confederation hoopla, Canadians felt the need to develop their own institutions, and the new and exciting game of lacrosse seemed to be just the ticket. Interest in the game exploded and soon almost everyone in central Canada had lacrosse fever. A special lacrosse game was played on that first Confederation Day, in which the Kanyen'kehaka of Kahnawake defeated the Montreal Lacrosse Club 3-2. Later that summer, a Six Nations squad defeated a white team in Toronto before a crowd of four thousand people, leading another six hundred white men to begin playing the sport. The first national lacrosse championship was held the following year, in which the Kanyen'kehaka of Akwesasne defeated a white team from Prescott, Ontario, by a score of 2-0 to win the title. That same year a team from Six Nations toured the United States playing exhibition games, while a squad of Kahnawake and Akwesasne players toured France and England, sparking the formation of the English Lacrosse Association. Within a few years, lacrosse had also spread to Australia and New Zealand.

In spite of its booming popularity, some places wanted no part of lacrosse. One city that rejected lacrosse, according to an American magazine of the time, was Boston: "It was considered too laborious, too exciting for our more nervous and delicate young Americans. Physicians described the dangers of such fast and long continued running, and anxious parents tried to smother the game in its infancy."

By the end of the 1860s, lacrosse had undergone major changes because the whites—the Canadians—had remoulded the game to their liking. After that, when an Indian team played a white team, the whites insisted that they play "by the rules"—their rules. At first the changes were innocent enough: putting boundaries on the playing field and limiting the number of players on the field at any one time. However, when the rules for the National Lacrosse Association were revised in 1869, the changes were clearly aimed at making lacrosse a white man's sport by minimizing individual Indian involvement. Rule IX, Section 6 decreed: "No Indian must play in a match for a white club, unless previously agreed upon."

Indian players were banned, in effect, because they were too good. The man who wrote the rule book was William George Beers, a Montreal dentist and a lifelong lacrosse fanatic. The changes he had wrought in the game, as he explained, were for the better: "The present game, improved and reduced to rule by the whites...is as much superior to the original [Indian game] as civilization is to barbarism, base ball is to its old English parent of rounders, or a pretty Canadian girl to any uncultivated squaw."

But the discrimination didn't end there. When white and Indian teams played exhibition matches against each other, the Indian team was often forced to play with one or two fewer players. And in 1880 the level of discrimination increased still further when the "gentlemen amateurs" who ran the sport banned Indian teams from playing for the Canadian championship because they were "professionals."

By the turn of the century, lacrosse was firmly entrenched as a white man's sport. In the 1904 and 1908 Olympics, Canada won gold medals in lacrosse, and the top lacrosse players of the day were being paid more than base-ball legend Ty Cobb.

After World War I, though, baseball's popularity soared while lacrosse went into decline. In an effort to rejuvenate the game, the lacrosse establishment changed the rules once again in the 1930s. They brought the game indoors, to be played in the confined space of a hockey rink. And it was at this time, when the traditional outdoor game that the Iroquois had played for thousands of years was being cast aside, that the ban on Indian participation was lifted and Indian players were allowed to play the radically new version of the game.

For the past sixty years the Iroquois have been playing the white man's version of our traditional game. They have been vastly outnumbered by white Canadian players, and Iroquois influence on the game has consequently withered to nothing. Over the past three generations, the Iroquois presence has been noticed only when an Indian superstar has occasionally risen from the ranks to dominate the game. One such player in the 1950s was a Six Nations Kanyen'kehaka, Ross Powless. His son Gaylord achieved the same pre-eminence twenty years later. They are now both in the Lacrosse Hall of Fame.

Even though Indian participation at the top level of modern lacrosse has consisted of a handful of the best Indian players being sprinkled among various teams, Indians have not been entirely assimilated into the "white" game, and in recent years, the Iroquois have begun putting their own stamp back on the game. Two years ago, a local team, the Six Nations Arrows, won the Minto Cup as the best Junior A team in Canada. Last year, a group of local men founded the Six Nations Chiefs lacrosse club and sent an all-Indian team to play in the Ontario Lacrosse Association's lily-white Senior A division, the top level of Canadian lacrosse. The Chiefs aimed to be the first Indian team to capture the Canadian championship since Indians had been banned from the sport more than a century ago. They pulled together a team of the best local players, including some of the cup-winning Arrows, and set out to prove that, despite all the changes to the game, despite the overwhelming numerical superiority of white players, Indians were still the best lacrosse players in the world.

They got waxed. The Chiefs won only one game all last year and ended up in last place.

The club owners regrouped, however, and engineered a remarkable turnaround. They began by hiring away the coach of last year's Mann Cup-winning team along with a rack of premium white players from across Ontario and New York. When they were finished, they had a team with a white head coach and an Indian assistant coach and a player roster that was 50 percent white and 50 percent Indian.

The team finished this season in second place and defeated teams from Brampton and Brooklin to become all-Ontario champs and play in the national championships.

I don't know why the Brantford Civic Centre wasn't packed to the rafters for this event. Lacrosse is, after all, a fantastic spectator game that combines the most exciting elements of hockey and basketball—fast-break action, end-to-end passes, ball-handling wizardry, dazzling passing combinations and ruthless defensive play.

Oh, did I mention the fights? And the unbelievable amount of pain and physical punishment the players have to endure? To say that lacrosse is a rough game is a colossal understatement. The plain fact is that lacrosse is to contact sports what King Kong is to monkeys.

What is truly mind-boggling is that the game was, by almost all accounts, far rougher when it was played only by Indians. For instance, the translation of the old Kanyen'kehaka name for lacrosse, *attsihkwa'e*, means "carrying a ball with a webbed stick while being chased by a howling mob of big ugly guys who try to beat you senseless with long wooden clubs." Okay, so maybe it's not an exact translation, but there's no denying that broken bones and deep gashes were commonplace in the old days and the occasional death was not unknown. One witness of a Cherokee game in the early nineteenth century reported: "Before I witnessed an Indian ball play, I did not know that the vertebral column possessed as great a degree of flexibility as was demonstrated on such occasions. The principal respiratory tube is handled in such a discourteous manner, that the jaws fly open involuntarily, followed by a protrusion of the tongue."

The old-time Indians played the game with such intensity that injuries inevitably resulted, but I don't think they set out to wound their opponents on purpose. In the Kanyen'kehaka–Seneca match in 1794, for example, in which a Kanyen'kehaka deliberately injured a Seneca, the Senecas immediately dropped their sticks, went to the aid of their injured teammate, walked off the field, packed up their things and went home.

The rules these days prohibit choking, tripping, spearing, slashing, butt-ending, high-sticking and cross-checking, and this, combined with the fact that players now wear helmets, face-masks, teeth-guards, gloves and armour-like padding all over their upper bodies, has led many old-timers to grumble that lacrosse has turned into a sissy's game. (Amazingly enough, though, lacrosse is still played bare-legged.)

A declining number of players, the older ones mostly, continue to use the traditional lacrosse stick, handmade from hickory and strung with leather and catgut. The younger players, though, have switched to machine-made sticks, which have an aluminum shaft, a plastic head and nylon webbing.

The rules still allow for a frightening amount of stick-work. It is permissible—expected, even—to slap, hammer and push an opponent harshly and repeatedly with a stick to force him to drop the ball or to knock him off his feet. The stick-work is such a natural and necessary part of the game, in fact, that coaches and spectators are constantly hollering a single command to the players: "LAY THE WOOD ON 'IM." Because a wooden stick is heavier than an aluminum one, it packs a bigger wallop and leaves bigger bruises. Players who use a wooden stick sneeringly refer to the plastic-headed sticks as "Tupperware."

Although the game today is nowhere near as tough or

brutal as it once was, the violence is a large part of its appeal, as evidenced by the T-shirts being worn by some of the fans: "Give blood—play lacrosse."

It may seem from all this talk about violence that watching a lacrosse game is comparable to watching a Newfoundlander clubbing seal pups surrounded by brawling Hell's Angels in the middle of a roller-derby. It's not. I watch lacrosse because it's exhilarating to see the way the game blends speed, strategy, strength and finesse. Lacrosse truly is a thrilling and beautiful game. But when the fighting and the rough stuff starts—when the sticks start flying and the bodies start falling—I don't look the other way.

And since such a large portion of the game is spent inflicting and enduring pain, I think everyone in the league—white and Indian alike—must be a sadist or a masochist. It has to be one or the other because these guys clearly are not playing the game for the money. It so happens that there was a story in the paper the other day about the salary demands of the professional baseball players who went on strike last month. Although the *average* baseball salary is already $1.2 million a year and superstars like Barry Bonds get paid $7 million a year, the players still want more. Among other things, they want baseball's minimum wage increased from $109,000 to $175,000–$200,000 a year.

By comparison, the average player salary for the Six Nations Chiefs is said to be just $50 a game. Lacrosse superstars, like the Chiefs' Paul Gait, reportedly get a couple of hundred dollars a game. What this means, then, is that the lowest-paid—and arguably the worst—player in professional baseball, a utility infielder no one has never heard of, gets paid as much money for playing one double-header as some of the best lacrosse players in the world get paid for playing all year. Even players like the Chiefs's John Tavares, who dominates lacrosse the way Wayne Gretzky once dominated hockey, has a day job—he works as a baker in Toronto.

The last and only other time a Mann Cup final was played in the Brantford Civic Centre was in 1971 when the Brantford Warriors, captained by Gaylord Powless, won the national championship. The turnout that night was 3,774—50 percent higher than tonight's attendance. Even though the number of people playing organized lacrosse in Ontario has tripled over the past ten years, the Chiefs drew 1,300 fewer people to the same building for the same event. During the regular season, the Chiefs' average attendance was said to be just 600. And the reason for the poor turnout, like the reason for a lot of other things around here, is political.

Looking around the arena tonight it was clear that more than half of the people were Indians. *Where were all the white people?* From what I've been told, most of the people who witnessed the Warriors' victory in 1971 were white. In that year, though, the vast majority of the players and owners were white, the team was headquartered in town, and it was called the *Brantford* Warriors. In 1994, by comparison, half of the players are Indian, all of the owners are Indians, the team is headquartered on the reserve, and it is called the *Six Nations* Chiefs.

Despite the hundreds of empty seats in the arena, tonight's game was close and exciting. Watching the action I could see that there were many trying moments when the Chiefs were exhausted and hemmed-in, when they had to exert a superhuman effort to outrun or outmuscle one of the Salmonbellies. I like to think that it was at just those moments, when the players had exceeded the limits of their endurance, that the Indians on the team were able to draw on the special reservoir of strength that lies deep within the heart of every Onkwehonwe who plays this game. After all, lacrosse is more than just an organized sport to our people. It is a game that children play without supervision, for the sheer fun of it. Iroquois boys and girls grow up playing lacrosse as naturally as inner-city kids grow up playing basketball.

The centrepiece of lacrosse—the wooden stick—also has special significance to our people. "Real" lacrosse sticks are not made of synthetic materials assembled in a distant factory. They are hand-crafted by people we know. They come from trees that grow in this territory, and as such, they contain the power and essence of Mother Earth.

Lacrosse is woven into the very fabric of our culture. It is a game that was given to us at the beginning of time by the Creator Himself. In the old days our people played lacrosse to honour and amuse the Creator. Playing the game, therefore, not only promoted physical strength and well-being, it also led to a state of spiritual peace. Lacrosse was also part of the healing rites our people used to cure illness—they prepared and administered the medicines to the sick and played lacrosse to give the medicine extra power. When the Seneca prophet Handsome Lake was on his deathbed, for example, he asked on his last day of life on earth that a game of lacrosse be played for him.

The memories and knowledge of events such as these are imbedded in the deepest layer of our being. We are bound with unbreakable ties of devotion to this game. I believe it was this knowledge and these ties that gave the Onkwehonwe players on the Chiefs an extra spark that was transformed into the adrenaline that helped them win.

When Rich Kilgour, a Tuscarora, scored the winning goal in the last minute of play, the crowd went wild, including me. I got a lump in my throat watching the players parade around the arena exultantly brandishing their trophy. As I watched the celebrations erupting in the stands, it was clear that the players had lifted the hearts of the people.

The people, in turn, showered the players—native and non-native alike—with praise and appreciation.

Standing there amid the cheers and confetti, I thought of the things that have happened to the Creator's game since the dawn of time. I thought of the sacred reasons we once had for playing lacrosse, and I thought of how the whites had taken it over, changed it and called it their own. But none of that mattered tonight because we went home knowing that an "Indian" team had won the national championship, just as an Indian team won it 126 years ago.

Let all our minds be as one

Now at this time we are gathered here and we have not heard of any unfortunate event occurring to anyone. We arrived here without incident because the Creator protected our journey. So at this time let us acknowledge each other and our good fortune by combining our minds as one and giving greetings and thanksgiving to one another.

Thus begins the *ohenton karihwatehkwen*, known in English as the Thanksgiving Address, the Sacred Address or the Opening Ritual. It literally means "the business that comes first." If the Rotinonhsyonni had a national anthem, this would be it, and more, because the Thanksgiving Address is "The Star-Spangled Banner," "God Save the Queen," "O Canada" and the Lord's Prayer rolled into one. But it's not about saving queens, standing on guard, forgiving trespassers or bombs bursting in air. It's a prayer of thanksgiving: it speaks of the way that human beings are related to everything in the universe and it gives thanks to all living things.

Every gathering of any significance in this community,

with the exception of meetings of the elected band council, begins with the recitation of the Thanksgiving Address.

The Address contains up to twenty stanzas and, depending on the speaker, can take up to twenty minutes to deliver. Each stanza pays reverence to, and gives thanks for, a different element in creation, beginning with the last thing that Shonkwaya'tihson created on Mother Earth—the Onkwehonwe.

At the end of each stanza, the speaker says (according to one printed version): *"Etho niyohtonhak ne onkwa'nikonra."* So now let all our minds be as one on this matter. The people, to show that they are in agreement, respond by saying, *"Yo."*

The Thanksgiving Address is more than just a list of thank-yous that have to be recited. It reminds human beings about their place in the realm of creation. It also dictates a code of conduct for the Onkwehonwe—to regard all life and all things in creation as equal. What's more, it does so in a touchingly beautiful way. This, for example, is how thanks are given for the trees:

> Now we turn our attention to the forest where
> grows all kinds of trees, both big and small. Of
> all these trees our Creator chose the maple tree
> to be the leader of all the forest. It is the maple
> whose sap is the first to run, to show that winter
> is changing to spring. From the maple comes
> the sugar and syrup our people cherish. From
> the trees come the fruits that our people need to
> survive. From the roots and barks of various
> trees come the medicines to heal the sick and
> injured. In the hot summer months it is a great
> comfort to sit in the cool shade of a big tree.
> From the trees of the forest comes the wood
> needed to provide shelter and heat so that our

smallest babies will not freeze in the cold of
winter. So we will now direct our thankfulness
and our acknowledgment to the life of the trees
as they are still producing the things necessary
to our survival as the Creator intended. We are
grateful, so we give thanks.

"*E'tho niyohtonhak ne onkwa'nikonra,*" the speaker
then says, and the people respond, "*Yo.*"
On any level, the Thanksgiving Address is an extraordinary invocation. The language, first of all, is uplifting. The
content, in which human beings are charted in relation to
everything else in the universe, is humbling. The message
of thanksgiving is reverential. And underneath it all is the
subtle psychology that unifies the listeners by focusing
attention on one subject after another and getting them to
voice agreement along the way. By the end of the address,
everyone is of one mind, allowing the business at hand to
proceed more smoothly.

I listened to the *ohenton karihwatehkwen* again today. The
occasion, appropriately enough, was a spiritual gathering
on the so-called Glebe lands in Brantford, said to be the
site of the original Kanyen'kehaka village on the Grand
River. The site is especially significant because the
Kanyen'kehaka longhouse is said to have been there. As
well, many Kanyen'kehaka people are still buried on the
site, including the victims of a cholera epidemic.
Today, though, most of the site is covered by fields of
soybeans drying on the vine. Part of it is scarred by a gravel
pit and bisected by high-tension hydro wires, and all of it
echoes with the not-too-distant roar of city traffic. The
Glebe is officially part of the Six Nations territory and is
the only link the Onkwehonwe still have to the original
settlement here. Squeezed as it is between a strip mall and

the shallow waters of Mohawk Lake, the land is coveted by the city for a highway and coveted by the band council for a casino.

The people who gathered at the site today, though, have other ideas. In fact, the gathering was born out of a campaign to stop the city from bulldozing a four-lane highway through the property. Some of the people behind that campaign then decided to hold an annual get-together on the site to socialize, to commemorate the people buried there and to give thanks. On the closing afternoon, the people took turns and spoke soberly of our culture and the special responsibilities it imposes on us, chief among them the obligation to give thanks for what we have received—an "attitude of gratitude" as one man put it.

The gathering began and ended, as it should have, with the Thanksgiving Address, recited by bear clan chief Richard Maracle. As I listened on this special day, in this special place, the words had special meaning because I was finally able to know what many of them meant. I'm still a long way from knowing what it all means and even further away from being able to recite it myself—but I'm getting closer.

After Richard Maracle had given thanks to the waters, fish, insects, plants, animals, birds, winds, the sun, moon and stars, he came to the last stanza:

> Our Creator asked that we, the human beings,
> be grateful and thankful to all the universe's life
> forms and to our Creator. And so in order to
> fulfil our obligations to our Creator, we will
> express our gratefulness through the yearly
> ceremonies, through the Four Sacred Rituals.
> Our Creator requested that we have love in our
> hearts and in our minds; that we carry each day
> and night thoughts of goodness; that we are

helpful to one another. Our Creator made the
universe and he created us. Our Creator left
nothing lacking as everything we need to have
satisfaction, peace and a good life is here on this
Mother Earth. So we are indeed blessed today as
we review the Creator's plan of land and life.
Now we the people using one mind will search
for the most humble, kindest words as we now
thank you, our Creator.

"E'tho niyohtonhak ne onkwa'nikonra," Richard then
said. And, feeling very grateful about the place I hold in the
Master of Life's scheme of creation, and feeling that I was
of the same mind as all the others, I replied as they did.
"Yo."

A plan of action

Some people say that the only way the political conflict at Six Nations can be resolved is by physically creating two separate communities. That way, everyone who wants to live under the Indian Act and be Canadians can live in one place, and everyone who wants to live under the *Kayaneren'tsherakowa* and be Onkwehonwe can live in another. That certainly would stop the feuding here, but the disruption would be horrendous.

There is, however, another less chaotic way to end the conflict. It was first suggested in the late 1980s by then band chief Bill Montour. He saw that the band council was overstepping its mandate, that its job was to plow the roads and not negotiate "treaties" with the federal government, as the elected council is trying to do now. He recognized that the conflict was paralyzing the community and he realized that there was only one solution, so he approached the Confederacy and proposed, in effect, a "peace treaty." This led to a historic meeting between the Confederacy and the elected councils of all the Iroquois communities at which the traditional chiefs gave the combined councils a list of nine areas of responsibility the Confederacy would handle, leaving the band councils to deal with everything else. Under this arrangement, the Confederacy would be responsible for things like land claims, taxation, treaties, membership, hunting and fishing issues, while the band councils would provide municipal services and administer government programs.

The Six Nations band council, however, has never responded to the Confederacy's proposal. But if the present council could summon the same vision and courage that Bill Montour displayed and accept the Confederacy's proposal, it would be able to concentrate on the civil administration of this territory and do it well, rather than trying to do everything and doing it poorly. More importantly, such a move would break the paralytic impasse between the two councils and finally bring a sense of peace to this community.

Even if this band council doesn't accept the Confederacy's proposal, the next one could. And until then, the present band council could still do a few things to earn a little respect. For starters, it could promote the use of our mother tongue throughout the territory. It could ban federal and provincial polling booths and census-takers, on our sovereign territory, as the elected band council at Kahnawake does now.

Just as a peace treaty would mean big changes for the band council, it would mean even bigger changes for the Confederacy, which would undoubtedly face increased demands from every direction. Presumably, and hopefully, the Confederacy and the band council would develop a working relationship based on mutual trust and respect. And with their respective roles clearly defined, the Confederacy's hand—the community's hand—would be strengthened immeasurably in dealings with government.

Even if the band council does not accept a diminished role for itself, there are still many things the people have to do to strengthen the Confederacy. The first item of business is to get the clans working again. This means charting family trees, drawing up clan lists and publishing them so people will know where they belong and who their fellow clan members are. Then the people will have to begin by acting in a clan-like fashion—by helping and supporting one another. They should also begin filling vacant chieftainships and clanmotherships, adopting clanless people and sorting out the duplication of titles. If the Jews and Arabs can kiss and make up, surely the members of the same clan of Onkwehonwe can come to one mind as to who their clanmother or chief should be.

My fondest wish is to see a Kanyen'kehaka longhouse built in this territory because we desperately need one. Most of the Kanyen'kehaka adults here did not grow up with the ceremonies, did not get an Indian name and did not learn the language. Yet these are the very things that give people a sense of identity and make them strong. The lack of these things is something that has weakened and impoverished the present generation. Clearly, we owe it to our children and to future generations to give them what we were denied, and a Kanyen'kehaka longhouse will help immeasurably in doing just that.

Most of the Kanyen'kehaka here who have traditional beliefs don't attend the longhouse doings because the longhouses at Grand River are all based on the Code of Handsome Lake. The obvious solution, then, is to establish a Kanyen'kehaka-speaking longhouse that would be based only on the Great Law, not on the Code. Such a longhouse, I understand, is already operating in the Kanyen'kehaka territory at Kahnawake. Such a longhouse here would allow the Kanyen'kehaka to conduct the ceremonies and give thanks in the proper way and at all the appropriate times during the year—just as the Creator and the Peacemaker intended. It would allow the Kanyen'kehaka to name their children, adopt outsiders, strengthen their clans and preserve their language.

If such a longhouse were built, the people would come. It wouldn't be easy to establish, given the shortage of people who speak the language and know what to do. But it certainly is worth doing and the good thing is that there are many people around who are willing to learn and willing to help.

And if none of the things I've suggested ever comes to pass, there are still many things that all of us as individuals can do.

On a small matter, I'd like to see the women here stop the practice of taking their husband's name when they get married. We are a matrilineal people and the women are the bedrock of our culture. For them to change their names is an affront to our matrilineal traditions. It therefore follows, in keeping with that tradition, that all children should be given their mother's last name and be placed on their mother's band list.

I'd also like to see every able-bodied person here plant a garden and grow at least some of their own food. This would do more to improve the health and well-being of the people here than all the government's health programs combined. In fact, in a rural area like this, with the cultural traditions we have, there's no excuse for *not* planting a garden.

In addition, I'd like to see the people here learn and use their aboriginal language. I'd elaborate further but I've probably said enough about that matter already.

Lastly, there are a number of interrelated things that people could do that would raise the level of spiritual fulfilment across the territory a hundredfold.

The people here, especially the Christians and the people who don't go to church or to the longhouse, should learn about the traditional ceremonies that are conducted throughout the year. There's no harm in learning about our traditional religion, after all, especially for people who take pride in being Onkwehonwe. In the same way, more people should learn about Indian tobacco so they can use it to offer prayers and give thanks, as the Creator intended.

Although it may seem as though we will never be able to settle the political turmoil that has plagued this community for so many years, I truly believe we could end the conflict, and achieve much more besides, if more people here used the traditional pattern of thinking and behaviour that once governed our lives—the principle of the good mind. In this regard, I like to think that we can find ways to focus on the things that unite us and put to the side those that divide us, and hold our tongues about each other's individual failings. If we root our minds in peace, harmony and humility and if we remain true to our traditions, we can achieve our goals and safeguard the future for coming generations.

I am more than a little uncomfortable making all the foregoing suggestions because I don't want to sound like a bossy, lecturing know-it-all. What I am doing is simply repeating instructions that originally came from the Creator and the Peacemaker, and I am not saying anything that I haven't already heard many other Onkwehonwe say many times before.

My first year back on the rez has confirmed my belief that conquering the problems we face won't depend on self-government, economic development, feasibility studies, framework agreements, surveys, reports, proposals, resolutions, consultants, conferences, committees, seminars, think tanks, government programs or government money. The only thing that will win our struggle will be our culture—specifically our clans, languages, ceremonies and traditions. We may never solve our legal, economic, social or political problems, but if we can fortify our culture at least we will be physically fit, morally strong, emotionally healthy and spiritually fulfilled. And we can then be at peace with ourselves, with each other and with our Creator.

Giving thanks

A year ago I had Thanksgiving dinner with a white middle-class family in suburban Ottawa, in a spacious, well-kept home that could have been featured in a magazine. We ate in the family's dining room, fitted out with fine furniture, on real china with real silverware. There were a dozen people at the dinner table. Except for my daughter Zoe and two others, they were all strangers to me. The other guests were dressed for the occasion: the women wore jewellery and make-up; one man wore a suit and tie.

At the time I was in the final stages of packing my belongings and preparing to move back here. I was unsettled, in more ways than one, and I really appreciated the invitation. My hosts were gracious and friendly and I spent a pleasant afternoon having a very enjoyable and typical Canadian Thanksgiving dinner.

Two weeks after that dinner I moved back to the rez and today, one year later, I hosted a Thanksgiving dinner of my own. My surroundings this year are nowhere near as expensive, stylish or tidy as last year's. This house will never be featured in *Canadian Living* magazine, but like an old slipper it's comfortable and it suits me fine.

What made this an extra-special occasion was the

company: it was a mini family reunion. My only disappointment was not having Zoe with me today because she is in Waglisla attending a ceremonial potlatch with her mother. But there were still twelve of us crowded into my kitchen, wedged together around a makeshift table. There was my mother Kitty and her mother Martha, my father Leonard and his mother Lillian, his brother Tom and his uncle Stan, Stan's daughter Linda, my sister Dennise, her boys Tom and Wade, my sister Marilyn and me. After we were seated, I looked around the table—at the beaming faces of my parents, grandmothers, uncles, sisters, nephews and a cousin—and I smiled too.

I couldn't help thinking about the events of the past year that had brought us together. Although I didn't have a job as such, I was incredibly busy. For starters, I had to do an unbelievable amount of work to make this old house livable. In the process I learned a lot about woodstoves, firewood and water pumps. I also learned a lot of things about this community, about the band council, the Confederacy and the Kanyen'kehaka Nation. I went to a lot of local activities—to a school sports day, a snowsnake tournament, an Iroquois social, Bread and Cheese Day, the local pow-wow, the Ohsweken Fair and a slew of lacrosse games. I stirred the ashes at mid-winter, listened to the Great Law and took part in *Noyah*. I was also much more physically active than I had been in the city. I split a lot of wood, cleared a lot of brush, cut a lot of grass, re-roofed the garage, planted a garden, pulled a lot of weeds and did a lot of spear-fishing. I've just taken a part-time job with the local university entrance program and have begun writing for a new local newspaper, the *Turtle Island News*. I've taken every Kanyen'kehaka language class that's been offered and I'm signed up for more. I've come to know a lot of people here, made a few new friends and spent time with my grandmothers, uncles, sisters, niece, nephews and cousins, several of whom were sitting at the table.

We had a typical Thanksgiving dinner. Except for the turkey and cranberries, which came from the supermarket, the rest of the meal came from my garden—the potatoes, squash, beans, carrots, tomatoes and pumpkin pie. As the heaping plates of food were being passed around, I took enormous pleasure in being able to share the fruits of my labour with my loved ones. As I listened to the grace being said, I whispered my own silent thank-you to the Creator for allowing us all to share this day in good health and high spirits.

It was a wonderful dinner. Even though we didn't have enough glasses or elbow room, the food was terrific and the companionship was even better. It was just like all the other Thanksgiving dinners I had while growing up. It was crowded and crazy, delicious and delightful, and the first of many more I hope to have here with my family. And that, after all, is what moving back to the rez is all about—living in the heart of the great family of Onkwehonwe.

Truly, it has been a wonderful year, and on this Thanksgiving Day, of all days, I felt especially thankful, humble and joyful. Earlier today, when I was in the garden harvesting vegetables for dinner, I expressed my own thanks to Shonkwaya'tihson. I offered tobacco for the life-sustaining food I had taken from the flesh of Mother Earth. I then made one more offering of tobacco to Shonkwaya'tihson to show my respect and appreciation for all the blessings of creation that He has bestowed on all His children, but especially on me.

I am ever so grateful for the chance to do and to learn all that I did in the past year. But the best gift of all was getting to know myself in a way that comes only from knowing that I am finally where I belong. I have found a place among my people.

I am home at last. And there is much to do.